OUT OF THE RAT RACE

The Quest for Financial Freedom

Eric DUNEAU

Copyright © 2019 by incubiq solutions ltd. All rights reserved.

All rights reserved. No part of this publication may be reproduced, stored in any retrieval system, or transmitted, in any form or by any means, electronic, mechanical, photocopying, recording or otherwise, except as permitted by the U.K. Copyright, Designs and Patents Act 1988, without the prior permission of the publisher.

Designations used by companies to distinguish their products are often claimed as trademarks. All brand names, product names, song titles, and song extracts used in this book and on its cover are trade names, service marks, trademarks or registered trademarks of their respective owners. The publisher, the author, and the book are not associated with any product or vendor mentioned in this book. None of the companies or individuals referenced within the book have endorsed the book.

Limit of liability / Disclaimer of Warranty: While the Publisher and Author have used their best effort s in preparing this book, they make no representations or warranties with respect to the accuracy or completeness of the content of this book, and specifically disclaim any implied warranties of merchantability or fitness for a particular purpose. It is sold on the understanding that the publisher is not engaged in rendering professional services. The advice and strategies contained herein may not be suitable for your situation. Neither the publisher nor author shall be liable for any loss of profit or any other commercial damages, included but not limited to special, incidental, consequential, or other damages. If professional advice or other expert assistance is required, the services of a competent professional should be sought.

Author: Eric Duneau

Title: Out of the Rat Race – The Quest for Financial Freedom

ISBN 978-1-9161145-0-0
version 1.02.79981

Subjects: Personal Finance | Money Management | Financial independence | Retirement Planning | Self-Help

"A bill is the most extraordinary locomotive engine that the genius of man ever produced. It would keep on running during the longest lifetime, without ever once stopping of its own accord"

Charles Dickens

Contents

ABOUT THE AUTHOR	XI
A LETTER TO MY YOUNGER SELF	XII

GROUND ZERO	**1**
STEP 1: WHAT WAS HE THINKING?	2
STEP 2: A FARM FOR A POT OF HONEY	3
STEP 3: INVEST LIKE A LADY	6
STEP 4: FOUNDATIONS ARE DUE A RESET	8

FOUNDATIONS – MONEY	**11**
STEP 5: THE INVENTION OF COINS	12
STEP 6: THE INVENTION OF NOTES	14
STEP 7: THE INVENTION OF LOANS	16
STEP 8: THE INVENTION OF TAX	19
STEP 9: THE INVENTION OF INFLATION	21
STEP 10: THE INVENTION OF INTEREST	23
STEP 11: THE INVENTION OF BANKS	29
STEP 12: THE INVENTION OF CREDIT	32
STEP 13: FRACTIONAL BANKING	34
STEP 14: AND MONEY BECOMES TRUST	40
STEP 15: DEREGULATION AND GLOBALISATION	42
STEP 16: THE ALCHEMISTS	45
STEP 17: INTO DEBT	49

FOUNDATIONS - ATTITUDE   53

STEP 18: DO NOT GET INTO DEBT   54
STEP 19: BE A BETTER PERSON THAN YOU WERE YESTERDAY   58
STEP 20: DEALING WITH STRESS   60
STEP 21: TWO BRAINS FOR ONE PERSON   64
STEP 22: POWER OF TRUST   66
STEP 23: POWER OF YOUR CIRCLE   68
STEP 24: DEALING WITH THE UNKNOWN   70
STEP 25: ALWAYS TAKE THE LONG VIEW   73
STEP 26: BEWARE THE SALESMAN   76
STEP 27: WHO ARE YOU?   79

FOUNDATIONS - FINANCES   81

STEP 28: NO TRICKS BEYOND THIS POINT   82
STEP 29: YOUR NEW ARITHMETIC TABLES   86
STEP 30: FINANCIAL CRASH COURSE   92
STEP 31: INCOME AND CAPITAL   98
STEP 32: FINANCIAL DASHBOARDS   100
STEP 33: KEY PERFORMANCE INDICATORS   103
STEP 34: TAXES AND FEES   106
STEP 35: MONEY AS WATER   108

A NEW DAWN   113

STEP 36: IN EMPLOYMENT   114
STEP 37: A RAINBOW OF MONEY   120
STEP 38: INCOME VS FREEDOM   130
STEP 39: DEBT FREE FALLACY   135
STEP 40: FROM HUMAN TO FINANCIAL CAPITAL   140
STEP 41: RISK ON CAPITAL   149
STEP 42: A FIRST INVESTMENT PLAN   154

ENTER THE PROPERTY GAME   161

STEP 43: ANATOMY OF A GOOD DEAL   162
STEP 44: WHAT YOU BUY   163

STEP 45: HOW YOU FINANCE	166
STEP 46: OPERATIONAL RATIOS	169
STEP 47: PROPERTY MARKET SLUMPS	178
STEP 48: OPERATING AS A BUSINESS	183
STEP 49: PRACTISE, JUMP, AND IMPROVE	187
STEP 50: INDEPENDENCE IN SIGHT AT 3+1	190
STEP 51: NO GOOD REASON TO SELL	200
STEP 52: IS YOUR HOME AN ASSET OR A LIABILITY?	202

REAL CASE STUDY — 207

STEP 53: IN NEED OF A MOMENT OF TRUTH	208
STEP 54: NEW BEGINNING	210
STEP 55: THE CASE FOR SELLING	212
STEP 56: CASH BUY FROM HOME LEVERAGE	217
STEP 57: HOME SWAP FROM HOME LEVERAGE	220
STEP 58: DREAM HOME FROM HOME LEVERAGE	230

ENJOY YOUR NEW FREEDOM — 237

STEP 59: LEVELS OF FREEDOM	238
STEP 60: LIFESTYLE	240
STEP 61: QUALITY OF ACCOMMODATION	243
STEP 62: QUALITY OF TIME	248
STEP 63: MONEY VS TIME	252
STEP 64: WHAT WAS THIS ALL ABOUT?	260

OTHER FINANCIAL GAMES — 265

STEP 65: WRAPPING-UP REAL ESTATE	266
STEP 66: MR MARKET	267
STEP 67: INVESTING	271
STEP 68: RETIREMENT ACCOUNTS	273
STEP 69: FINDING YOUR PLACE IN THE WORKSPACE	277
STEP 70: FREELANCE OR SMALL LIFESTYLE COMPANY	279
STEP 71: MONEY PRINTING VIA INTERNET-BASED VENTURE	282
STEP 72: MONEY PRINTING BY GROWING A START-UP	284
STEP 73: MONEY PRINTING BY FLIPPING LAND	290
STEP 74: OTHER OPPORTUNITIES	291
STEP 75: TO PARADISE WITH SIMULATORS	293

LEVERAGE YOUR LIFE! 295

STEP 76: LIFE IS A JOURNEY 296
STEP 77: BUT WHAT A JOURNEY! 299

APPENDIX 305

THANK YOU 306
ADDITIONAL RESOURCES 307
SOLUTION TO THE INVESTMENT CASE 308
GLOSSARY 310
REFERENCES 313
INDEX 314

About the author

Eric Duneau is a 50 years old French citizen, married with two children now at University.

Eric moved from France to UK in 2000. He has spent most of his professional life working in CxO positions at Technology companies (start-ups). Eric has ramped up a tech company from 3 guys in a garage to IPO in Europe within 6 years, and then successively managed up to 12 companies in western Europe, USA, and South Africa. This has exposed him to a lot of diverse challenges and cultures worldwide.

Eric has also succeeded to get out of the Rat Race through mainly two "financial games": investing in real-estate and investing in start-ups. This book explains most of the knowledge and tricks he has gained and used, with a strong focus on real-estate, to get OOTRR!

A letter to my younger self

My dear friend,

You are about to embark on a journey, you have no idea! Do you really think it is plain sailing ahead? It is by struggling and failing and falling and getting back up that you will achieve your most ambitious and dearest projects. You think you know what they are? You have no idea! Life will change them, and life will change you.

Sit down a moment. Give me just a few hours now, for a lifetime of learning. Here is the deal and my present to you. This book is for you. It is a condensed story of the most important lessons I learned in the last twenty-five years. Some experience and wisdom that can make the difference to your very own next twenty-five years. A promise to make you a better person in a few hours' time.

As you are clearing all hurdles, fast and furious, without any second thought, just pay attention for once. You will have plenty of time in your life to achieve what you want and more, but first and foremost, you need to understand the world around you and the world inside you. What do you stand for? Which achievements will stand true to your values? Can you engineer your future life? I know, you think you should not bother with these questions. But that's exactly why you need me now. Getting clarity on such simple questions will determine the direction of the track on which you run. And let me tell you this right now: it's bloody important to run on the right track!

Listen carefully my friend: there are many things you take for granted, but you should not. Even the little spare cash you have in your pocket, you think you know what it is, but really... you have no idea!

Let's cut to the chase. I will now give you all the material you will ever need on your arduous journey to pause, reflect, analyse, take action, succeed, accept failure, learn, and improve beyond all your expectations, so that you get financially free, out of the Rat Race, and become the best possible person you could ever be. This book is your guide. As you mature and understand the world better, open it again and in the light of your new experiences and wisdom, you will be surprised to discover a treasure of new valuable lessons.

So here it is. Do you really want to get out of the Rat Race and be financially free starting from nothing and nowhere? I am afraid there is no shortcut. Only your best friend's advice.

What are you waiting for?

Sit down, relax, and turn the bloody page!

Yours truly

Eric

1

Ground zero

Welcome to the world...

...there's no turning back

Tears for Fears

Indeed, welcome to the world!

Before we can even make sense of the scale of our mission, we need to confront the reality.

My friend, I am afraid that we both have to go through a total reset of beliefs, attitude, principles, and knowledge. If you don't, it is unlikely you will be allowed to fulfil your dreams.

From now on, there's really no turning back.

Step 1: what was he thinking?

I once was on the bottom rung of financial independence. First salary, first rent... A first taste of freedom and full of dreams!

I was 25 years old and living in a suburb of Paris, France. Everything seemed clear and simple. I knew what I wanted, and I knew I would achieve it. The details were not that important. Bah! They were just details... My plan was simple:

```
"I will work very hard for a few years, and then I
will have enough money to do what I want."
```

To be honest with the 25-year-old me, had you probed a bit more about the details, you would have had this improved version:

```
"I will work at least 12 hours a day, six days a week
for at most 5 years in the start-up I just co-founded.
Then we will sell it. I will get at least 10m Francs¹ so
that I will not have to work anymore. From then on, I
will play music or do all the other stuff that I like..."
```

Looking back with a bit more wisdom, this improved version is still riddled with bad assumptions and even worse conclusions. If I wanted to play music, I could have done it without the ordeal. It looks like I did not know much about myself and even less about money. In addition, I was free from any concern that I could end-up struggling in life.

Have you had, or do you still have your own simple dreams? Are you ready for them to be shattered? I will tell you one thing: better face the music right now than in 25 years!

So, what are you thinking?

Are you ready to embark on this journey with me?

---

[1] This was in France in 1995, pre Euro. Translate the sum at the time into £1m or 1.5m Euro.

Step 2: a farm for a pot of honey

Just a century ago, my great-grand-parents bought a farm in rural France. They paid 4,000 Francs[2] for it. In today's value, it is worth 40 Francs (post 1958, but pre-euro), which converts into €6.10. Today, that's the cost of a small pot of honey...

Now I hear you say, there have been 100 years of inflation at work here. Indeed! Cumulative inflation over the last one hundred years was just over 100,000%[3], so that's not a small variation! In other words, the 100-year-old honey has not only crystallised, but also costs one thousand times more.

Fig 2.1 A farm for a pot of honey

Applying the official inflation rate, we now have an "inflation indexed price" of the farm, which is close to a large barrel of honey, or to be more precise, a whopping €6,250 and change (that is around $7,000 or £5,500).

If you are still reading casually, it is time to pause and reflect. I should hear you scream:

"What? I could pay €6,250 today and acquire a farm in France?"

Let me rephrase. Today's average salary in France is €2,200 per month[4]. We just worked out that, according to official inflation, we should be able to buy this same farm for around three months gross salary. Of course, we know it does not work like this, and you have to work for a damn more than three months to be able to buy a farm in France! So where is the trick?

---

[2] That's "old" French Francs. In 1958, a devaluation turned 100 old Francs into 1 new Franc.
[3] Calculated from https://france-inflation.com/calculateur_inflation.php, inflation in France from 1919 to 2018.
[4] The average gross salary in France in 2017 is €26,500 ; €2,200 is around $2,500 or £1,900.

A little research showed that back then, my great-grand-parents must have been earning around 100-120 Francs a month. Just for the fun of it, we are talking about €0.15 per month in today's money! Or £0.13 per month, or $0.17 per month... well you get the picture! On that basis, my great-grand-dad had to put aside the equivalent of around three years of gross wages to buy his farm.

The same farm today would actually cost around €250,000. That is around nine years of current gross average wage. The chart below highlights the trick.

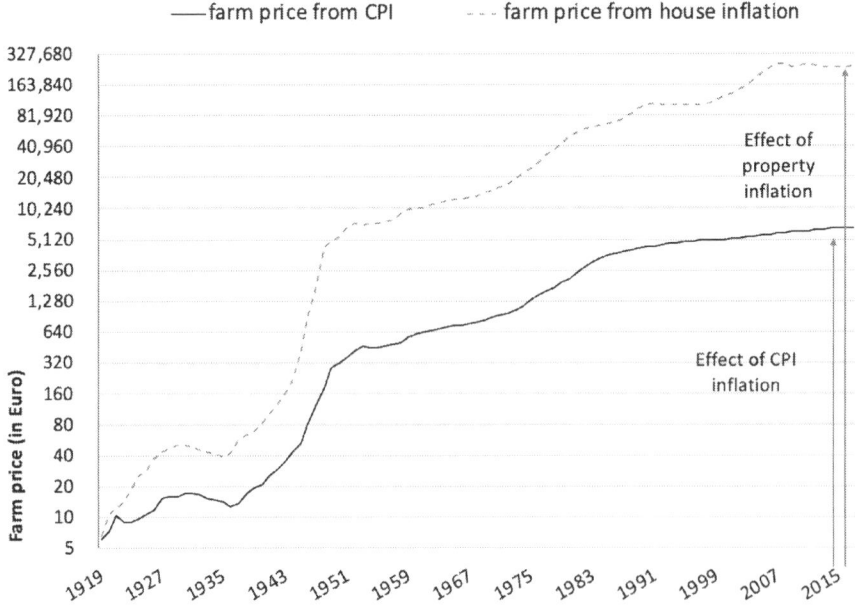

Fig 2.2. Farm price inflation over 100 years (rebased in Euro) using a log scale

The Consumer Price Index (CPI) is the officially measured inflation rate, according to which the farm should be worth €6,250 (black line) if it followed CPI inflation. In reality, the farm is worth around €250,000 (dotted line), or 40 times more than CPI would suggest.

Oh, and just this little detail: saving an entire nine years of wages is not going to be very practical for one person who also has to live and pay tax. Therefore nowadays, the farm is more likely to be bought by a couple both in employment. If both are on similar average pay, that reduces the need for accumulating only four and a half years of income each. But that's before tax! Let's not forget that in the world we live in, we are subject to gravity and tax. I don't recall the formula for gravity, but for sure the tax one looks like this:

$$Net = Gross - Tax$$

Therefore, our couple will need to put aside at least 6 years of net income each, not just four and a half.

Can we make sense of all this?

- 100 years ago, one could buy a property by saving three years of income as a labourer.
- Today, for the same (but modernised) property, you will need to save twelve years of net income, or four times more than your great-grand-father had to[5].
- If you are unfortunate to have followed family tradition and kept your great-grand-father's job as a farm labourer, the property is simply unaffordable.
- Over a century, the value of money was deflated by a factor of x1000. A variation of this magnitude is at the very least deceitful. For me, it has to be called theft. I will call it "The Accepted Theft".
- Another invisible theft accounted for around x40. If you think it's a rounding error compared to inflation, think twice. It means that the total theft over a century was x40,000.

This is not some conspiracy theory. It's not even a theory, it's reality. It's a fact. Over one hundred years, the state deflated the value of money by a factor of 1,000. On top of that, an invisible man pocketed a further factor of 40.

---

[5] As you also need to live and pay for your food, travel, lifestyle, local taxes, and more, it means you may need to work from 15 up to 30 years until you own your home.

Step 3: invest like a Lady

> "Who lives to one hundred years?"
>
> "France was bound to have hyper-inflation, they always go on strike!"
>
> "And who wants to buy a farm anyway?"

OK then... Let's move to U.K. and slice the duration in half to 50 years. And let's make it public so that anybody will be able to check all the facts.

In 1965, a Lady named Margaret Thatcher bought a house in Kent[6] (U.K.) for £8,000. In today's money, taking into account compounded CPI inflation, the old £8,000 is worth around[7] £150,000. That's a good bit of inflation already! However, the same house is valued today at £1,500,000, or 10 times its "inflation related" value. Doesn't this smell fishy to you?

Let's do it again! In 1972, the same Lady bought another house[8] for £30,000, in London. Again, compounded CPI inflation tells us that it should be worth around £380,000 today. But the house is now worth... a whopping £6,500,000. Now, that's 17 times more than its "inflation related" value. I can accept that the current owners have improved the house, modernised the electricity, the plumbing, added more bathrooms and toilets, but surely not at a cost of over £6,000,000!

In the end, we've got to admit that there's something just not right with these numbers...

- A house which should be worth around £150,000 according to CPI inflation measure is in fact worth £1,500,000 (a factor of 10 over 53 years).

---

[6] From https://www.standard.co.uk/lifestyle/london-life/margaret-thatcher-and-her-property-ladder-8576063.html
[7] From https://www.bankofengland.co.uk/monetary-policy/inflation/inflation-calculator
[8] From https://www.standard.co.uk/lifestyle/london-life/margaret-thatcher-and-her-property-ladder-8576063.html

- A house which should be worth £380,000 by the same CPI measure is now worth £6,500,000 (a factor of 17 over 46 years).

The invisible man is back, and he is shifting value (stealing or giving, depending on which way you look at it) at a faster pace, way beyond official inflationary pressure.

When I look at the astonishing facts of French CPI inflation being more than ×1,000 over one hundred years, then of house inflation being 10, 20, or even 40 times more than CPI, leading to totally unreasonable and seemingly unexplained price explosions, I can only ask myself these fundamental questions:

- What is money?
- What is the value of money?
- Can I trust money?
- Can I trust something else better than money?
- Who is pocketing the difference in value?
- Why is this so?

Step 4: foundations are due a reset

For a good part of my younger life, I thought that money represented a fair and real measure of compensation for my work and effort. I could then exchange money, either now or in the future, for some products which I could then consume, or for someone else's effort spent for my benefit, or against larger spending such as a house.

This belief assumes two fundamental principles: fairness and trust.
- Fairness: the monetary value I receive is a fair measure of my effort and skill.
- Trust: what I received today can be used later in time without much prejudice.

Do you share the same belief? I would not be surprised if most people on this planet do. For all of us, money is engraved in our mind as a true representation of value, on the same line as a unit of measurement, like you measure distance, volume, heat or decibel.

Well, I have some very bad news. You, me, and most of the people in the world are born and educated to be suckers! We are naïve in the extreme. I will give you a hint…

The bucket measuring a pint of milk does not give a different value if you change country, go back in time, or fast forward into the future. One pint will always be one pint, and the bucket can be trusted. But the tool measuring wealth will indicate that for one unit (Euro, Dollar, Sterling or any other), you can buy a farm in a certain location at a certain point in time, whereas at the same place but another time, the same one unit only buys you a pot of honey.

We must accept that we cannot place much trust in the bucket that measures wealth.

Let's review for a moment what money really is. Let's try to understand how and why we came up with our current monetary system.

Let's find this invisible man and make friends with him. Only then, when we have a better understanding, can we start playing the game with a more than 50/50 chance of winning.

Let's embark on the journey!

2

Foundations – money

Money's too tight to mention

Simply Red

So, you still think you know what money is?

The next few steps are slightly romanticised for entertainment purposes, but still very close to what really happened. After this, we jump into the hard facts of money in modern times. This is where you are in for a surprise.

My friend, money is not what you think it is…

Step 5: the invention of coins

Way back in time, around 5,000 years ago, another of my ancestors was roaming the great plains of land-with-no-name-and-no-lord with his tribe, collecting fruit, and hunting small animals.

One day, my great-grand-tribe came in contact with another one, who had a special delicacy never seen before: honey. At first, it was offered as a welcoming present. A special treat for special guests. But, as my ancestor's tribe started to appreciate this mysterious honey, they debated and haggled until it was settled that one hare was happily exchanged for 4 pots of honey.

Both tribes were satisfied with this transaction. They both found the exchange of value was fair, and trusted that the hare was recently killed, and honey tasted as good as the first time.

Barter was born, by necessity and through the establishment of trust.

As centuries passed by, small tribes started to settle together. Dozens of individuals, then hundreds, and progressively even a few thousands gathered together to form villages and towns. This allowed a more predictable and secure life, and therefore the interest of the individual was better served in the community.

But bartering was reaching its limits. It was failing to satisfy the wants and needs of so many people every day as they were trying to exchange goods which were either perishable, or not available at certain times of year. Another form of exchange was required. One which would be easy to use, and easy to recognise and trust.

Physical coins, made of metal, appeared to fit the job description. They had the right attributes for what was going to become money:
- Portability: a high value in a small volume makes it easy to transport, store, or hide.
- Durability: not perishable, not easy to destroy, acts as a good store of value.

- Rarity: not so easy to fake or find, only available in limited supply.
- Divisibility: small coins can be melted into a bigger coin, which in turn can be melted again into the same original small coins.
- Uniformity: coins are easy to recognise, and a mental value can be associated to each variety.
- Acceptability: the honey guy, the hare guy, and all other guys in town will readily accept it against any other guy's goods or services.

Now we can exchange the hare for a few coins, and later when needed, exchange some of the coins for honey.

Indeed, the invention of coins is the invention of money!

From this point onwards, and until now, this invented money serves two purposes:

- A means of exchange: you and I work to exchange our time against money, which we then exchange again for necessities (hare, honey, or other useful goods or services).
- A means of storing wealth: we can also accumulate capital (here coins) to use it later either for investment purposes or for enjoying the sweet things in life.

It is very important to make the mental difference between both these purposes at this very early stage:

- Either working for money for the present life necessities.
- Or accumulating money for either investing and acquiring other assets, or for securing a lifestyle in older age.

Step 6: the invention of notes

Around 4,000 years ago, all was good and well in the little city of Mesopotamia. The invention of coins made of metal had a positive impact on most people.

Now, of course, a few people started to collect a bit more coins than others. Also, for all those who had discovered the benefits of agriculture, the reward came mostly all at once by the end of summer, whereas one needs money throughout the year.

At that time, those who enjoyed a better education and greater wealth were the priests. And the priests started to store their coins of copper, silver, or gold in their temples, where it was assumed that no common man, woman or child would venture and steal coins, as God would surely inflict unto them a disproportionate eternal punishment!

By the end of the summer, the farmer sells his fruits and veggies and receives too many coins in relation to his short-term needs. Hiding them is a risk not worth taking. The farmer talks about his problem to the priest, and the educated priest, in his wisdom, finds the solution.

```
"Farmer, you just have to give me your coins. They
will be safe in the temple. If you give me 16 coins, I
will give you a receipt for 10, a receipt for 5, and a
receipt for 1. When you need some coins, give me back
one of your receipts, and I will give you back as many
                coins as written on it."
```

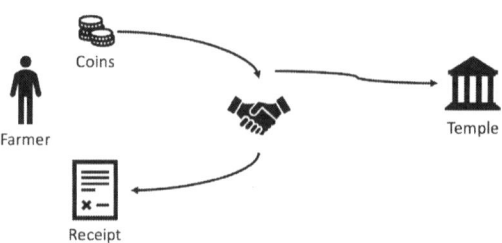

Fig 6.1 Farmer stores coins at temple

The farmer cannot be happier. His coins are safe, and he can draw them back as he needs to. The farmer also soon realises that he can pay someone with a receipt, instead of having to collect the coins at the temple himself, and then pay with the coins. The payees will collect the coins at the temple with the receipts themselves.

Without anybody really noticing, the priest has just created his own little bank, and is issuing his own bank notes (the hand-written receipts). Still, the priest is a good man, and the cumulated value of all bank notes is an exact match with the cumulated value of all coins which belong to others and are stored in the temple.

Money, as coin or as receipt, has become a trust-worthy measure of anybody's wealth in the city.

Step 7: the invention of loans

So, the year goes by, and the farmer pays with receipts and draws coins, week after week. Until that day when, well, he has no coin and no receipt anymore. The last coin is spent. However, the next harvest will arrive very soon. In just two months. So, the farmer pleads with the priest.

```
"I will pay you very soon with all these coins that I
am about to receive, but I really need a few of your
        coins today to get by for a few more weeks."
```

As it happens, the priest has collected coins from many other people in the little city. He's not really short of coins in the temple…

```
         "Hummm… should we help this farmer?

He is a good man. He works hard. I will make sure he
understands that if he does not pay me back, God will
       not only punish him for eternity, but also all
                descendants for 100 generations.

               That should make it safe enough."
```

The generous priest gives a coin to the farmer and this time, he keeps a receipt where he writes: "farmer owes temple one coin".

After a few other villagers hear about this (free money at the Temple?), the priest starts to find himself in the business of loans. And as he quickly learns, issuing loans is risky business. Risk to him if those people do not repay in time, die before being rich enough, or encounter any of the other hazards that mother nature throws at the mere mortals every now and then.

That little favour to the farmer is getting out of control… So, the priest starts recruiting disciples, who will worship God, build and maintain more temples, and keep track of all those loans and deposits. With their help, the Priest-Bank-Manager signs all receipts, which from now on, we will call notes. He sets his basic principle as follows:

Out of the Rat Race

For all incoming coins: keep receipts of the deposit by the depositor in a ledger at the temple + give the depositor signed notes of equivalent value.

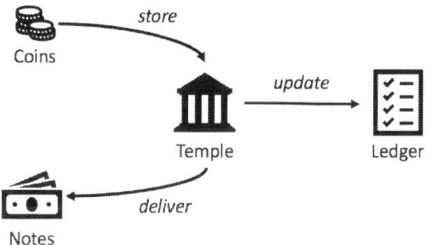

Fig 7.1 Incoming coins

For all incoming signed notes: keep the signed note at the temple (to reuse when a new depositor comes) + give back the equivalent amount of coins + update the ledger.

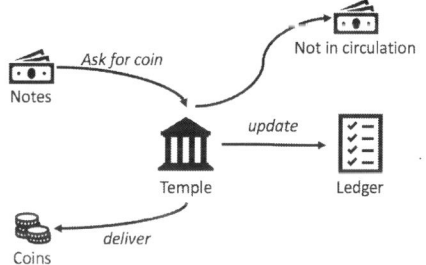

Fig 7.2 Incoming notes

For all incoming pleas for coins: assess risk, and if OK with the risk, keep the receipt of the loan at the temple + ask the loanee to sign a debt contract + give the loanee the equivalent value in coins.

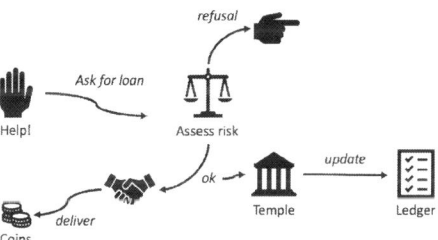

Fig 7.3 Assessing loans

Chasing debt: the priest has the good fortune of seeing everybody at the place of worship on very regular basis, so he makes it a habit to chase debt repayments every week.

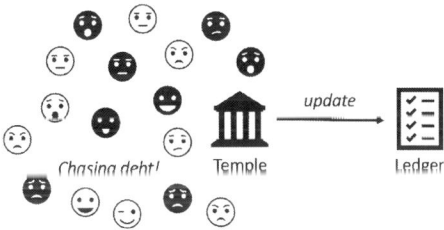

Fig 7.4 Chasing debt

The loans in circulation cannot be of greater value than the amount of coins in the temple. If there are no more coins in the temple, the priest cannot issue any new loans. However, the coins in the temple don't all belong to the priest. Remember, they were deposited by all those who had a surplus. It would be bad for the priest's reputation if a villager came to redeem a note and the temple was empty at the time of such request. Therefore, a wise and risk averse priest would add a rule to never accept a new loan if the amount of debt in circulation (i.e. the value of all cumulated loans listed in the temple) is greater than, for example, the amount of coins at disposal in the temple. In other words, in this example, the priest keeps at least a 50% reserve to swap coins for notes, to whomever wants their coins back.

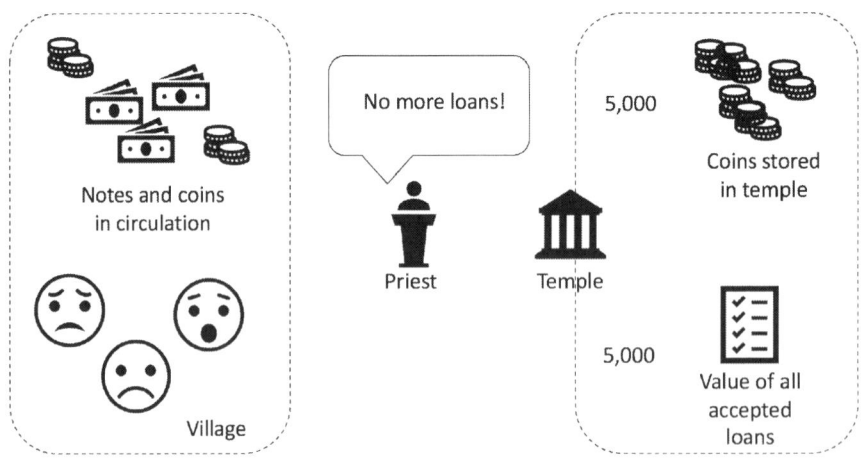

Fig 7.5 Controlling risk when emitting new loans

An even wiser priest could add rules such as, when operating above 90% reserve, the risk assessment on issuing the loan is minimal, if in the range 75-90% reserve, the conditions gets stricter, and if in the range 50-75%, it has to be exceptional circumstances for the loan to be accepted.

So long as the pressure is kept up for repayments to be made on time (God's threat over the next 100 generations), and so long as our Mesopotamian priest keeps on top of risks and holds a healthy reserve, these short-term loans are a good thing for the community, helping those villagers finding themselves in momentary need.

Step 8: the invention of tax

Mesopotamia was destroyed by a King who had an army strong enough to eradicate it. The King took all the coins, melted them and re-issued his own. He then paid his army with these new coins. In turn, the warriors bought goods with the coins, which ended in circulation in a far larger territory than their small city of origin.

King after King, war after war, more coins were amassed, melted again, circulated again through the warriors needs and wants.

But wars are costly. Even more when a battle is lost. As a result, to finance their ever-expanding quest, the Emperors and Kings invented a legal way of recapturing those silver and gold coins.

They called it taxo[9].

At the time of Julius Caesar, an inheritance "taxo" was collected throughout the whole Roman Empire to fund the military. In addition, a sales "taxo" was collected, to fund his growing "administration". Of course, more taxes were invented and enforced over the centuries which followed. For its own prosperity and survival, an evolving and expanding society will always have needs which can only be funded by plundering others. That leaves very little choice: either declaring war on neighbouring but independent tribes or states, or collecting taxes on its population.

At its origin, taxation could have appeared as open day theft, like a powerful bully taking part possession of your hard-earned coins hidden under your mattress. Indeed it was, and still is, forcefully imposed by a powerful authority, against which ordinary citizens are rather powerless. As communities of people got more organised, and as the control and collection of tax got exercised by powerful administrations backed by laws, tax got more entrenched in people's ordinary life. To the point that it has progressively been turned into a citizen's moral duty to benefit higher social objectives.

---

[9] Yes, we are now talking about Tax…

Still, as good or as bad as it can be perceived, tax on its own does not remove trust from the monetary system. Whether it belongs to me or to the King, a silver coin is still a silver coin, and has the same buying power.

Step 9: the invention of inflation

But taxes were not enough. And they were too much "in your face" of the people they were collected from. The Kings and Emperors had to find another way of collecting money and financing their wars. Necessity being the mother of invention, they soon found a way…

The first coins issued had a very large amount of intrinsic value. By this, I mean that a 5 Gram coin of gold, had 5 grams of gold in it. Same for silver coins. The coin's value was directly derived from the weight of the precious metal it contained. That sounds a pretty good idea to have linked the value of the coin to the value of the precious metal it contained. Since Mesopotamia, commerce had thrived thanks to this assumption.

As the powerful state extended further across new lands and seas, it had no other choice but to issue many more coins. It needed to pay for so many more soldiers, and circulate the coins to so many more people, at the far reaches of its empire. The state required the establishment of a seemingly rich economy, where everybody had a share of the empire's generated wealth. All these new coins could not be made out of the gold and silver acquired by painful excavation or wars. There was simply not enough gold and silver to put in the hands of such a large population.

If Julius Caesar found tax to be an interesting proposition, another Emperor got another idea: introducing new silver coins, similar in shape and size to the ones in current circulation, however made with slightly less silver. With time, more wars, more financial needs, and more uncertainties, the debasement of the silver coins continued until the point where a silver coin, initially containing at least 98% silver, was made two centuries later of only 2% silver. But why stop there? Indeed, silver coins soon stopped containing any silver at all!

I believe debasement is the right word from the point of view of the authority emitting the coin, hoping that nobody notices. But from the People's point of view, once they notice, the consequence of debasement is inflation. The coin in your hand, this trusted measure of your wealth, does not seem quite as trustworthy as the one you had in your hand a year ago, a month ago, or a day ago.

Because today's coin is not the same as yesterday's coin (let's say it suddenly has 10% less silver in it), the first user of the new coin, in general a person or an organisation of power, will buy goods from someone else, cheaper (here 10% cheaper). This is the point where the original theft happens, but not too many people noticed. As time passes and new coins replace old coins in the economy, some merchants figure out the value in silver they are paid is less than they used to get, and therefore slowly increase the price of their goods to compensate for the loss of silver. The issuing of the new coins has created inflation. At last, the common people start to notice. They are paying a little more every day to compensate for the unhappy first recipients of the new coins, who want their 10% back.

With inflation, for the first time, trust is broken. What used to be our trusted measure of wealth, our Holy Bucket, has now become just a holey bucket: a bucket with a hole in it.

With inflation, money is not the same. Money today is not the same as money yesterday. It is imperceptible. We all act as if it is the same, because frankly we do not want to worry about one more thing we can neither control nor vividly perceive. But it is not the same, and it will never be the same again.

Trust has been broken.

Step 10: the invention of interest

Back in Mesopotamia, our priest was giving out loans to help citizens in need, and was doing it with restraint, and not for profit. However, an unintended consequence was the increase of the supply of money in the city's economy, as loans were granted, and then the corresponding decrease as the loans were repaid.

Let's say that the whole city had 1 million identical silver coins, and 10% of these coins were deposited to the temple by savers. As a consequence, the temple had 100,000 coins safely stored, which were not for use. They could only be redeemed against the equivalent 100,000 notes in circulation. In summary, the city's economy ran with 900,000 coins, and 100,000 notes. This is the same value than the original 1 million silver coins.

Now, a poor lad begs the priest and asks for 100 coins. After due diligence and risk assessment, the priest agrees to give the 100 coins, against a promise to repay the debt. The new situation is: there are 99,900 coins safely stored not for use, the same 100,000 notes in circulation, but now 900,100 coins in circulation too. The total value of the city's economy has just been inflated by 0.01%.

Repay the loan, and we are back as before. If the priest permanently lends around 15% of the coins deposited, that amounts to 15,000 worth of loan, or in our example, 1.5% inflation. It looks marginal, and indeed, probably nobody will notice. However, businessmen do not necessarily come with the same restraints.

In the middle ages, Religion was still bigger than States. Your city could possibly be destroyed, your nation be taken over, but your God would still exist until the last surviving worshipper. Over long periods of time, all religions have defined many life principles. For example, in explaining good vs evil, they defined their expectations of good behaviour, which have been passed over many centuries from generation to generation, in powerful stories. One such common exert is made of many variations on the theme: "you shall not lend with interest". As a consequence, interest bearing loans were not a very common practise of lenders back then.

However, as trades expanded further, between people of different origins, different nations, and ultimately different religions, there came a point when some travelling merchants got teased and deviated slightly from the original principle.

> "Lending without interest to people of my country and my religion is fine. But I have journeyed so long into this remote country. Look at these people around. They know nothing about my god. They have their own god which I know nothing of. Surely, I can lend to them with interest, and not be damned!"

That's it!

A few traders become lenders, and a few lenders lend with interest. The practise becomes more and more common place, and some religions start to accept that they had better accommodate with the changing nature of human life, and "legislate" that... maybe the interpretation of the text... after all...

It is OK to lend with interest!

Let's visit a fictitious remote village, which has 100 families, and 10,000 silver coins, all of same size and value. We can picture the economy of the self-sufficient village. On average, each family has 100 coins, and uses the coins to buy or sell stuff to others.

A merchant-banker discovers the village. He arrives with 1,000 coins of similar value to those of the villager's coins, as well as loads and loads of pots of honey to sell. He sells one pot for 1 coin, or three pots for 2 coins, but he is willing to lend the extra coin to those buying the three pots.[10]

It's a big success. The transaction looks as follows:

---

[10] You already guessed that it costs him less than one coin to produce, store and transport the three pots, but that's by the by...

Out of the Rat Race 25

- A villager gives 1 coin to the merchant for buying one pot of honey.

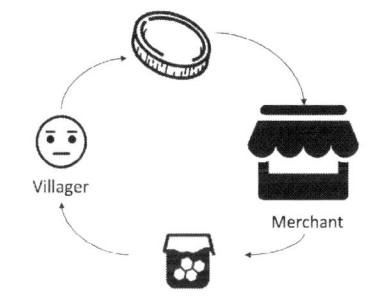

Fig 10.1 Villager buys one pot of honey with one coin

- The merchant lends one coin to the villager, at 1% interest per month, and secures the deal with a right to own some properties of the villager if the coin is not repaid in full and with interest, within 6 months. The villager signs the agreement and gets the coin from the merchant.

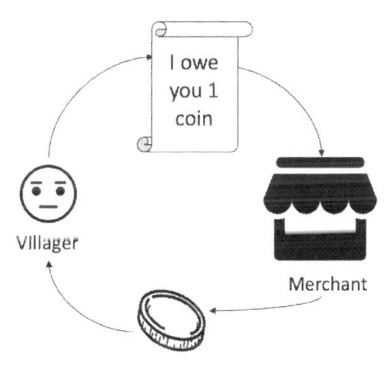

Fig 10.2 Merchant lends one coin to villager

- The villager gives back the lent coin to the merchant in exchange for two more pots of honey.

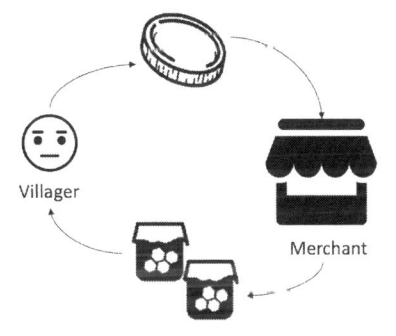

Fig 10.3 Villagers buys two pots of honey with one more coin

The merchant now has:
- Three less pots of honey.
- One new coin.
- A promise to receive another coin within 6 months or earlier.
- A promise to receive 1% of a coin's value for each month passing with the promised coin not yet paid back.

And the villager has:
- One less coin (the original village's coin).
- Three pots of honey.
- A debt of one coin to pay back to the merchant.
- Another debt of 1% of a coin in interest per month, to the merchant, for each month that goes by and the loaned coin is still not repaid.

The merchant plans to come back every month to settle the debt and sell more honey.

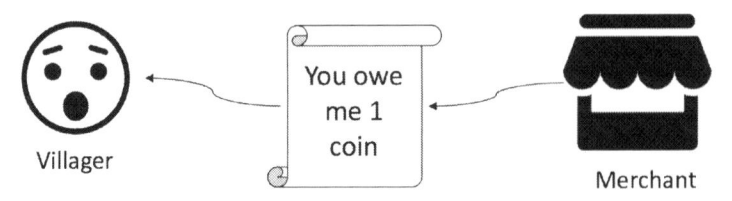

Fig 10.4 Merchant asks for debt settlement

As months go by, and as more pots of honey are bought by packs of three, the village's economy gets depleted. The honey was delicious, but the original village coins are getting spent, and the debt must be settled.

The villagers have the following options:
1. Sell goods to people in other villages in exchange of their people's coins.

2. Default on the debt and see their possessions being taken away by the merchant.
3. Dig into the earth, find metal, melt it, and make new coins.
4. Pillage nearby villages and steal their silver and gold.

Option 4 may have been very tempting back then, but even in our fictitious village, it is likely that most villagers would fear god to the point of acting decently and would therefore choose option 1.

> "Let's work and sell our hours and stuff we produce!"

And so they work, bring home more coins, and pay back the debt.

After a few years of being in the honey-loan business in this little village, the merchant has accumulated promises for over 5,000 coins that are still owed to him. These coins earn him 1% per month, so that is 50 new coins per month. And perhaps there are 9 other villages around too... We are now speeding towards 500 coins a month. Not from the sale of honey, but from the sale of loan contracts bearing interest. It's not so important that these loans helped buy honey, as they could have been issued to buy anything else the merchant had in store.

As we saw in this example, the merchant was never really in the honey business, but more in the very lucrative "loan with interest" business.

Let's pause for a moment. It is important to note that interest do not only come from loans. They can also take the form of dividends or rents which get regularly extracted from a capital working for you. What is interesting to distinguish, even at this early stage, is the merchant's two sources of income: working for income (selling pots of honey) vs getting a passive income (the interest on the loan).

Clever guy!

Finally, let's remind ourselves about the effect of inflation. The coins the merchant will receive in 6 months may not have the same value as the coins he lent today. And the merchant has no idea when the King is going to debase the coinage. The merchant might earn a 6% return within 6 months, but the inflation rate could be 10% in the same 6 months.

The lesson is this one: interest is powerful and seems like free money to the lender, however the real question is:

```
Who has the better deal after inflation?
```

We will have to remember this. In our world, sometimes there is free money on offer.

But not that many people take advantage of it.

Step 11: the invention of banks

As time passed, the inhabitants of the villages, towns, and cities progressively feared their Gods less. As a consequence, the temples slowly stopped being such a safe place to store gold and silver. The priests moved back to their monasteries and churches, and in exchange, we got Goldsmiths. Not just the metal worker goldsmith, but more like the secure-storage-banker type of goldsmith.

Goldsmiths had a tendency to be slightly more business oriented than priests. And in their world, 1+1 is not merely 2. It can be a lot more!

Like the priest in the temple, the goldsmith has lots of silver and gold at his disposal. The coins have been deposited by savers, who in exchange got their banknotes, which can be redeemed later and exchanged against the same original value in coins. Nothing new. Like the priest, some of the stored coins can be lent to others in need, provided a good check on the borrower. Now, unlike the priest, the goldsmith wants his risk covered by more income, and the past is a good indication that lending with interest is a good practice for the lender.

At this stage, the goldsmith issues banknotes to savers, and lends coins to borrowers with interest on top. More and more of these savers-borrowers' dance, and the goldsmith sees that there are coins which never leave the safe. Savers tend to pay more and more with banknotes, and never redeem them against coins. The goldsmith wonders...

> "These unused coins could be lent to generate more interest."

After having loosened the lending criteria, there comes a point when the last coin is lent. Interest payments are flowing in.

And now what?

If savers are feeling happy enough to pay their wants and needs with banknotes, why would it not be the same for borrowers? Why not give borrowers a banknote, instead of a coin? And ask for interest on the loaned banknote? And at the same time, why not repatriate as many coins as possible back into our safe, against our banknotes?

At this point, we will call the goldsmith a banker. Because clearly, the guy is not in the business of melting gold, or safely storing coins, but more in the business of printing paper, and collecting interest on the newly printed notes.

So, here is the short formula for starting a bank, way back then:
- Find a goldsmith with a good reputation.
- Find enough savers who feel secure enough to deposit their coins in the goldsmith's safe, against his promise to give them back the coins on demand at any time.
- Make sure those savers asking for their money back are happy to get banknotes instead of their original coins.
- Make sure borrowers are happy to borrow banknotes on the spot against a debt payable in the future and interest on the outstanding debt.
- Allow the goldsmith to issue as many banknotes as he is comfortable with. It could be five times the value of coins in his safe, it could be ten times, or more. It all depends on his appetite for risk.

From this point onward, the main problem for our banker is not finding savers or borrowers. With a bit of a reputation built-up, there will be many people willing to save and borrow. No, the problem is more fundamental, and inseparable from the way he operates, at the heart of which is the promise to return a saver's funds at any time and on demand. Our banker has to balance the risk of a large number of savers coming back in a rush and asking for their original coins. This is because at this stage of operating as a bank, the value of all bank notes in circulation is vastly greater than the value of the coins he holds in deposit. Yes, our banker printed paper money out of thin air. Sometimes, 1+1=5, 10, or more...

For a nation, even a century or more ago, the risk of a bank run was never something that those in power were happy to entertain. Somehow, they needed to control the big banks, the ones which could cause havoc if they were to fail. Therefore, each nation seeing commercial banks popping up in street corners had to start thinking about limiting risks by regulating and policing their nascent financial sector. They had merely two choices: either slowly create their own central bank, or nationalise a large bank to this effect. Then, it was up to those central bankers to establish the rules that would still allow the bankers to defy arithmetic, but within a degree of restraint.

One such happy rule is called Fractional Reserve Banking. This is where money is not the same money anymore.

Tax? Inflation? Interest? Nah... this one is not just about making a bigger hole in the wealth measuring bucket. We are about to discover a siphon...

If you still think you know what money is, sit down and read on!

Step 12: the invention of credit

My grand-parents came into this world just before World War I. As they grew into adulthood, they grasped the basic concepts of money which were inherited from the past centuries. You needed to find yourself useful to somebody else, to exchange your time against coins or notes. You could save your money, under your mattress or in a hole, or if you had too much for comfort, you would go to town to deposit the money on your bank account. Once a year, you paid taxes, and once in a while, you would find that your hard-earned money did not buy as much as it used to. When you wanted to buy a farm, you had two choices:

1. You could work for 5 or 10 years and save your money under your mattress. As you were saving towards your goal, there was always the risk of a war or something that could generate 50% inflation or more[11], and within a couple of years, you could lose nearly everything you had saved, and you had to start again.

or...

2. You could ask for credit.

Like most in their generation, my grand-parents thought credit was bad, on the basis that it was debt to be repaid later. Nobody in their right mind wants to be burdened by debt. We all understand instinctively that debt means adding a burden on your future self. However, if in your family someone worked for a few decades and had nothing to show for it, apart from buckets of worthless devalued bank notes, one can hope that a lesson would be learned.

```
"Never store the cash under the mattress ever again."
```

The new mantra becomes: if you have cash, invest it, if you do not have cash, ask for credit.

---

[11] After the war, inflation in France was 29.2% in 1918, then 22.6% in 1919 and 39.5% in 1920.

Rampant inflation, devaluation, and other similar inflicted pains forced past generations to adopt credit and accept it as the best of two evils. Today, it is unthinkable to buy a property without a mortgage. Therefore, we all ask for credit.

```
"But what is credit?"
```

Let's start by introducing two types of money. We have money that has, let's say, a physical representation: coins, bank notes, precious metal… And we have the other money: credit.

Early on, when my grand-parents were paid a salary, or were buying goods, they were using physical money. Then, commercial banks introduced credit, and slowly but surely, they flooded the economy with credit money. To the point where nobody knows the difference. My credit becomes your physical money, and nobody minds.

In truth, credit cannot be the same as money. It is just a promise to repay a debt. A promise from you to repay your bank in accordance with the conditions of your mortgage. The bank gives a big number on your behalf to another person (the seller of the house you are buying), you add your signature at the bottom of a mortgage contract, and the same big number appears now in negative value onto another bank account of yours (your mortgage account).

This is a big turning point. I am afraid that you will not become financially free, until you understand well this credit money. And to do that, we first need to dig into fractional banking, and then into the world of central banks.

Step 13: fractional banking

Fractional banking is very similar to how our goldsmith-banker was operating, but a tiny bit more regulated. A commercial bank holds in reserve a fraction of the total amount of deposit it receives from savers. To start with, let's make the simple assumption that the bank knows from history that on average, its clients never ask for more than 10% of the total deposited amounts. As a consequence, the bank decides that it can keep 10% of cash deposits in its safe to satisfy incoming customers and use the remaining 90% to offer loans.

A quick example shows the money creation inferred by this simple rule.

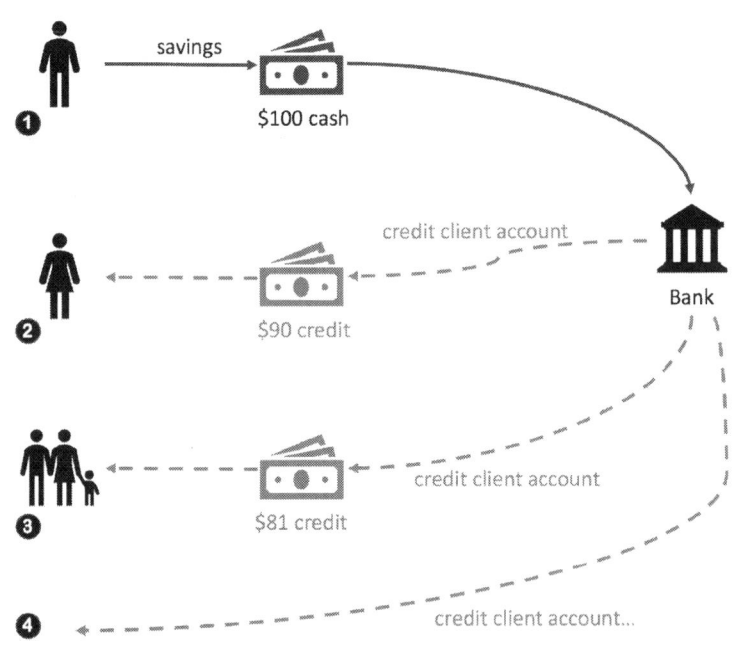

Fig 13.1 Creation of credit under fractional banking

If a customer deposits $100 cash at the bank, the bank can then decide to lend $90 to another person. Now, the other person needs a bank account to receive this $90 credit money. Let's open the account in the same bank, so that our bank sends the $90 and receives it on its new customer account. Now the bank keeps again 10% in reserve (that's $9) and loans $81 to another customer. We do this until the last dollar, and what we get is that from an initial $100 cash deposit, the bank kept a $10 reserve, and created $900[12] of new credit money which got deposited on its many other customers' accounts. In short, they just created credit money up to 90 times the initial reserve, or 9 times the initial deposit.

At this stage, my hope is that we have acquired enough background on financial practises over the past millennia and centuries to dismiss the otherwise very natural idea, that the mortgage money you get from your bank comes directly from the money deposited by another person into the same bank. No, we are not at the temple anymore...

In a fractional banking world under the supervision of a Central Bank, a commercial bank deposits physical money at its Central Bank, in exchange of a right to issue credit at will, proportionally to its deposit. The Central Bank defines a reserve requirement to allow the friendly bank to create x times more credit money than they had physical money in the first place.

Let's say that a very successful commercial bank has one billion US Dollars in deposit from its customers, and its Central Bank has set a reserve ratio of 10%[13]. As you would expect, the commercial bank sends 10% of their deposit to their temple, the Central Bank.

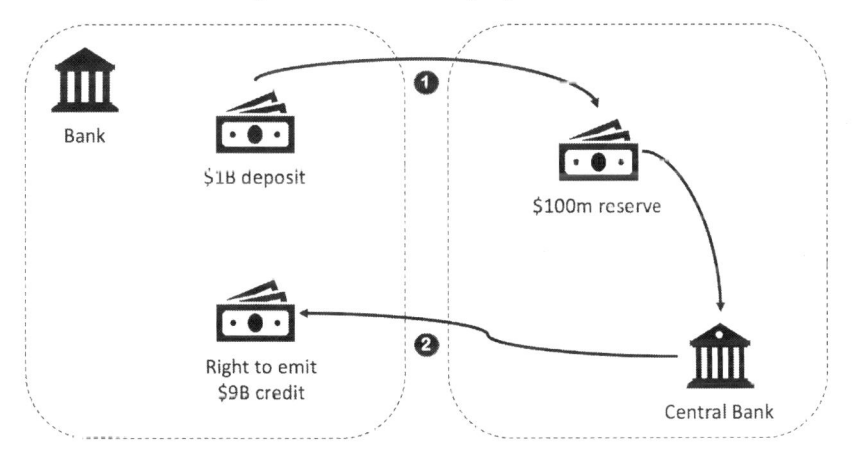

Fig 13.2 Fractional banking under a Central Bank

---

[12] $90 + $81 + $72.90 + $65.61 + $59.05 + ... which in the end makes $900
[13] A reserve ratio of 10% is actually the requirement of the US central bank for its largest commercial banks, although smaller banks can have a reserve ratio of only 3%

The Central Bank stores the $100m of physical silver, gold, coins, bank notes and other valuable sweeties, and in exchange, allows the depositing bank to issue credit, which in our case happens to be the same ratio as in our previous example. From its $100m reserve deposit, the commercial bank has the power to create $9b of new credit money.

But it can only create credit when a customer comes to ask for it.

We need a simplistic example to see how this works in practise. Your friend Joe is considering buying a house.

1. The bank accepts a loan of $500,000, with various conditions of duration, interest, loan to value and more... At the date of signature, the bank creates[14] $500,000 of new money and writes it as:
   - a liability for Joe (who will repay slowly over time, plus interest).
   - an asset for themselves (the loan is the bank's asset).

2. But Joe does not buy the house from no-one... He pays the $500,000 to the seller, Susie, who bought the house 10 years ago.

3. Let's say that Susie made a nice profit on the transaction. For example, after the successful sale transaction, Susie:
   - paid $50,000 in fees and taxes.
   - repaid her $200,000 mortgage.
   - saved the remaining net profit of $250,000 at her bank.

Thereafter is the complete transaction, starting from the bank issuing the new credit, and ending with the bank receiving the past debt repayment and the new savings.

To simplify matters, we made Joe's and Susie's bank the same.

---

[14] I would love to write it differently, but there is no other word... it "creates" the new money into existence, and this new money is also a promise to repay later.

Out of the Rat Race 37

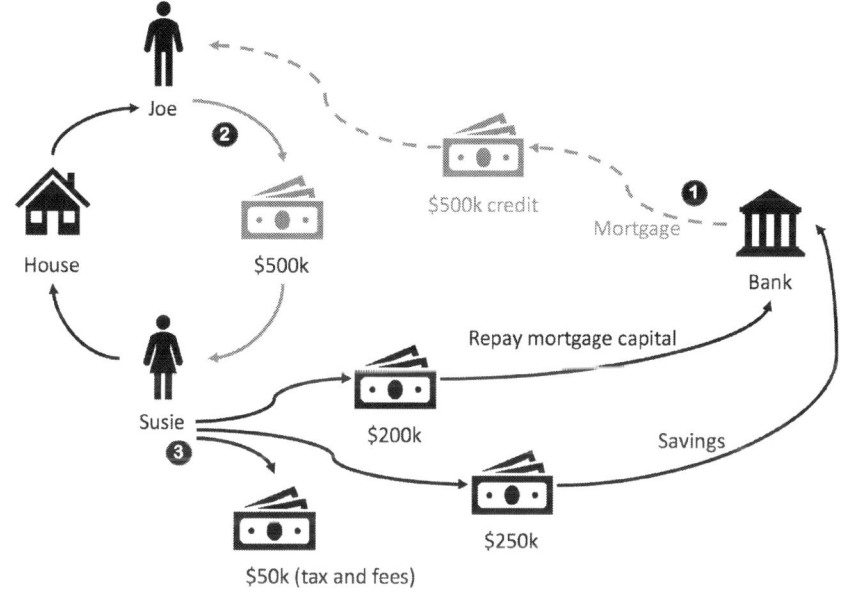

Fig 13.3 Money creation when a property is acquired

Let me tell you right now that this picture smells dead fish from a good distance! In truth, Joe's credit becomes Susie's money and nobody minds...

Look at the same transaction from the point of view of the bank.

1. They offered a $200,000 mortgage to Susie a long time ago.
2. They just offered a $500,000 mortgage to Joe.
3. Susie transferred $450,000 to the bank, split in $200,000 repayment of the loan and $250,000 saving.

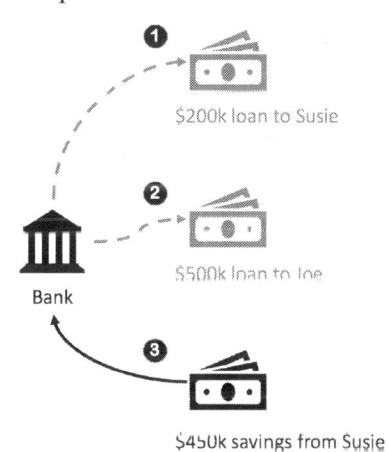

Fig 13.4 A view from the bank

The $200,000 credit that the bank created a decade ago must now disappear (poof!) as Susie repays the capital. But, as luck would have it, this $200,000 crunch is compensated by $500,000 new credit money (Joe's debt) and $250,000 of recycled money (Susie's profit), which now sits in her bank account.

The bank will place again 10% of the sum with the Central Bank (the bank assumes that surely Susie will not spend it all now), and in exchange, they gain a right to create an extra $250,000 x 10% x 90 = $2,250,000 of new credit money[15]. Not too bad a transaction! Of course, Susie could also use 20% of her profit as a deposit, take a new mortgage of $500,000 as well, and consequently contribute to another merry-go-round of new money creation. Loop ad infinitum...

When I think of credit money, my head gets dizzy. Within certain constraints set by its Central Bank, a commercial bank can create new credit money pretty much as they please, or more exactly, as they can find customers (savings and loans) and keep on top of their risk. This new credit money will disappear again when the loan is paid back, so from this point of view, it is rather neutral. However, three more incidental things happen:

1. The credit money generates monthly interest which stays with the bank (their payback in very real money)

2. The very inflationary nature of this process means that apart from during rare and brutal crisis events, this money creation, mostly used for financing real estate assets, grows rather exponentially

3. When inflation, time, and other magic tricks have done their job, the seller of the mortgaged property makes a profit, which now becomes real money (the credit of the buyer partly turns into real money for the seller)

The last point is the most significant. It feels like pure alchemy, so I need to repeat. The bank creates new money from nowhere-land (or Central Bank Land if you prefer), lends it to a buyer, who pays you, to acquire your property, and the credit money the buyer received becomes new real money to you, after you have repaid your mortgage,

---

[15] The same 90 multiplier on 10% reserve on deposit, as we saw earlier.

taxes and fees. You then recycle this real money in the system by buying goods, properties, or making other investments. It is in the utmost interest of your bank that more money gets created this way, that the Lady's property gets so vastly overvalued, way beyond normal inflation, because it transforms temporary credit money into new forever real money, that the bank can leverage again.

Oh, let me write this again!

```
"It transforms temporary credit money into new
forever real money that the bank can leverage again"
```

Now, can you start spotting our invisible man in the shadow of the Central Bank's leveraging system? Do you feel dizzy too?

But we are just getting started! The last half century of human financial invention and intervention did not stop with the invention of credit.

There is more dead fish perfume ahead!

Step 14: and money becomes trust

By the time my grand-fathers were playing with wooden sticks in the French countryside, world export and import had grown from not much at all to an estimated 25% of global world output. In itself, that's a lot of exchange and activity developing from next to nothing in just a few centuries. It required an international monetary system which could be trusted anywhere in the world, and there was nothing better suited for that than using gold. The gold standard allowed countries to settle their relative deficit and surplus through the movement of part of their gold reserves, instead of using their own currency.

World War I brought down the gold standard, and then after a collapse in world trade, a Great Depression, and another World War, world imports and exports were reduced to a mere 10% of global world output. Facing chaos, the old (U.K.) and new (U.S.) financial powers of the world gathered in 1944 to put in place a new monetary system, which required all the currencies in the world to have a rather rigid exchange rate against the world winner's currency, the US Dollar, otherwise known as USD. In exchange for this new status and the promise to keep the exchange rates very tight, the US central bank would guarantee any foreign Central Bank, the conversion of $35 cash into one ounce of gold. As a consequence, all foreign countries had a huge interest in keeping lots of USD reserves, as they could be transformed into gold at will.

The problem is that you cannot create gold out of nothing. In general, you have to dig it from far below the surface at high cost. At best, the world produces each year an extra 1% or 2% of gold, above the reserves of past centuries. After 25 years of worldwide average economic growth of 7-8%, we got to a situation where the cumulated reserves in USD from all countries except the US, has a higher value than the gold reserves, valued at $35 an ounce, held by the US central bank. Soon enough, the USD reserves held by all foreign Central Banks could be valued more than the entire gold reserves of the planet! If all countries were to ask for the settlement in gold of their USD, that would be the mother of all bank runs. Therefore, in summer 1971, the

US president in power announced to the world that the paper that once could be transformed into gold, could be transformed no longer!

As a consequence, all the currencies in the world were now worth... exactly what people thought they were worth! They could float or sink relative to the trust they conveyed.

Trust in the financial system, trust in the Central Bank, trust in your bank, trust in the tax system, trust in the economy, trust in the ruling political elite... Today's money is a leap of trust, more than ever.

That trust in the financial system may be a problem if you are a bit like me. I do not trust politicians who change their views as soon as the wind changes direction. I do not trust that my bank has my best interest at heart and will offer me a better deal each time it advertises a better offer to the market. I do not trust that the Central Bank has a complete control of all future consequences when it prints gazillions of dollars, euros, or pounds. I do not trust that the tax rules will be kept unchanged long enough for me to make a proper plan. But... these thoughts get me nowhere.

I have no other choice than to play this game.

And neither do you!

Step 15: deregulation and globalisation

By the time import/export had come back to 25% of global world output, my grand-fathers had already reached retirement age. The change in the global monetary system progressively triggered a return to globalization. In turn, it gave birth to an even bigger change in a rather boring and stable financial industry, which was mostly restricted to their country of origin, and made of three distinct sectors: commercial bankers, investments bankers, and insurers. The traditional model was known as 3-6-3, meaning that commercial bankers took deposit at 3%, lent it back at 6%, and were on the golf course at 3pm... Boring and stable.

Earlier, we encountered Lady Margaret Thatcher, who invested wisely in homes of highly appreciating value. She was a leading figure in this change, as she deregulated banking and finance in the U.K., as part of the free market revolution of the late 1970s.

As a result of these deregulations in the western world, banks grew larger and became global. In many cases today, ex local banks have grown much larger than their nation of origin. Their activities extend beyond deposits, loans, and golf, to a soup of financial activities such as acting as advisors, underwriters, insurers, traders, market-makers, and other creators of financial weapons of mass destruction, as they became known after the subprime mortgage market collapse. Another consequence of the deregulations: their ability to create money out of thin air expanded to the limit of their creativity. Instead of operating under a multiplier of savers' deposited funds, the banks can now tap into funding from the money markets, hence don't have to bother about enticing savers anymore... In good times, that pretty much removes the cap of the central bank on money printing, as they can raise zillions on the market, send 10% to the temple, and print gazillions of credit money. They also got into the fishy practise of repackaging collections of contracted mortgages to resell them as a single product on the market, to other financial institutions. Now, instead of 1+1=10 in their backyard, the largest global banks start thinking 1+1=100 on the world stage...

As we see, there is no denying that in this game, the cards are dealt by the banks. It is the role of a commercial bank to create money out of thin air, within a set of restricting parameters, and to pump it into the real economy, through credit. In good times, commercial banks pump a lot of cheap credit into the economy.

At this stage, it is good to pause and reflect for a moment. Banks issue credit. The credit of the bank is your debt. This debt is nothing more than a promise from you to repay capital and interest as per the contract signed with the bank. This promise is materialised by a new account, a mortgage account, which is created with a big negative number in it, and an equivalent amount of money that in general you will never see for more than a few seconds, as it immediately funds the acquisition of the property used as collateral of the debt.

We can feel again that somehow, the credit money of the bank, which is underpinned by the promise you made to the bank, is not like the "normal" money, which is underpinned by the promise that both the Government and the Central Bank made to you as the owner of a coin or bank note. A private promise vs a public one.

Then, when you save or invest "normal" money, the risk on this investment is either:

- to be taxed (the government's decision).
- to be eroded by inflation (the Central Bank's decision).
- or to be mal-invested (your own decision).

The risk on invested credit money however, is all of the above plus the additional risk that the private promise to repay the debt gets broken. Initially, we could see this last risk as a risk on the bank growing from two sides:

- Their assets may shrink as some past borrowers are no longer able to repay their loans anymore, so the bank has to write off the loans.
- The market may stop providing funding, and with savers wanting their money back, the deposit used to leverage the creation of new money evaporates.

When commercial banks are under such pressure, they stop issuing credit. As they stop the credit tap, or as the interest you have to pay on the loan gets too expensive (which is a bit the same as a bank can stop lending by making interest go through the roof), we start to find that the house we were ready to acquire at whatever inflated value the seller wanted is now a bit more risky, a bit more unattainable, a bit more not possible to fund with debt at current conditions. As we refrain making the big lifetime purchase, and the sellers cannot find another buyer (everyone feels the squeeze and no-one can borrow), sellers may start to experience problems repaying capital and interest on their own loans, putting more pressure on those sellers to sell their assets at a firesale price, pushing down the house price. But again, if nobody can get credit at good conditions, the house price continues to fall... until the price is low enough that somebody will find the opportunity to invest too good to pass. Or until the bank, who was initially dead certain you would repay as per the agreed conditions, now sees that you are in such financial troubles that you will probably not repay anything at all. So, they repossess your house and sell it at whatever price they can get, in compensation for your broken promise. If it happens in cascade all over the market, many people may see that the wealth they thought they had was built on shaky grounds. It evaporates fast as in fact their wealth was mostly made of other people's debt, or in other words, other people's promises.

Let me repeat it.

```
"Most assets bought on credit have a price which can
vary substantially with the market confidence in the
zillions of underpinning promises to repay their debt"
```

It is paramount to remember this:

Credit money is debt.

> Debt is a promise.

>> A promise can be broken...

>>> ...and then all Hell breaks loose.

Step 16: the alchemists

As we just saw, we live in a world where the supply of money (both real money and credit) expands and contracts, subject to many forces. And when it gets really out of control, the mother of all forces, the big economies' Central Banks, step in with their bazookas.

The Central Banks can become very inventive when faced with life or death situations. During the depression which started in 2008, wave after wave, they stepped in and they created money out of thin air under operations known as Quantitative Easing.

Take note: Central Banks do not issue credit money. Instead, as our Central Banks are the true alchemists of our modern times, they print real money. They flood their friends with real banknotes.

In the aftermath of the 2008 financial crisis, they bought financial products from banks at face value where the book value was not even half that. Through commercial banks again, they bought so much debt in their respective countries that, for example, mid-2018 five-year bonds issued by the German state cost money to the lender, instead of paying them interest[16]. When it looked like there was nothing left to buy, they financed massive loans issued by large public companies, thereby giving these companies (and their shareholders and top brass) near free money to play with. They bought everything they could find until there was nothing else to buy in their respective parts of the planet. The total of new money created is estimated at over $7 trillion.

Let's get our measuring tool here: that's $7,000,000,000,000. Yes, it's a very large hole in the money measuring bucket. To put it in perspective, in less than a decade, they printed a value equivalent to all the gold ever mined on earth since our ancestors roamed the great plains of land-with-no-name-and-no-lord. And that's not gold at $35 anymore, but at today's average of $1,300 an ounce[17]!

---

[16] Mid 2018, 5 year German bonds are paying negative interest ; it makes no sense but lenders pay to have the privilege of lending their money to Germany over 5 years.
[17] Average price of gold in USD early 2018.

In the end, here is the situation. Globalisation is very deflationary on goods we consume as it finds places where those goods can be produced cheaper than close to home. Technology and innovation are deflationary too, again on the goods we consume, as for a fixed cost, both conspire to deliver more, better, and cheaper goods. The growth in population is inflationary, both in Consumer Price Index (CPI) and in housing index, as more people chase less goods and not enough houses. And then, banks and Central Banks add their own spin within the power conferred by their greed and regulation (banks) or science and remit (Central Banks). In good times, commercial banks create credit money, which is very inflationary on most financial assets, such as property and company stocks. When a black swan moment happens, it can feel like the earth will collapse on itself, but the Central Bank heroes duly step in and repaint the whole planet with new shiny money. Over time, that is also inflationary on everything that has a price tag on this planet (goods, services, and assets).

I hope you noticed the difference of recipient (goods and services vs assets) on which inflation and deflation forces are exerted. But let me dig a bit more into the CPI before we come back to this key point.

The largest Central Banks (US, EU, UK, Japan) have a remit to keep CPI inflation in check at around 2%. The reason is, they do not want rampant inflation, and will do whatever it takes to not have deflation. Deflation is too bad for their nations and governments who need at least a moderate level of inflation to eat into the monster debt they have allowed to accumulate over the years. Indeed, all governments need inflation to continue financing, with more debt, all the promises they make to their citizens[18]. They do not want too high a level of inflation either, because it can get out of control very quickly. Extreme inflation is the best way to ruin everybody in the country. So, they will not let this happen either.

---

[18] Like the debt you take from your bank is a promise, you should also see as debt some of the promises your government make to you. A debt drawn on the future you, and on your children.

I will trust that most of the agencies calculating inflation via the Consumer Price Index method do it to the best of their knowledge and ability. However, as we saw earlier, it does not accurately represent how certain assets inflate over time.

Indeed, CPI measures how a defined average person (their persona of choice, let's call him Average Joe), is impacted by price changes on a monthly, quarterly, or yearly basis. Average Joe's spending is mostly a daily, weekly and at most, monthly spend. He spends most of his money on goods and services for basic necessities. That is why he is Average Joe, and not Billionaire Joe. He can afford to pay the basic necessities with his monthly paycheque. The same should apply to you. You do not need to take up loans to support similar spending. However, the large investments of a lifetime, typically your house, is only represented in the CPI as a very diluted monthly mortgage repayment. Average Joe's monthly mortgage repayment is not yours. In addition, it may be diluted by 23 years of other past different Average Joe's unique mortgage situations and actual repayments[19]. As a consequence, the 2% CPI does not reflect much of the house price inflation at all, and even less of the general asset class inflation.

Central Banks have a mandate to keep inflation in check at 2%. But as we now understand, the inflation they track, this CPI measure, does not reflect the price inflation of most asset classes, including real estate. However, these same asset classes are at the core of how commercial banks make money.

If a commercial bank's raison d'être is to make money by charging interest on credit, you can be sure they will want the issued credit to be as large as they possibly can. For this, they need the underlying assets, the real estate market in general, to continue growing, if possible disproportionately to the commonly accepted growth measures (GDP or CPI inflation).

---

[19] CPI calculated in UK includes housing expense such as a mortgage repayment but smooths it over 23 years which dilutes massively any variation of price in real estate. See http://doc.ukdataservice.ac.uk/doc/7022/mrdoc/pdf/7222technical_manual_2014.pdf

If at the same time, the commercial bank's master, the Central Bank, through its 2% CPI narrow mandate, turns a blind eye on how fast these underlying assets grow, and let the commercial banks issue credit money at will, we should be wise to do everything we can to get invited to the party.

Surely, we will find our invisible man dancing there.

Step 17: into debt

There is apparently $1.7 trillion of physical USD money in circulation. Whatever it means...

Well, to help you make sense of these mind-boggling numbers, have this in mind: if "one" represents one second, or just enough time for a brief passing thought, then a thousand would be more like a long TV advert, and a million like a good holiday break. Now, a trillion is more representative of an entire working life, and the quadrillion is like the entire duration of mankind since the Neanderthals disappeared.

Are we in sync? One dollar, one second, and one trillion dollars, one working life... Now, let's re-read this $1.7 trillion cash in circulation in light of the following numbers[20]:

Market	Value
Cumulated value of stocks on the US stock markets	$30 trillion
US private real estate (excluding agricultural and commercial real estate)	$32 trillion
US national debt	$20 trillion
Cumulated debt of all countries in the world	$63 trillion
Government, corporate, and personal debt worldwide [21]	$250 trillion
The derivative market [22]	$1 quadrillion

Table 17.1 Comparing physical money with other markets

As we saw earlier, the entirety of gold ever mined is close to $7 trillion at $1,300 an ounce. The gold standard as exchange of value is

---

[20] Rounded but actuals as of 2018
[21] Yours and mine are in there!
[22] The largest financial market, which nobody seems to be able to estimate properly, but slowly approaches the $1 quadrillion

long gone and would not even begin to support today's financial world. So much for gold! And cash?

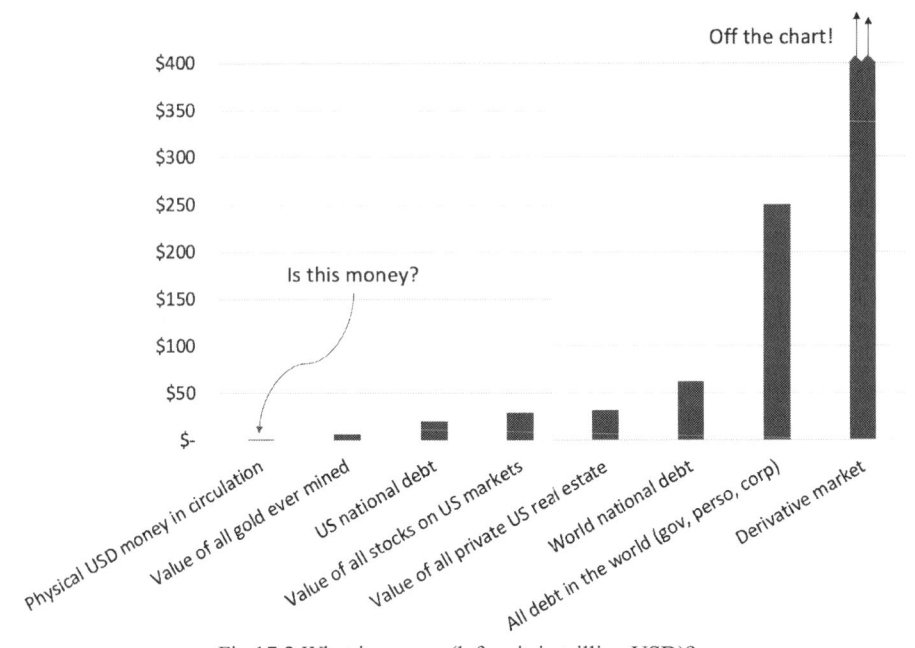

Fig 17.2 What is money (left axis in trillion USD)?

If you were still wondering what money is, I hope you can at least find in these numbers, what it is not. Money is certainly not cash or cash equivalents! Money is not backed by gold or any other physical asset.

Money is credit. Money is debt, massive amounts of debt, and therefore promises, that we cannot begin to comprehend. These promises are created faster than we can start counting what they represent. And then there is this derivative market. How shall we call this one? Bets on promises? Leveraged promises? If all the USD cash in the world is a long working life, then these leveraged promises will swallow all our common ancestors, back to the Neanderthal!

Only if and when you understand this, can you start making workable plans for being financially independent. Knowing what money is and how it works will significantly improve your chances.

In conclusion, to reach financial independence, our goal has to be the control of enough cash generating assets, so that we can live off the "real" money these assets will generate, in the form of interest, dividend, rent, or other payments. Starting from nothing, or not much, these assets can only be acquired by debt. Savings from working in normal employment will never be enough to catch up with the capital required for these investments.

As counter-intuitive as it may seem, I believe that financial independence starts by putting a bigger burden on your shoulders.

Therefore, we have two rules:

1. Get into debt.
2. Invest wisely.

3

Foundations - attitude

*And you fall, and you crawl, and you break
And you take, what you get, and you turn it into...*

Avril Lavigne

As the pace of life tends to get faster and faster, from time to time, we like to take shortcuts.

My friend, you may think you can allow yourself to skip over this chapter and take the shortcut. Of course you can, but as we lay the ground with another foundational topic, let me tell you one thing: if you do not get your life on the strongest foundations, you will pay the price later. I cannot conceive how to drive the long journey to financial independence without at the same time improve oneself as a person.

Ignore this section at your own risk.

Step 18: do not get into debt

> "what are you saying now? Two minutes ago, debt was good, and now it's bad?"

Well, there is good debt, and there is bad debt. We want to carry as much as possible of the good debt, so long as the conditions are favourable. But we do not want to touch bad debt, even with a bargepole.

The good debt is the one you contract to secure the control of an appreciating asset which, as far as your due diligence can demonstrate, can and hopefully will produce post-tax profit much in excess of the interest you pay on the debt. We will study this in more detail later.

The bad debt is pretty much anything else, such as debt that you contract to acquire a depreciating asset (a car, a computer, or anything that you know has already lost its value the minute after you bought it new and shiny), or credit that you take to finance day-to-day spending. Oh, and it would be a very bad debt if you were to contract a loan to finance your next holiday!

Not incurring bad debt is an attitude challenge. Yes, it's hard. It may sometimes feel impossible. I never said everything would be easy. We want our financial independence as early as possible, and if you are starting from nothing and nowhere, there are no two ways about it. Do not get burdened by debt that does not produce more profit than it costs. Live within your means. If it means being frugal, then you have to be frugal.

It's so long ago that I find it hard to remember when I last had a credit card. I think it's 25 years ago. There are no good reasons that I know of to exchange a peace of mind for living permanently on credit for weekly and monthly expenses. A debit card is very good. You spend what you have, not more. And just in case you need this confirmation, you shall never ever put your bank account in negative territory.

A very long time ago, at one of my first real jobs (I mean, a job which was in line with my future aspirations), I was placed on contract for a year in the IT department of a mid-size European bank. My boss there jokingly told me this:

```
"the best customer of the bank is the one who is
always overdrawn, month after month, but is just
managing to catch up and regularly pays the fees and
interest charged for his or her own negligence"
```

I am not sure if this is the profile of a good customer, but I certainly do not want to be this kind of guy. And you should not either. This is a no-go territory, with really no good reason for exception.

Now I understand that life may have thrown various curveballs at you, and you may have accumulated such "bad debt". On the very likely assumption that its interest cost is higher than inflation, you have to get rid of the bad debt as fast as you possibly can. First, if you have affordable tiny chunks of debt, pay them off now, to reward yourself and encourage your new attitude towards eradicating your debt. Then, consolidate all the rest into one single pot of debt with the lowest interest rate that you find available, but still with correct exit conditions that do not lock you up. You want the freedom to repay early without being punished for it. Finally, find ways to pay the damn debt back! Note that if you happen to have a property not mortgaged to the maximum loan to value, it may be more interesting to re-mortgage it to the maximum at a rather low rate of interest, and with the extra money, pay back as much as you can of all other debt, which may incur a higher rate of interest. That's a better way of consolidating, at least temporarily.

There is also the question of paying for education with debt. I would treat it as coldly as business investors would. You need a good and fast return on your investment in your education, otherwise it may not be worth getting so much into debt for it. Venture Capital firms want a return on their investment within five to seven years in general. Why should it be any different with your education? Make a simulation (more help about this later) to check how soon you can repay your debt after graduating. If you can demonstrate that you will pay it back within five years, go for it. If you cannot, start asking questions. If you cannot honestly prove that you will pay it back within twelve, fifteen or twenty years, I think you should not see it as education, but more as semi-educational leisure time that you agreed to burden yourself with for a good part of your future life. And then, when confronted with this reality, will you re-train for another job? That is not really efficient if you are looking for early financial independence. Of course, what I write is mean and hard to stomach, but your future life in such an indebted condition is going to be a lot more mean than my writing. If you want your financial freedom way before you are too old to enjoy it, ask yourself the right questions now!

There are many ways to get into bad debt and feel that you have a clear conscience. I think one of the worst one is the car loan. It is not because there is a car loan industry that it is fine for you to take a loan. It is not! For six years, our family managed without a car. Everybody on foot or bike! When we started to need a car, mainly because of our rental businesses, we bought the most ridiculous model[23] at a local dealer for £2,000. It then got bumped into a few years later, and the car being what it was, a cheap shit-box, we just had to write it off. The insurance paid us back more than we paid for it. We took the money and bought another one on eBay for the same amount. This second car lasted eight years, and we finally sold it for the price of its tyres. They were not fancy cars for sure, but if you need to get from A to B and cannot do it any other way, it's good enough. No car loan!

Not incurring bad debt is an attitude question. It's a way of life, and you need to be comfortable with it. Your neighbours or colleagues will show off their latest holiday on the other side of the planet, their fancy car, their whatever else that you really think you cannot afford but would like to. Keep your focus. You are planning your financial independence in ways that they probably don't. You are in a different game. Don't be jealous of their fancy stuff.

---

[23] In case you want to know… https://en.wikipedia.org/wiki/Daihatsu_Pyzar

You can be sure of one thing: you will never have enough money to buy all the fancy stuff that you don't really need. So don't even compare. Stay true to your more restrained lifestyle, and don't get into bad debt.

You are doing great!

Step 19: be a better person than you were yesterday

What has this got to do with financial independence? Well, a lot. On this journey, you are going to be pushed around quite a number of times. More often than you would like, you will have to think and define your position. You will need to find the principles which will lead you to the better path among all choices. Where do you stand? Where do you draw the line? This journey will define you more than you can imagine.

So, where do you really draw the line? For me, it goes with truth and trust. Not much else matters more. For sure, I did not know this 25 years ago.

I have learnt to know that every morning, as I wake up, the "Me" who starts going into the motion of the daily routine is a slightly different "Me" than the one who went to bed the night before. This new "Me" can build on the experience lived by yesterday's "Me" and become a tiny bit better. But I make no mistake: yesterday's "Me" is dead and has been replaced by today's "Me".

I have also learnt that comparing myself with others is natural and good for a brief curiosity check of where I am and where I want to go, but when it becomes an obsession, it is a recipe for making my life depressing. In addition, one will mostly see the happy life of others, their perfect success, perfect achievements, perfect family, perfect smiles et al. It can only generate more stress if you constantly set such an unattainable benchmark. The only person you should compare yourself with obsessively, is the "You" of a few hours, days, weeks, months or even years ago. If every day, you become a tiny bit wiser, a tiny bit better, there is no limit to where you can go. It's like a compounding interest effect on yourself. "You" becomes incrementally better with each passing day.

Another important learning is that it is not worth banging your head against the same wall every day. Stop bothering about and stop getting bothered by things which are totally out of your control. Act upon what you can change and control. Let go of the things you cannot control.

It may sound like restricting your final potential, but I see it as directing your focus and effort on what you can influence and change, so that you can learn and move on to bigger challenges. Maybe the big wall you are banging your head against today will be a soft breeze in two years. But for this, you must first refocus your attention and give your best shot at passing the smaller wall. Bit by bit, take on the right challenges, the ones that will make you a better person, and improve many aspects of yourself, irrespective of you winning or failing.

As I was not achieving my early goal (of financial independence) year after year, ever postponing the moment of liberation, I slowly started to realise that my focus was the wrong one. It took me many years to understand this. More than a decade for sure. One day, as I explained my journey to a friend on a rare week-end trail, it made me realise how the journey itself was rich and enriching, and how it made me a better person day after day.

If other events had unfolded very differently, maybe I could have reached financial freedom by more luck than wisdom, within four or five years. Had I taken this short road, I would possibly have become a jerk not knowing what to do with people and money. And with such lucky money in my bank account and no wiser head, I would still have needed to go through a similar journey to improve myself, so as not to lose what I had so easily acquired.

But an easier life may not have given me the chance or the will to go through any difficult choices. It was not allowed, and it is probably better this way.

A long road full of a multitude and diversity of challenges ultimately leads you to become a better person.

Step 20: Dealing with stress

My grand-mother's name is Alice. In 1940, during the war, she was twenty-eight. As the German army was invading inland, she decided to move south into non-occupied territories with three toddlers, a horse, and whatever little necessities they could afford to travel with, across rivers and fields. An exodus alongside a few other millions of people. A few days later, realising that life on the road with constant bombardment was worse than staying at the farm, they came back home. Life went on. Later, she gave birth to three other children. One child died young. How much stress can she have suffered from?

Stress is not a good state of mind or body. Nevertheless, for sure you will be stressed. Placing financial burdens on yourself and your family is going to be stressful. There is no denying it.

But life is sacrifice. Life is suffering. Life is stress. Anyway!

Therefore, the challenge is more how you deal with stress, rather than how you avoid it. As human beings, we are a very adaptable species. We adapt to a good life, and we adapt to a tough life. I will not consider the case of permanent life-threatening situations, because one needs to get out of this intensely stressful pit first, before hoping to think clearly about financial freedom. But for others, I am pretty sure that one can be very stressed or depressed despite living a good life, whereas another one can live relatively stress free in a tougher environment. Jet-setters consume drugs too, and many shanty town dwellers live their lives as normal.

Therefore, it is how you deal with stress that matters.

It probably takes time to train the brain, but I have a found few tricks that worked rather well for me. Let me give you my 2 cents.

1. Flatten the excitement curve.

    I cannot really tell you how I have trained myself for this, because it's been after years and years of being confronted with stressful situations. But basically, the first step is to position the stressful event in relative order compared to others and let the better "Me" deal with it later. Worst case of all, if you are totally overwhelmed with the event and this is the worst that happened to you ever, compare it to the deported Jews of Auschwitz. Is your problem still so stressful?

Once it is relativised, it does not mean it goes away. Of course, it will stay at the back of your mind for most of the day. But it re-calibrates the pain and allows a more cartesian analysis to take place. Do not try to resolve your problem yet. Only think about the anatomy of the beast. How big is it? What collateral damage could it cause? What weaknesses does it have? What triggered it? What would have prevented it? Etc... Only allow yourself to think about it in small periods of 5-10 minutes. Do not get mad about it. Only allow yourself to think about it a few times during the day. And unless it's an immediate life or death situation, no decisions on the spot. Refuse to take any action. Then, the "You" of the day will go to bed and will refuse to contemplate the damn thoughts during the night. Yes, it's hard, it will come back, but each time you will push it back and think about something else. Always something else. You can do this, because you know that the "You" of tomorrow is a slightly better version of the "You" of today, and this guy will find the answers. Let the "You" of today have a good sleep. And if tomorrow is still not good enough, the "You" of the day after will find it. The problem will slowly resolve itself and its strangling arms will slowly get untangled. For most problems, it should not take you more than a week or two to find a resolution and take action. Because within a week, the many "You" have been working on it from all angles, have been getting better and better at it, have had good enough sleep and rest, and have found the best solution to it.

2. Project yourself in the future

I do not deny that some pains are more long-term ones. If you suddenly get divorced or widowed, you are not going to get over it in a week. I found that the best way of dealing with these situations is to picture yourself far enough in the future, say three years from now, where the pain has been mostly replaced by a new situation which brings peace and happiness. Picture it clearly in great detail. See the film of "You" in three years' time, in the best possible situation. When you have the clear picture, go back in time by six months. Now you are two and a half years from now, and you have a new picture of the situation. It is slightly less peaceful, less than your best wish, but trending towards it. You want to examine what happened in between, what virtual steps you took to go from there to the ideal situation. And then you move back again 6 months, and you examine again the virtual steps you took, and do it again until you reach now. All these virtual steps you pictured are your plan. You have the blueprint to get back to a long-term peaceful state of mind. You will achieve it, or you won't, but at the very least, you are on the right track, and your condition of stress will resolve slowly as you progress.

3. Sport

With hindsight, I cannot imagine how a week of excitement, stress, adrenaline, and testosterone pumped confrontations can be evacuated without a dose of physical activity. Sport is a must do. For the first fifteen years of my stress-filled adult life, I thought that my stamina and energy were a good enough compensation for sport. How wrong! Do not make the same mistake. Include sport in your weekly routine. No ifs, not buts, no lame excuses. As someone told me once:

```
"Since I started running most mornings, I am no
longer the one barking at others during daily
meetings, and I can take their gibberish all day"
```

4. Meditation

I cannot say I have been very good at this, but I can see that many people in stressful positions use it, and I also think I used it without really knowing it was meditation at certain times. Anyway, as I am not the expert, I will leave it to you to find out more, but this is a must try.

You will have to find your own ways to deal with stress, but I hope I have provided enough good starting points to get you on the right path of a life with managed stress.

Step 21: two brains for one person

I am not going to lecture you about the left and right brains. I do not know what a hypothalamus is. And why should I want to know?

What I know, is that a part of me is analytical, and another part of me is emotional. And they do not always appear at the same moment.

Let's put it this way. I would go to bed after a long day of many excitements and probable frustrations, and I will start thinking about many challenges and opportunities. Suddenly all seems very simple. Blue sky! I have many solutions to many problems, even some that don't exist. There, lying in my bed, I can picture 80% of the next big thing that will surely make me the next billionaire. And no, I am not dreaming yet, I am just thinking intensely. Everything looks so fantastic. I take paper or mental notes of all, and I conclude that after all these new discoveries, I will have so much to work on tomorrow, that I'd better start sleeping a bit now.

The morning after, the new "Me" wakes up, and takes over.

> "Let's review all these exciting ideas. Oh! this is so good, the old "Me" did not just leave me with ideas, but an 80% plan to finish up. Let's have a look."

And there and then, the excitement does not even take off. The new "Me" is very analytical in the morning, by opposition to the old "Me" who had gone through a full day of excitement and was left in a very emotional state of mind.

> "what a load of crap! OK, I will just take note of this little idea here, maybe tonight it can transform into something better. But the rest, come on, who had those thoughts? Fire him!"

I feel this was an important realisation as to how I operate, and very probably, many of you will find sooner or later that you work in similar ways. As a consequence, my rule is that I shall never let the emotional Me take very important decisions alone. I need the analytical Me to counterbalance the rushed shortcuts coming out when my adrenaline-filled self takes over.

Do not take big decisions after mid-afternoon. Wait until the morning. Maybe the new "You" will find a better option, or even write-off the entire plan.

As we will see later, this can create a problem when assessing deals. Committing to a deal always has to balance between emotions and hard figures.

Now, in the many years I have spent seeing, participating, discussing, negotiating, or signing deals, I am very clear about one thing: deals are signed first based on emotions. You want the deal or you don't. You like the contracting party or you don't. You want this house, or you don't.

Once your guts have worked and decided, then the only thing your biased self wants, is to hear that the hard figures do not spoil the party, and that you can proceed. To such an extent that I regularly see buyers acting deliberately blind so as to not see certain figures at face value, or to not ask any difficult questions, or to shortcut the process of due-diligence, just to satisfy their gut, and close the deal. This can be dangerous to them. Or useful to us.

Learn how to deal with the emotional minds, yours included!

Step 22: power of trust

When dealing with others, I fail to see what is more valuable than trust. When trust collapses, everything else gets very shaky. Without trust, there is no firm ground on which we can plan a sound relationship, or even a short one-off business transaction.

Seeking trust in others is fraudulent if you do not clean up your own self first. We will come back to this later on, but you have to consider yourself as the CEO of "You". As a consequence, "You" have a brand. "You" have a reputation. The way that you conduct yourself, in private or in public, is how "You" will be perceived and remembered by all those you encounter.

For many years, my business motto has been this simple one:

```
"I say what I do ; I do what I say"
```

Pretty simple, and at the same time, pretty powerful.

"I say what I do" means that I will communicate as clearly as I can, the promises I am about to undertake, so that they are in the open, most likely in written format, and detailed to the best of my abilities and knowledge of the situation. The "detailed" part is very important. Not being specific leads to not being trustworthy when situations change.

"I do what I say" means that I really try to implement what was agreed, and so long as I do not require a change of plan, I am working on the plan. It's an implicit "trust me". In case the plan has changed (for many possible good or bad reasons), then we are back to explaining the situation (what changed? ; did the details cover it? ; if not why?), discussing options, negotiating the best retained option, and taking a new promise which loops us back to the same motto.

So far, this motto delivers a good background in trustworthiness:
- Ability to make a promise.
- Ability to be specific and remove ambiguity from the promise.
- Ability to communicate the promise.
- Ability to fulfil the promise autonomously.

- Ability to deal with hazard and anticipate, to convert a currently risky promise into a new and better promise.

With time, I have found that others acting rather in line with most of these abilities were, from time to time, still not very much trustworthy to my eyes. As a consequence, to make sure I do not end up on the wrong side myself, I have added the following values to "Me", to my brand.

- Truthful: never lie, always speak the truth. On the rare occasion that I am asked a question and I do not want to answer it, I will just say "I prefer not to answer". But I will not lie.
- Ethical: there is probably a lot to cover here, but I will keep it to applying the biblical golden rule "Do to others as you would have them do to you".
- Consistent: It is all well and good to act like a Mesopotamian priest for a week, a month or a year, but trust should be built forever. It requires consistency in the values I care for, for how long I apply them, and despite how severely they are tested, to the limit of my coolness, by life's trickeries.
- Authentic: I am not mimicking somebody else. I am "Me". I ooze the brand of "Me". I am the real "Me", and in case you like to interact with me, it is likely in part because you saw "Me" as authentic and trustworthy.

Trust is slowly acquired, constantly tested, and will take an awful lot of time and effort to heal if broken. Make sure that "You" oozes trust. Work on it. Keep the smallest of promises to get into the habit.

As an added benefit, the more you become trustworthy, the more you will detect others who are not, including their hidden agendas, and their bullshit!

Make sure that you ooze trustworthiness!

Step 23: power of your circle

I grew up on a farm. No animals, only vegetables. I could sense from a very young age that growing potatoes was not going to push my limits of intellectual challenges. The people you meet on a farm are farmers, workers, and from time to time, salesmen coming to advise on materials, fertilisers, or weed killers. That is the close circle from which you develop.

As a consequence, there was no better alternative than working as best as I possibly could at school, and progressively discover and get closer to like-minded people, some of which would enter my close circle. Rinse and repeat this for several iterations (years) and as my network grew in number and quality, there came a time when new opportunities presented themselves. What you would have called an unbelievable luck a few years before became the new normal.

I believe that a good way to develop your own circle is to take responsibility and move away from the place where the future looks like a Groundhog Day of growing the latest breed of turnips, or whatever equivalent is on your horizon. What will your future network of reliable friends and advisors be made of? Those living a few roads around you? People from your city? From your country? A select group of people living all over the planet? Which network is likely to make you a better person?

Your close circle shall only be made of people you trust, and who trust you, irrespective of their sex, religion, race, place of living, and background. That's probably not going to reach a few dozens, but it does not matter that much. Networks are very powerful and transform the whole planet into a little village. The Six Degrees of Separation is a concept by which you are only six steps (or links) away from anybody, or anything, in the world. Through the friend of a friend of a friend of a friend of your friend, you can reach anything you want. At the very least, one thing is sure: through your improved close circle, you will get exposed to more opportunities which are likely to be more in-tune with your aspirations.

The role of your close circle is also and prominently to pull you in directions that you would otherwise have not even considered. They allow you to bounce ideas, have them dissected and either killed or improved, so that you can progress faster with than without these people around you. For this to work well, I find it important that most of these people share some of the profound core values that you have chosen for yourself.

Where are your opportunities going to come from? Luck is not going to knock on your door in a vacuum. You make a good part of your own luck, and this happens because you set the scene for opportunities to arise regularly, through your network of relations, starting from your trustable close circle. Then from time to time, when it feels right, you look at one opportunity more closely and decide to take the challenge.

Your close circle has to be one of your most precious assets in life.

Nurture it with care.

Step 24: dealing with the unknown

As we start to get to know each other, it's time for me to take a risk. The risk is that you dismiss these ideas and put down this book after reading the following lines. In the end, I need to write what I think will help you on the road to financial freedom, and part of this is how to deal with the unknown.

I have had many roles in the last 25 years. The last one was Chief Technology Officer of a medium size software company. Yet, when asked what I did for a living, most of the time I said this:

> "I solve problems which got completely out of control for others"

Unfortunately, when a problem is already at this stage, it has grown out of the comfort zone of normal management. The good news is that because the problem is very visible, I will be able to redirect the focus of many staff members to help resolve it.

So here we start. The first few days are dedicated to establishing a credible plan as to when normal order will be restored and all parties will be sufficiently happy that life can go on as usual. I will assemble a team of let's say 5 people (those I think are the best ones for solving the problem at hand), and we will split the challenge in many parts, define and assign tasks, to build a credible plan. Each individual in the team will define with the most precise analysis and experience, how long their assigned tasks will take. We will add them up, draw a detailed project diagram, and end up with a good idea of the time and effort it will take to resolve this damn hazard which makes everybody else fear for their life, job, pay or commission. For good measure, I will add a 15% effort for project management, and we have our final plan with the estimated date of delivery.

Experience has taught me that things are never going to happen like this. The project has risks. In addition, it will be delivered by a team of very confident folks who plan for winning[24]. On top, for sure the end-client will be picky and will not accept the first delivery as final. As a consequence, I take the delivery date as our internal commitment. To the world outside the team, those mostly in fear for their life, job, pay and commission, I communicate a new high-level plan with another delivery date.

In the process, I have inflated the effort by Pi.

Yes, Pi is roughly 3.141. In a complex and highly testosterone-driven project, Pi is a good factor. In a less complex or less male-dominated project, I will use Phi, which is 1.618.

All right, at this point, you want to have a laugh. But let's go past this for a moment. My point is the following one. You and I certainly do not know the future, and we are taking assumptions, making predictions, so that we can be financially free way before normal age of retirement. The laws, including those impacting taxes, fees, cost of living, and more, are spun-out in an ever more complex, ever-changing world. They are made by testosterone-filled and short-term driven politicians who have less clues about the consequences of their actions than my team mapping their tasks in a complex but rather controlled environment. In this context, can you take your own financial plan, floating in a sea of unknown future regulations, at face value without a risk factor?

Let me give you a real-life example.

I started worrying about university fees for my children when they were around 8 years old. Apparently, I was reckless because most British plan it at child birth! Anyway, after all these years it took me to understand that university is not free, back then in 2007, the fees were set at £3,000 per year. So that's my careful planning in motion, nearly 10 years ahead of the kids starting "Uni". I even added inflation at 3% to plan for the risk. Now, fast forward to 2017, and my kids are,

---

[24] The main problem with "planning for winning" is a scenario based on a happy path all along, where not one thing will go wrong. But of course, many things can and will go wrong!

at last, going to Uni. Ten years is a lot of free time for politicians who cannot help but change, tamper, tinker and then rewrite order and disorder... As a result, in 2017, university fees were set at £9,250, or a Pi factor away from the original plan, blowing out of the water my careful 3% inflation consideration for risk.

As for Phi, it has long been used in stock market graphs technical analysis, under the name "Fibonacci retracement". In this case, instead of using the raw Phi (1.618), the custom is to use Phi as a percentage (I will call it Phi%). This translates into using 61.8% as the "golden ratio", and then a few derived and less prominent ratios such as 38.2% (which is 100% - 61.8%) and 23.6%. Many traders and trading programs rely on these retracement ratios to win (but sometimes lose) money.

If you are planning for long term, taking into account inflation alone is unlikely to cover all your risks. You need a larger margin of safety. You can use Pi, Pi%, Phi, Phi%, or you can use anything else you feel comfortable with. However, be very aware that your planning is likely to be a happy path, and many surprises will take you off-road. When you start venturing off-road, it's a lot more expensive to finance the trip until the end of the journey.

Do not take your happy path as your final financial planning. As you are going to load debt on your shoulders along this journey to financial freedom, never forget to factor risk.

Consider using Pi and Phi on all your most risky assumptions.

Step 25: always take the long view

A goal will never be more than a milestone in your journey. You reach it, or you don't. You change it, you tweak it, complexify it, simplify it, and then you wave it goodbye. It's gone! But the journey is still here, part achieved experiences, part unknown and expectations.

So what do you think matters? The goal, or the journey?

It is easy to be tempted and care more for short-term goals than long standing principles. And it is also easier to set goals relating to material possessions (I want this fancy toy, I want this holiday, I want this house, I want this job, ...) than to plan for a meaningful journey. If you only set materialistic short-term goals, your journey will happen by accident more than by design. It does not mean it will be less rich, but for sure you will be less in control, and more subject to surrounding forces.

Sometimes, these surrounding forces are just like punches in your face. Then, it's what you do about it, and how you react that matters. You set a new goal, you prepare yourself as much as you can, you put in place a credible plan to achieve it, and you jump again. And along the road, you get punched again! This process can only re-enforce the reality that the goal was just a milestone and nothing more than this.

Only the journey matters!

For all these good reasons, you want to design as much as possible your own journey and run your race on the best possible track. Want it or not, there is a very high likelihood that you are in a Rat Race. Every working day of your life, you wake up, and you run on the same track. Same known hurdles, a few new unexpected ones, and a short-term finish line in sight by the end of the day, week or month. One more pay cheque. Instead of working to pass the same hurdles, at some point, ask yourself a few questions. Come-on! Ask the right bloody question!

"What about running on a different track?"

When you start asking this type of question, you start seeing the world in a different light. A world where all is possible, but at the same time, a world where all is relative, and all has its place, based on priorities, values, principles, and lines in the sand.

It is important that you know where your lines in the sand are, as they help define who you are. Let me give you an example.

You walk down the street, and you see a little insignificant plastic wallet. There is nobody around. Your curiosity makes you pick it up. You open it briefly, and you see a credit card, an ID, and few other cards. And there is cash too. Like a thick layer of folded bank notes. Not sure how much yet, but you know there is a lot. What do you do? You take over this wallet owner's identity? You take the cash and throw the wallet? You put back the wallet in the middle of the street? You take the wallet to the police? You make a point to find the owner and return the wallet untouched? It looks insignificant, but it is not. What you do then shows who you are.

This is why lines in the sand are important. They give substance to your identity. They define what is acceptable and what is not. And they help define your principles. These principles are of even higher value than the simpler lines in the sand. This is because a principle should not be bullied or torn apart just for a short-term gain. These principles help define on which track you want to run your race, and who you will have alongside during your journey. Hopefully, this close circle will share fundamentally the same principles with you. If not, you risk running on a different track than what you think it is...

With good values and good principles, you should be able to establish good priorities. And when in doubt or bullied by the short-term ordeals, these principles will help you take the long view, and see what's right to do.

When in doubt, I look at what I have and cherish. And most of this does not have much to do with straight financial gain. I am healthy, I have a wonderful family, I have a few close friends with whom I share reciprocal trust, I have beautiful flowers in my garden, and I have a million ideas in my head. Is the nasty bastard between myself and my next goal going to separate me from this? If not, then call the bastard what he is, and move on. I will take the long view, reassess the goal, but not change the journey.

In case of pain or doubt, always take the long view.

Step 26: beware the salesman

Family rumour has it that just before World War I, Alice's father invested a few years of savings in Russian bonds[25]. It is hard to imagine how large a sales and marketing operation it must have been at the turn of the 20th century, to convince some French peasants from nowhere-land to part with their savings and invest it in a leap of faith in the Russian state.

For sure, if there is a profession that understands the duality of the brain, and the tendency to buy first from the emotional side, it must be that of Sales and Marketing.

On our quest for financial freedom leveraged by debt, we become prey, simply because we find ways to temporarily control lots more money than we would ever have under our normal work conditions. But it is debt and it is not entirely ours yet. However, in a salesman's eye, it is money you could be separated from, with a bit of skill.

As a consequence, the financial industry at large is full of people who want to give you their advice... for a fee! You want to sell your property? An estate agent will tell you that it is the best moment to do so, as the market is peaking. You want to buy? The same agent has the deal of the century waiting for you, and there's so much potential to be added, you would be mad not to take it. And anyway it will be gone tomorrow, so you have a few hours only to decide! You want to buy stocks? So many "experts" will sell you their recommendations for a subscription fee that you will for sure compensate with all the profit they will help you collect over a few weeks. I could go on and on.

Over 25 years, I have not met many people who could give me a valuable unbiased advice. But I still receive ten solicitations a day for pseudo-advices from salesmen.

---

[25] Russia defaulted on its foreign bonds repayment by the end of the war.

Therefore, it would be of great advantage that you train yourself to recognise salesmen and decode the value of their "advice". Here below is a starting point to spot a salesman:
- People sending you unsolicited emails.
- People you meet at trade fairs.
- People who put pressure on you to sign now.
- People who want to help you without listening much to you.
- People who get a commission on the deal you are about to sign.
- People who use emotional strategies or even lies.

Over the years, I have signed up for a few stock market advice newsletters. Some of them, I am pretty sure, have more than 1,000 subscribers, suggesting that the "advisor" makes already in excess of $1m in fees (our subscriptions). For example, one such expert advisor was sending emails with deep analysis of junior gold miners. Very detailed and compelling analysis of a very imminent "break-out" which will juice several hundred percent of profit for the "sophisticated" buyers. Way back in time, I bought a few of his recommendations. I lost everything I invested in, way faster than those Russian bonds turned to rust. With tightening regulations, this "advisor" had to provide a bit more transparency, and a "disclaimer" link to his website appeared at the bottom of his emails. Of course, we know not many people would click. When I did, I discovered the small print: his research was paid for by "sponsors". Those sponsors were the companies he recommended we, the sophisticated investors, should buy. This salesman "limited" the sponsors to 25 a year at $18,000 each. Yes, he got paid $450,000 a year by sponsors, to advise us to buy shitload of stocks, on very lightly regulated markets. This paid service helped the sponsors' main shareholders sell their stocks to a captive market, until the value had disappeared into pennies, and everybody (advisor, main shareholders, and sophisticated investors, otherwise now known as suckers) move to the next one. One more lesson...

A salesman never has your interest at heart.

Now, when I read an article which captures my interest, after the first ten lines, I pause and check who the author is. What motivation does the author have to write this? It then becomes astonishingly revealing to have this context in mind, and either stop reading, or read with new lenses.

On our quest towards financial independence, our rush to make it faster than planned will sometimes lead us to take shortcuts. Around those faster corners, there is always a salesman waiting and weighting the commission value of his "advice".

Remember that the large majority of people giving you advices are salesmen. Then consider this:

- Salesmen are not impartial advisors.
- Salesmen are not your friends.
- Salesmen are in it for their own interest, and that is all there is to it!

Learn to make independent judgments and avoid relying too much on the next random person you meet.

Step 27: who are you?

I'm not joking! Who are you, really? Do you know yourself and do you know your strengths? We have touched a bit on the brand of "You" earlier, but now you really need to sit down, think, and make it clear. What projection do you want to reflect onto others?

There are a few easy actions that you can take to help understand yourself better.

The first one is a personality test. You can find many such tests on the internet. I used the 16 personalities[26] test to know more about myself. I am categorised as an "Architect", and it reflects pretty accurately who I am. It helps understand more why you think or work in certain ways, and why people with other personalities seem so alien to your reasoning or actions.

Second, you may not be totally aware of your strengths. You may think that things which you find easy to do can be done by anyone else. But that is not always the case. They may be easy for you because they fall under your strengths. The best way to know is to ask people who know you well, either because they are close to you, or work alongside you, or have a relation of power over you. They will know what your strengths are. Just ask them. If they all give the same picture, you can be quite confident it's an accurate version of the truth.

Your strengths can change dramatically as you learn on your journey. As you encounter difficult situations in life, you have opportunities to learn and improve. This in turn helps forge your personality. But as you grow older, this personality, who you are, will change less and less. That leads us to the other immovable piece at the core of who you are: your set of values.

Therefore, in third you need to understand your values. Yes, I am back to this again! Guess what: it's because it is very important. You need a clear view of what is acceptable and what is not. Earlier in life, it is easy to think that values are not so essential. But they are. Values

---

[26] https://www.16personalities.com

are the core of what makes you tick. Dealing with people who have similar core values makes it an enjoyable experience, even in case of dealing with trouble. Dealing with people of opposing values makes it awkward and unpleasant, even for unimportant matters. Research your inner-self and write your values on a piece of paper.

Lastly, you will not know who you really are unless you find ways to push yourself. Whatever your personality is, you have to push the boundaries. To give you an example, my personality test says I am 83% introvert. That does not leave much of a socially confident extrovert person in me. Nevertheless, for months and years, when faced with danger of not putting food on the table, in a crammed but quiet office with other people relying on my performance to get their pay cheque, I forced myself to cold call total strangers to find business opportunities. If you don't totally get it, let me tell you that for me, it's the equivalent of going to hell twenty-five times a day! Well, I am sure you can find equivalent "push the boundary" types of challenges to help you grow and become a better person.

Look back at who you were two or three years ago. Are you a better person now?

If you cannot see yourself as a much-improved person, either you have not learned much, or you have not pushed yourself enough.

In both cases, wake up and start being the "You" that you can and deserve to become.

4

Foundations - finances

I think there's something you should know

George Michael

This third and last foundational section establishes a minimal common background necessary to approach the rest of the book. It also gives a good peek into the way I structured regular reviews of my personal financial situation.

Step 28: no tricks beyond this point

You could be presented with false information. You know, the salesman's type of information. In that case, it would be your job to detect the bullshit. But you could also be presented with correct information in a devious way. This one is harder to decipher and arbitrate if you are not trained.

The graph below shows the progression of the DOW Jones index over 100 years. In 90% of the cases, this is how information is presented to you.

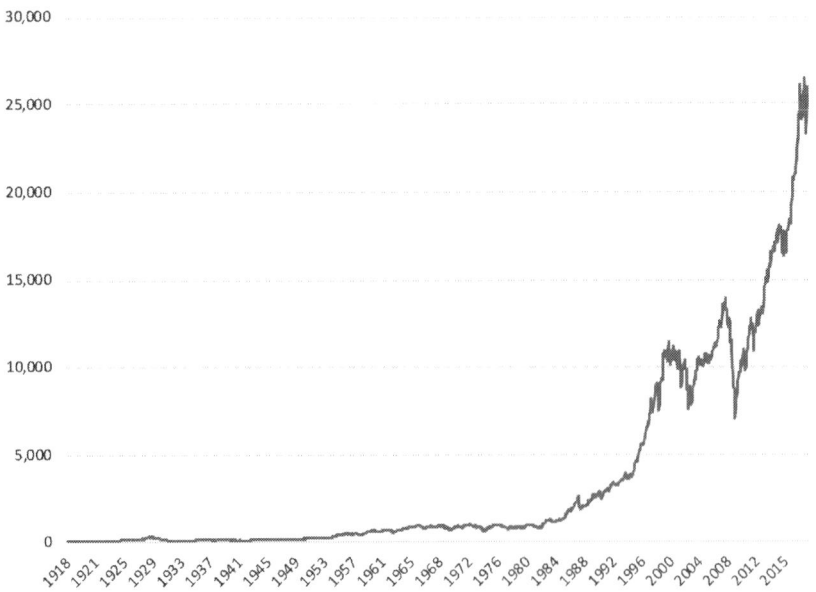

Fig 28.1 A salesman's graph depicting the growth of the DOW index over a century

Of course, when you see this, you wonder why your great-grandfather did not invest a mere $100 in the stock market one hundred years ago. But this is just a salesman's graph, not a proper representation of the reality. Now, just pause a few seconds, and ask yourself:

```
"why is this graph tweaking the reality?"
```

Give me two reasons.

Go on... two reasons!

I wait...

It does not matter too much if you did not find them this time. However, I hope that once you see the next two graphs, you will always remember how to detect the salesman's graph and dismiss it as pure propaganda.

So! The graph is indeed very misleading for two main reasons...

First, as we know, the past 100 years have seen quite some inflation, so $100 back then is not the same as $100 now. Therefore, this graph needs to be presented adjusted for inflation, which is what we now have below.

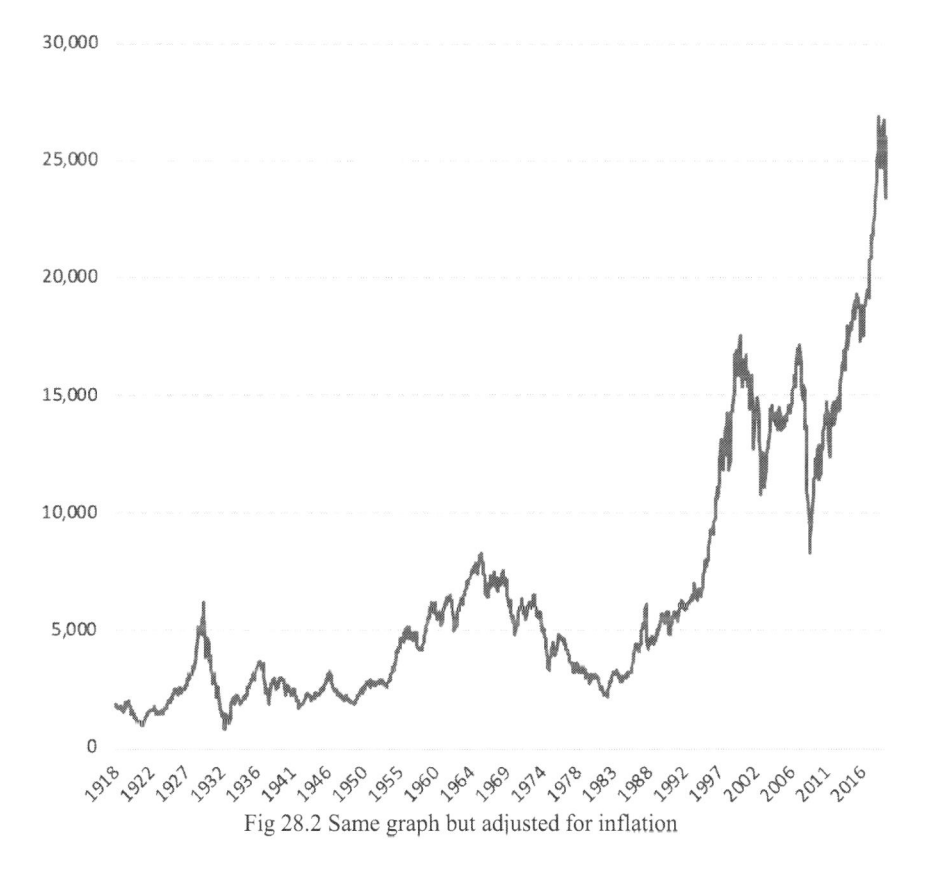

Fig 28.2 Same graph but adjusted for inflation

It is still quite a steep progression, but not as flat for 75 years and then Boom! I concede that adjusting for inflation does not seem necessary for short periods of time, but it's a very good practise to always think that what you are presented with is being eaten by inflation. Therefore, you need to take this inflation into account.

Second, you shall never forget that when dealing with strong growth, a linear representation is always flawed. When you double the value from 5,000, you get to 10,000. When you double the value from 10,000, you get to 20,000. The height of space between 5,000 and 10,000 needs to be the same as between 10,000 and 20,000, because in both cases, it is the same challenge: double the value.

Each time I am presented with a linear scale graph, I force myself to refuse that it depicts the truth. I want to see the logarithmic scaled graph, which is much closer to the reality. This is not easy, because most of the time, we read a report and there is no alternative, as it is provided with a graph not adjusted for inflation, and with a linear scale. I view linear scaled graphs as a trick to force a conclusion in line with the author-salesman's view, which is generally a partisan view of the reality.

To stay closest to the truth, we need a logarithmic scale. It avoids the otherwise natural and inevitable conclusion that there is a logarithmic progression of the value at the end of the graph. The following graph is adjusted for inflation and with a logarithmic scale.

Fig 28.3 same graph, adjusted for inflation, on a logarithmic scale

I want to stress again that all three graphs depict the evolution of the Dow Jones over a century. However, this last graph is more truthful. Here we can see that it took 30 years to come back to the same level of value after the 1929 depression. Yes, 30 years in the doldrums, totally invisible in the first graph, and now we see them! Or, the seemingly unique and parabolic growth post 2009 on the linear graph is nothing extraordinary now. Indeed, it is not more impressive than a few others which occurred in the past.

Do not be tricked by salesmen's pitches and salesmen's graphs. Have a critical eye, and probe everything you see.

Always adjust for inflation!

Always adjust for the parabolic growth effect!

Step 29: your new arithmetic tables

In our quest for financial independence, there are new basic laws that we need to have permanently in the back of our head. It's a bit like your addition or multiplication tables. Just another set of mathematical truths.

Note that exceptionally in most graphs below, I have kept a linear axis as I am mostly interested in discussing the lower parts of the charts, not the hyperbolic progression.

Inflation

Let's start to get a feel for inflation over a long term. Starting with $100, what amount do you need in x years to keep the same buying power, after inflation?

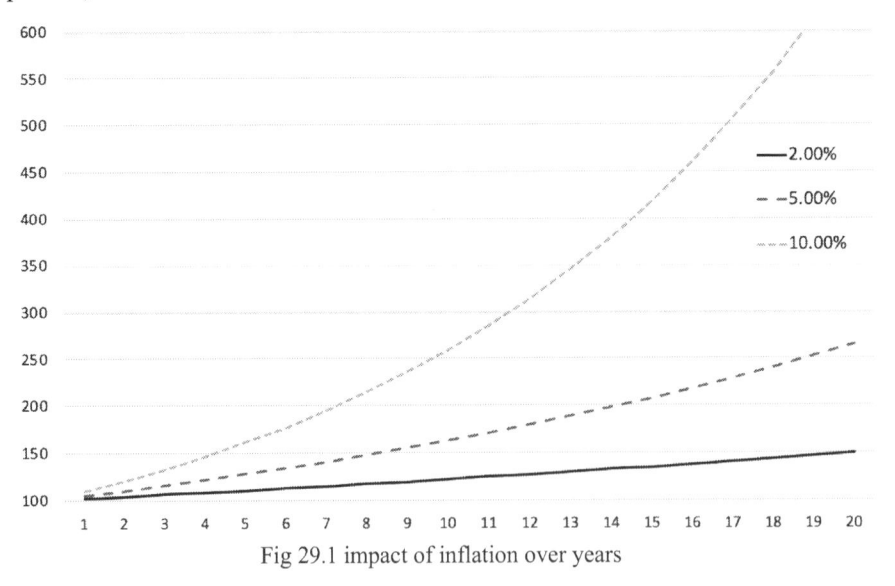

Fig 29.1 impact of inflation over years

The interesting findings are:
- At 2% inflation we have a very manageable situation. We cannot see all details on the chart, but an initial $100 inflates by around:
    - 22% after 10 years.
    - 35% after 15 years.
    - 50% after 20 years.

- At 5%, inflation requires you to double your capital after 14 years to keep the same buying power.
- An inflation rate of 10% is a very different game. For your capital to keep the same buying power, you need to:
  - Nearly double your capital after 7 years.
  - Quadruple it after 15 years.

Another interesting fact is that we can see the effect of the difference between two inflation rates. For example, if CPI is constantly close to 2%, but housing inflation is close to 5%, the area on the graph between the solid line (2%) and the first dotted line (5%) is the playground of our invisible man (you know, the guy who thrives in between CPI inflation and asset inflation).

I also like to have a long-term perspective on inflation. It helps put in perspective that even a fairly mild inflation rate, such as 3%, will do a big damage over the long run, in this case 1,922% increase over 100 years.

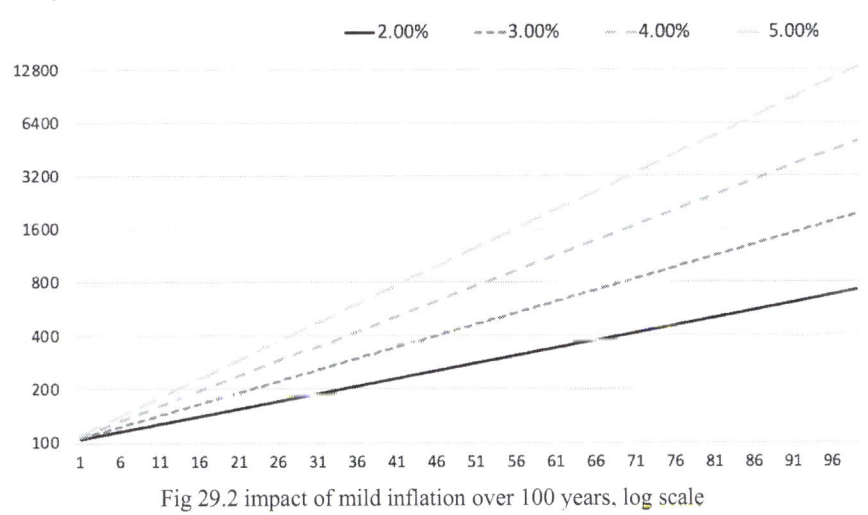

Fig 29.2 impact of mild inflation over 100 years, log scale

And as we can see, for a seemingly tiny 2% points more (going from 3% to 5% inflation), you take off to a 13,150% increase over the same period. Inflation over time is a very powerful force, which is why the invisible man needs just a tiny 2% difference over a long run to gain over 10,000%!

Compounding

Now with compounding. If you save at 5% per annum and you started with 100, at end of year 1, you have 105. If you reinvest your extra 5, at beginning of year 2 you have 105 invested, which means at end of year 2, you have 110.25. The 0.25 is the result of the compounding effect.

With this in mind, it does not take 10 years to double your money at 10% interest. Maybe you are already familiar with this table:

Interest per annum	# of years to double initial investment
2.0%	35
5.5%	15
7.0%	10
10.0%	7
12.5%	6
15.0%	5

Table 29.3 Compounding interest

Note that below 7% interest, it will take an awful lot of time to double your investment.

Ever since I was exposed to this information many years ago, I have kept the following in mind: it takes 7 years at 10% to double your money, or otherwise 10 years at 7%.

But that's unfortunately another salesman's pitch…

Yes, the salesman happily forgets to factor inflation. Money in 10 years is not like money today. Therefore, if you factor a 2% inflation, your 7% required interest should in fact be 9% required interest. It is indeed harder to make money in the real world, a world made of inflationary forces, than in much simplified versions of it!

Out of the Rat Race

The next diagram shows the effort required to double, triple, or quadruple an investment, but this time, taking a moderate 2% CPI inflation rate into account.

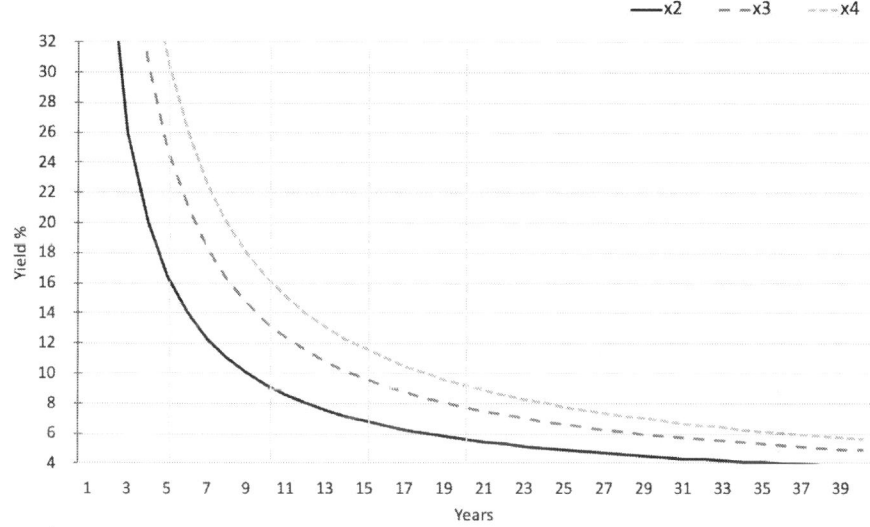

Fig 29.4 how long to double, triple quadruple your buying power with inflation at 2%

You can double, triple or even quadruple your money in a few years at over 20% interest, but that benchmark is not going to be realistic to achieve, at least within an acceptable risk. By the same token, hanging on for over 20 years is an awful lot of waiting time.

So we want to concentrate our focus on the elbow, between 7% and 11% yield. The next table shows exactly this. As we can see, saving at 7% in a world of 2% CPI inflation rate takes a lot more than 10 years to double your money... Damn salesman again!

Yield	Years to wait for doubling your money
7%	14.2 years
8%	11.9 years
9%	10.2 years
10%	9 years
11%	8 years

Table 29.5 How long to double your money with an inflation of 2%

Cost of interest

You also need a sixth sense for the cost of interest. The next table gives an idea of the cost of a $100,000 interest only mortgage with set duration and fixed interest. Inflation is again assumed at 2% pa.

Duration (years)	Interest	Cost (nominal)	Cost (inflation indexed)
10	2%	$20,000	0
10	4%	$40,000	$20,000
10	6%	$60,000	$40,000
10	8%	$80,000	$60,000
15	2%	$30,000	0
15	4%	$60,000	$30,000
15	6%	$90,000	$60,000
15	8%	$120,000	$90,000
20	2%	$40,000	0
20	4%	$80,000	$40,000
20	6%	$120,000	$80,000
20	8%	$160,000	$120,000

Table 29.6 Cost of interest

The interesting findings:
- When your interest rate is close to inflation, the loan costs you nothing in real money (after inflation). How good is that?
- 20 years at 4% costs you the same as 10 years at 6% (again, after inflation).
- Do not touch anything that would cost you in the region of 100% of the debt you agreed to take. In a low inflation world, that would be signing up for slavery!

Back from losses

Then, let's imagine you lost 75% of your capital on a deal. That hurts, but how much is required to get back to break-even from such a hole? Look at the following table.

Loss	%gain to get back to breakeven
10%	11.1%
20%	25%
25%	33%
50%	100%
75%	300%
90%	900%

Table 29.7 Back from losses

The interesting findings:
- A 10% loss can be compensated with a fairly similar effort.
- A 50% loss requires you to double your money just to break-even.
- Way above 50% loss looks like mission impossible to get back on track.

You can play with all these simulations and more on the website www.intheRatRace.com which I maintain for you.

Step 30: financial crash course

This book is not intended to become your reference for accounting practises. However, we need a minimum of common ground and understanding. I will try to make accounting so fun that you will consider it has a new hobby!

Let's go through a little game together. I give you this choice: today, you can either get $1,000,000 cash tax free, or a guaranteed and inflation indexed passive income for life of $70,000 per year (unfortunately a taxable income, like most). What would you choose?

This is not a toss a coin type of answer. It requires applying a lot of the knowledge we have acquired so far and is also related to your personal circumstances.

Take a few minutes and ask yourself the question. Go on, take a pen and paper. Which one would you choose, and why?

I wait for you here.

Are you back?

Let's see... how could we make the best choice?

I would choose the $70,000 pa in either of the following conditions:
- I am close to retirement age and want safety of income, in this case $5,833 per month before tax.
- I am after a long-term safety net allowing me to pursue other rewarding projects.
- I want to do many other things with my life and not have to manage my finances too much.

I will put aside the solution of taking the $1,000,000 and blow it out in a year or two on personal vanity projects. That's not financial planning.

If you take the $1,000,000 cash, it has to be because you think you can get way in excess of $70,000 per year, with a controlled risk. For this, we have to start planning.

My first back of the envelope plan would look like this:
- Investing in the stock market will give me on average 7%. Trying to achieve more without having an unfair advantage (skills or other) is likely to lead to ruin. Not much point taking those risks for the same return which is otherwise guaranteed.
- Investing in one or several ventures is even riskier and may stay illiquid for a very long time.
- Investing in property generating a monthly stable income… Let's explore this further.

If I invest it all in a property, I can get one in the region of $900,000 and leave 10% ($100,000), for covering various fees, taxes, and other expenses incurred by the acquisition.

I summarise the capital operation in the following table.

Property value before acquisition	$900,000
Property value after acquisition	$900,000

Table 30.1 Capital table

At this stage, I do not have a precise idea of the fixed costs to operate this rental business, so I will assume operating cost of $500 per month and then multiply by Pi to cover my unknown risk. I will assume I am able to rent it at 7% gross (not that easy to do), and a 20% tax on gross profit.

Income (at 7% of property value)	$900,000 * 7% / 12 = $5,250
Operating costs	$500 * 3.14= $1,570
Gross profit	$5,250 - $1,570 = $3,680
Tax	$3,680 * 20% = $736
Net profit	$3,680 - $736 = $2,944

Table 30.2 Income table (per month)

$3,680 per month net is around $44K per annum (a yield of around 4.9% pre-tax on the $900,000, but of only 4.4% on the $1,000,000 total investment). That's not even reaching two thirds of the otherwise guaranteed income. Not worth it. The table below summarises the operation.

Gross profit (before tax)	$44,160
Net profit (after tax)	$35,328
Yield before tax	4.42%
Yield after tax	3.53%

Table 30.3 Performance table (per year)

But wait… Should we not try to get into "good" debt?

Let's try again. I can probably get 80% loan to value mortgage. If I can find a $3,000,000 property, I can buy it with a $2,400,000 loan, $600,000 cash, and still have $400,000 to use as follows: $300,000 (same 10%) for house acquisition costs, and $100,000 leftover for improving the property and starting the first year of operation.

Property value before acquisition	$3,000,000
Property value after acquisition	$3,100,000
Loan	- $2,400,000

Table 30.4 Capital table with mortgage

As it is a larger property, we may now operate at say $750 per month[27], also multiply by Pi for the moment to cover the risk, add a 2.75% mortgage interest on the $2,400,000 and similar other conditions than the previous one (rent at 7% gross, tax at 20%).

Income (at 7% of property value)	$17,500
Operating costs	$750 * 3.14= $2,355
Mortgage interest	$5,500
Gross profit	$9,645
Tax	@20% = $1,929
Net profit	$7,716

Table 30.5 Income table with mortgage interest (per month)

Our gross profit is over $115,000 per annum, or around two third more than the guaranteed one. But there is also an extra upside. If the value of the house increases beyond inflation, I will keep the difference, as an increase in the value of my property. That's not yet cash, but it can be turned into cash, as we will see further on. And this potential house price increase is leveraged at three times the initial amount ($3,000,000 vs $1,000,000), as opposed to the previous deal where it was not leveraged at all.

This is only a very brief back-of-the-envelope calculation, but it already feels like it is a better deal for the long term. I can get 65% more income than the guaranteed deal, and I have the upside of

---

[27] Operating costs can vary a lot, as you may include in there some utility bills for your tenants, and depending where you operate, you may have various regulatory requirements.

property inflation: an annual 2.3% increase in property prices in the neighbourhood will generate an extra $70,000 of capital appreciation. Win on income and potential win on capital.

My performance table starts to show a few more indicators. As I have a loan, I can track a few more ratios which will be useful to me later on. Note that the yield appears lower than in the previous operation. It is normal, as we have to pay the bank for interest. The cash on cash ratio shows me how much return I would get on the cash I invested. Here I invested the full $1,000,000 so the return is 115,000 /1,000,000 = 11.57% per annum.

Gross profit (before tax)	$115,740
Net profit (after tax)	$92,592
Yield before tax	3.86%
Yield after tax	3.08%
Debt ratio	77.4%
Expense coverage ratio	222%
Cash on cash	11.57%

Table 30.6 Performance table with mortgage (per year)

I would not be happy with the current yield and cash return. I will not pretend that this is a good deal, or an investment you must make. This is only for illustration purposes, to introduce the power of leverage by debt. We are only getting started. Do not buy a $3,000,000 property just yet!

As you may have noted in this fictional scenario, I did not evaluate a capital gain option. In this business of property investment, it would have meant investing, adding value, selling, and pocketing the profit. My main reason for rejecting it is that it would have left me in the same Rat Race, possibly with a bit more capital, but for sure requiring me to "make another deal" or spend my capital.

This is important!

The option of leveraging my capital and generating an income from it was more interesting. I exchanged locking my liquid capital against a more illiquid one, but as a result, I got the benefit of a new permanent revenue stream. Incidentally, I also placed a bet on my new property increasing in value over time, although that was not the main purpose of this virtual transaction.

We don't get out of the Rat Race by making a deal which puts us back in the race right after it is closed.

Remember this: we only get out by generating enough long-term passive income.

What a nice idea! A long-term passive income…

Step 31: income and capital

As we saw earlier, it was useful to track some investments and income figures in tables. Slowly, we are going to track our financial performances just like a company tracks its own, although a bit simpler. But before we jump into tables, let me make very clear at this early stage that income to your life is like blood to your body. It is not wise attempting to live without it.

Like the 25-year-old me, you may be tempted to set the day of your financial independence at a net worth number, such as $1m, $5m, or $10m. This is where we get it wrong. Financial independence-day comes when you generate a permanent passive income in excess of your current and projected spending needs.

It is worth repeating and rephrasing:

```
"you will never get poor or insecure if you have
secured a long-term inflation proof passive income in
    excess of your current and future spending."
```

If you think you necessarily have to acquire a large capital by working and saving before you can enjoy life, it is only going to send you on the wrong path. The path of never having enough and always chasing more. And even if luck happened to give you enough capital in a record time, this is not the end game. You will have to manage it, invest it, spend it, or lose it. If you got unfortunate or not wise enough, you may quickly find yourself back to square one. Albeit with one essential learning: the capital was here for generating security and income, not to be spent.

In our world of Rat Racers laser-focused on financial freedom, our capital should not be used to fund our lifestyle. Only our income is meant to do this. Therefore, in order to build a solid stream of income, you need to be very clear in your mind about the difference between capital and income. The way I see it is fairly simple. Income is the reward coming from capital. No capital, no income.

Let's review a few examples. You want to receive income from a tenant; you need a property (your financial capital). You want to receive a good salary from an employer; you need skills in demand to sell over time (your human capital, we will come back to this later on). You like when your grandma gives you a cheque over Christmas, which after so many years of regularity feels like an income; you need to show her love (your social capital). It is that simple! No capital, no income!

However, the good news is that acquiring capital is not solely a game for workers and savers. As we advance through this book, the picture is getting clearer and clearer. Capital can be acquired by debt and leverage. Generating income is therefore reserved for those who know how to do it, not just for those who have saved during a lifetime, or who got lucky.

Finally, a last word on Capital. When investing, it is a very good idea to invest in assets which appreciate beyond the rate of CPI inflation. When looking for a job, it is a very good idea to select one that will also improve your future value on the market (not just a pay-cheque).

Yes, we want to control appreciating assets. When we do so, the rewards generated from those assets, our multiple streams of income, also automatically appreciate with time.

A regular and appreciating reward is what we want!

Step 32: financial dashboards

I started piloting my finances through a yearly financial dashboard the day I discovered Excel. That's a very long time ago. Of course, back then my dashboard was very basic, not always coherent, and lacked many indicators. But with time and newly acquired knowledge, each year, I would reformat the data in light of a new and better presentation. To this day, I continue to tune it at least once a year, adding a few more indicators or projections into the future.

The dashboard is useful for many reasons. It indicates the progress I made over the years, it highlights where I have to focus next and gives me a goal to reach. Once or twice a year, I have a meeting with myself, and I review my dashboard, its data, and its various indicators.

I will share with you a synthetic and simplified view of my current dashboard[28]. As you will see, I track my personal situation like a business. Let's have a look first at a very simple tracking sheet, which we will call the Balance Sheet.

	Year 3	Year 4	Year 5
Assets	**$30,000**	**$165,000**	**$194,000**
Cash	$30,000	$15,000	$32,000
Property	$0	$150,000	$160,000
Shares, bonds, gilts	$0	$0	$2,000
Liabilities	**$0**	**$120,000**	**$120,000**
Mortgages	$0	$120,000	$120,000
Equity (net assets)	**$30,000**	**$45,000**	**$74,000**

Table 32.1 Balance sheet

In the top part of this table, I track any significant capital that I own. I consider that a car, a TV, a guitar, a painting on the wall (at least my type of cheap paintings) are going to depreciate so fast in value that in

---

[28] The figures in the tables are illustrative only.

a few years they are worth zero. So I do not burden myself to track them. In the middle part, I track all liabilities. By the same token, I only track large liabilities such as mortgages, and I do not track any short-term ones. For example, my next council tax bill does not belong here, but in a different table.

Note finally that the most important information in this table is the equity (assets minus liabilities), which is a measure of the wealth created over the years.

Let's move to another tracking sheet, the Income Statement.

	Year 3	Year 4	Year 5
Gross revenue	**$60,000**	**$72,000**	**$74,100**
Salary	$60,000	$62,000	$64,500
Interest & Dividend	$0	$0	$100
Capital gain	$0	$0	$0
Rent received	$0	$11,000	$11,500
Cost	**$36,000**	**$42,940**	**$42,390**
Cost of living	$35,000	$36,000	$38,000
Home mortgage	$0	$0	$0
Over exceptional costs	$1,000	$2,500	$0
Cost of B2L operations[29]	$0	$4,440	$4,390
Gross profit	**$24,000**	**$30,060**	**$33,210**
Tax[30]	$12,000	$13,712	$14,222
Net profit	**$12,000**	**$16,348**	**$18,988**
% Tax vs income	20%	18.78%	18.81%

Table 32.2 Income statement (all costs per annum)

---

[29] Includes an interest only mortgage on the rental property (B2L means Buy to Let).
[30] Assuming a simple tax of 20% on salary and 20% on profit from B2L activity.

The income statement consolidates all my streams of income, identified separately, all my costs, separating the cost of living from costs incurred by other income generating activities, and finally the gross profit, net profit, and the ratio tax vs total income, which I try to control within a reasonable limit as much as possible.

Measuring my net profit at regular intervals was the first baby step towards keeping my finances under control. Note that I also keep track of the detailed income and the various associated costs of each activity in a separate spreadsheet. This income statement is only the consolidation of all the detailed information.

One last spreadsheet before wrapping-up, the Cashflow Statement.

	Year 3	Year 4	Year 5
Net asset variation	N/A	$15,000	$29,000
Net income	$48,000	$59,288	$61,378
Net profit	$12,000	$16,348	$18,988
% Capital appreciation	N/A	+50.00%	+64.44%

Table 32.3 Cash flow statement

I do not use my cash flow statement to predict future cash flow needs. Instead, it tracks the variation in capital from the previous year, the income for the current year, and the profit from my activities.

In addition to this, I also track in another table, some off-balance sheet items, which I call Intangibles. They are mostly very long-term assets which are unlikely to convert to cash rapidly, or unlikely to impact my lifestyle in the short-term. They are currently made of my private pension plan, some illiquid assets (such as shares of the company I co-founded, at current value then divided by Phi), and some inheritance assets[31] (at current value, then divided by Pi).

---

[31] Dear Mum and Dad, I indeed track inheritance, but only once in a long while!

Step 33: key performance indicators

The data entered in my financial dashboards allow me to calculate automatic financial ratios and compare their progression year after year. I can also compare these values against similar ratios taken from real successful businesses. Indeed, I compare myself to a business, and I analyse my performance as if it were that of a business. For example, the table below shows a few ratios I track.

	Year 3	Year 4	Year 5
Property debt ratio	N/A	80.00%	75.00%
Debt ratio (debt / capital)	N/A	72.73%	61.86%
Debt / Equity	0	2.67	1.62
% Cost of servicing mortgage	N/A	3.20%	3.20%
Rental activity gross yield	N/A	7.33%	7.19%
Rental activity net yield	N/A	4.37%	4.44%
Passive income ratio	0%	8.99%	9.54%
Expense coverage ratio	N/A	248%	262%
Net cashflow pm	$1,000	$1,362	$1,582
Net passive income pm	$0	$437	$480
Net cashflow excluding salary, pm	-$3,000	-$2,771	-$2,686
Freedom ratio	0%	13.63%	15.18%

Table 33.1 Financial ratios

The property debt ratio defines my ratio of property debt vs property capital. When I started tracking, it was approaching 70%, whereas currently I am fluctuating above and below 30%. To gain an efficient leverage, I try to keep my debt ratio around 30%.

The second ratio is all my debt divided by all my capital (not just properties). It defines my financial health. There are market guidelines for good debt ratio. Good companies generally have a debt ratio between 30% and 60%. For individuals, it is preferred that these sit within a lower range, around or below 30%. Don't be afraid to blow out this recommended value when you start. I surely did.

The debt-to-equity ratio is another variation on the same line. Companies like to see this ratio at a maximum of 1.5 or 2. Apart from some rare occurrences, I never got above 1, which means that I make sure I always have more equity than debt.

The rental activity yield indicators are tracking the performance of the rental business. The gross yield is all rents divided by property capital, whereas the net yield is all net income (rent minus costs) divided by property capital. I like to compare the net yield to the CPI inflation, and want to see it come significantly above inflation.

Then, another important ratio is my passive income ratio (cumulated net passive income, such as rent minus costs, divided by total income, which includes my salary). It gives me a good indication of how dependent I still am on my employment, or at the very least, how much of an income ratio I would lose if I were to move out of employment.

The expense coverage ratio (income from rental activity divided by cost of rental activity) is also an important one, as it reflects the type of risk I incur in my operations. I like to see this ratio above 200%, which means that my income from rental activities covers twice my costs from the same activities.

For convenience, I have added the net cashflow per month, net passive income per month, and net passive income excluding salary. They don't normally belong to this financial ratio table, but it is simpler to keep them here for reference. As it says on the tin, the net passive income excluding salary is all cash I generate per month, excluding salary (I track only per year, and then I divide by 12). To calculate it, you need to know your total annual income, annual salary, total annual spending excluding any other income generating activities, and how to recalculate tax post change of income. So long as this net cashflow excluding salary is negative, you cannot be totally financially independent, unless you reduce your spending, potentially dramatically, and as a consequence probably also your lifestyle.

Finally, there is the Holy Grail of financial independence: the freedom ratio. This ratio is a variation of the net cashflow excluding salary. It is the result of my total net passive income divided by my total living expenses. Of course, the goal is for the freedom ratio to be permanently well above 100%.

I track many other sub ratios which are not include here. Once you have the data, you can automatically generate all sorts of graphs and derived ratios.

Tracking these key performance indicators regularly is the best way to keep you motivated and geared up towards the exit.

Step 34: taxes and fees

There cannot be an introduction to finance without mentioning taxes and fees.

As we know, we should not avoid tax, only sensibly minimise it. Therefore, make sure you minimise your taxes, in a way that will not be qualified as avoidance in many years to come. That's how easy it is! I will not say much more on taxes, as my lack of any certified qualification and lack of insurance protection stops us here. Get tax advice and review the situation regularly.

But as for fees... where do we start? Probably with this picture:

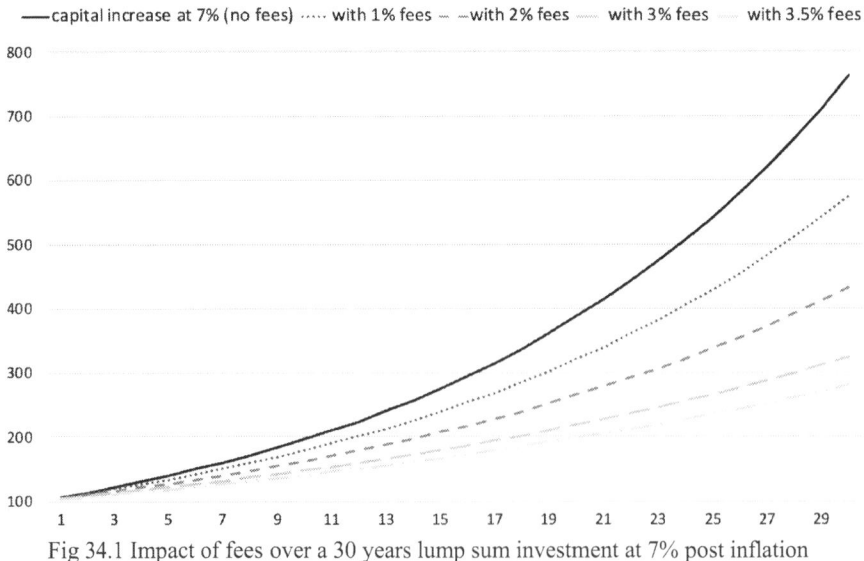

Fig 34.1 Impact of fees over a 30 years lump sum investment at 7% post inflation

The graphic shows the performance of a lump sum investment over 30 years. We assume the investment will return 7% post inflation[32]. Then we look at the impact of fees on the capital increase.

I hope you noticed the linear scale of the graph to impress the fact that fees are not good for you (yes, this is turning into a sales pitch)!

---

[32] At this moment, we do not want to bother about inflation on top of fees.

To turn this into an even better sales pitch, let's focus on the loss of gain instead. You see[33], if you have a return of 7% in a year, but you have a 3.5% fee, you will lose 50% of your gains to fees, right?

Except that we need to compare over time with 7% (the capital increase with no fees) at compounded interest[34]. This chart shows the percentage loss of capital gain that you surrender over time to the fees.

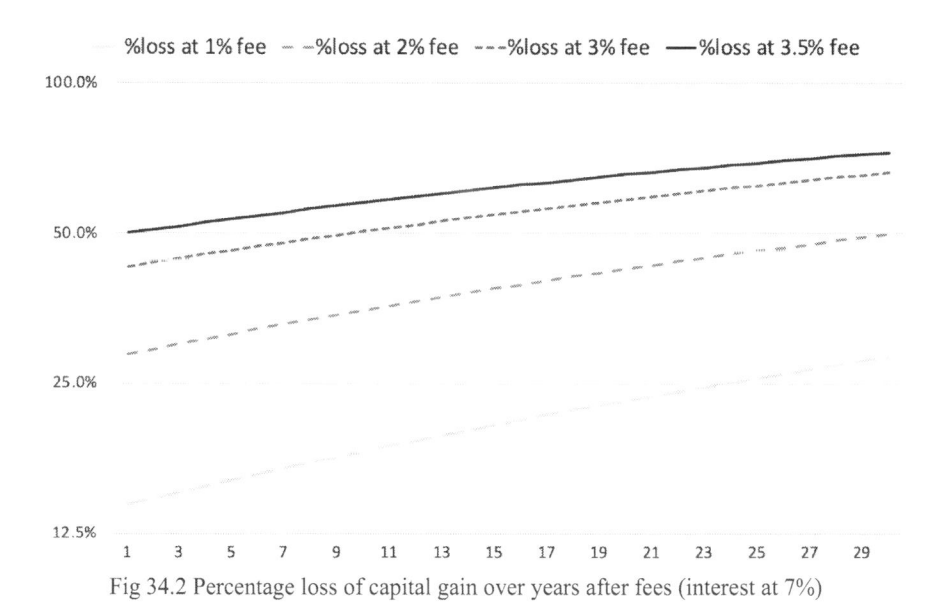

Fig 34.2 Percentage loss of capital gain over years after fees (interest at 7%)

Any way you look at it, this is really bad. At 3.5% fee, you start with giving up slightly over 50% of your gains. But after 30 years, before you know it, you have been separated from 72% of your gains. At a small 2% fee (what is 2% fee, nothing to worry about?), you will have surrendered around half your gains after 30 years, and a third of your gains after just 8 years.

I sincerely hope I made a good sales pitch impression on you, because if you do not pay attention to fees, you get taken for a ride by

---

[33] Real sales pitch, I hate this when people do this to me!
[34] In year two, the compounded gain at 7% would be 14.49, but the compounded gain at 3.5% (7% minus 3.5% fees) is 7.12, hence the loss after year two is not 50%, but (14.49 − 7.12) / 14.49 = 7.37 / 14.49 = 50.86%, and it grows with years.

an industry that thrives only on other people's fees. Don't become the goat that they milk!

Fees should not just be minimised. They should be avoided at all costs. Clear and simple. Fees eat into your profitability way beyond their innocent near-nothing percentage headline. But at least you can have a say as you can shop around for lower fees. You can avoid contracting third parties for those tasks you can do yourself. You can act to defend yourself! Oh joy! Let's list some of those costs we can avoid or reduce.

Type of fees	What to do about it
Fees on purchase with credit card	Send back the credit card and use a debit card
Fees on buying / selling shares	Change broker, negotiate with your broker, reduce your trading activity
Estate agent fees (sale)	Put them in competition, argue your case, negotiate something
Estate agent fees (rent)	Can you do it yourself instead?
Accountant fees	Learn to do your accounts yourself until they become too complex and the risk is higher than the cost of hiring an accountant
Anybody's fees	Negotiate before accepting the contract
Private school fees	If you cannot or will not avoid them... Pay and pray they don't increase next term!

Table 34.3 Fees to avoid

Fees eat into your capital way beyond their innocent headline. Beware the fees!

Step 35: money as water

I can already hear you say…

```
"What has water got to do with finance & accounting?"
```

Nothing at first sight, I admit. I just see it as a convenient way to picture capital, income, and our overall financial strategy to achieve financial independence. Hang on!

We will start with the holey bucket. The bucket has many holes. As many as you agree to punch. Some are by design. You need to eat, travel to work, heat your home, and a few more. Some other holes are by convenience, such as going to the movies. Worst case, some are by your own negligence, or your bad habits. Anyway, the bucket is full of holes. You regularly pay your council tax ; you punch a hole. You subscribe to Netflix ; you punch a hole. It leaks good and proper, and no matter what, it will continue to leak.

Therefore, you know you have to top it up regularly!

The bucket should be large enough to keep you going for up to three months, not more[35]. In other words, you need enough money in there to support your short-term living expenses.

Fig 35.1 Holey bucket large enough to sustain three months of leaks

When your short term is secured, we move to the mid-term by extracting savings out of the holey bucket, in a regular manner. For

---

[35] For those purists of risk management, you could use 3.14 months instead ;-)

this, we need to create another larger bucket. But this time, we create one which does not leak: a barrel. To keep the mental division between living costs and savings, open a new bank account which will hold your savings.

Any extra income (bonus, sale of goods, etc...) goes directly into the savings. In addition, it is important to implement a systematic saving habit. You should start with a minimum of 5% of your employment net income, more if you can[36]. Keep it regular: the day after you get paid, you transfer the money from your bucket account into your barrel account. Better even: make it an automatic payment. This is called "paying yourself first". If you do not know how you will afford to save 5% of your regular income, imagine that the taxman has raised taxes on your income by 5% and you have to deal with it. Then move this undue tax into your savings.

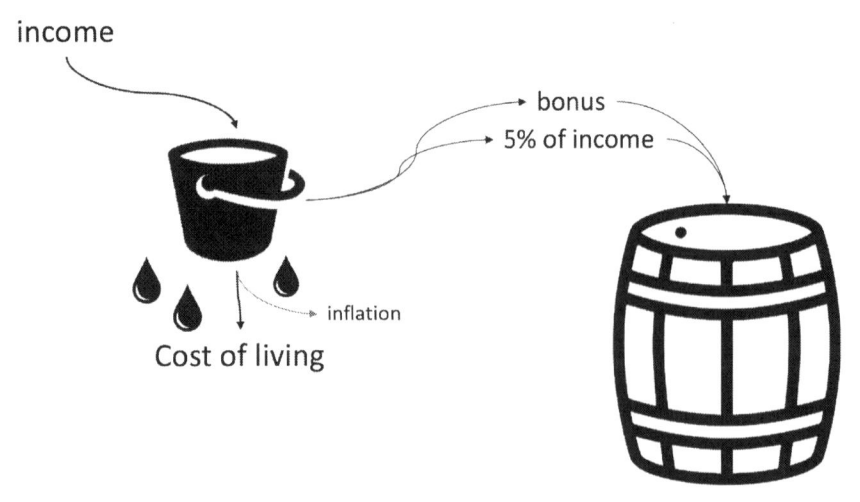

Fig 35.2 Automatic savings system

The barrel of savings should contain up to three years of cost of living[37]. More than this would be wasted investment opportunities.

---

[36] As we will see later on, financial freedom is acquired by saving, investing, and reaping the rewards. For this to happen faster, it requires saving more, such as 15%, 25%, or even more...
[37] Or in keeping with our strict rules, 3.14 years to me more exact ;-)

Less than three years is possible, but it depends on the opportunities you can find out there.

Now let's look at a long-term strategy. Investing is like pouring the water from your barrel into a small pond, which you fully intend to grow into a lake. Each time the barrel is close to being full, invest the money, and expand the lake of your financial independence.

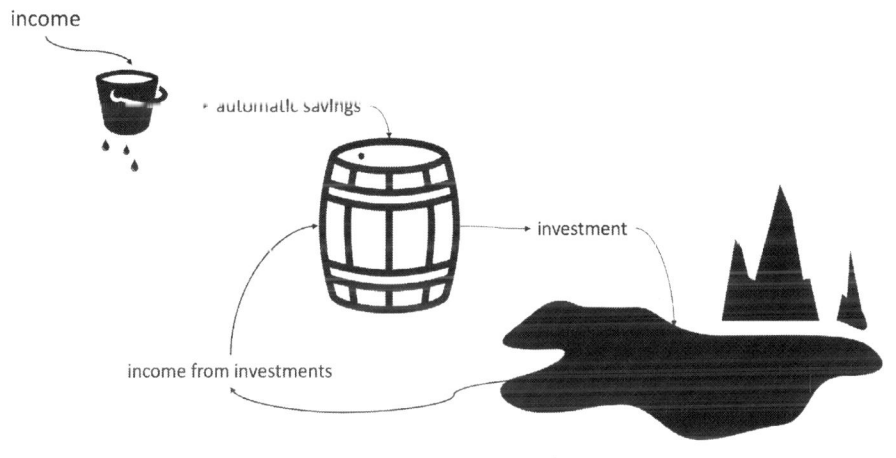

Fig 35.3 Investment for life

Now that we have the full picture, there are a few important rules to add:
- As much as we can, we want to control the leaks in the holey bucket by living within our means.
- The barrel should not have leaks.
- To secure filling up the savings barrel, automate pouring water into there every month.
- There is no moving back savings from your barrel into your holey bucket.
- Do not add another barrel when the barrel is full.
- As much as possible, the investments are for life, not for months or years. Be an investor rather than a trader.
- Income from investments either stays in the investment lake (one river stream per investment) or goes back into the barrel to fill it up faster, until financial independence is in sight,

when a few income streams are then allowed to pour into the holey bucket.
- The lake should not dry up, so we have a managed risk approach to keep water despite evaporation (inflation, fees, mortgage costs, taxes, and others).
- In case of disinvestment, the excess water (return of initial capital and profit) goes back into the barrel, ready to be invested again.
- As the lake grows, accept a few more drips in the holey bucket and reward yourself from time to time.

There is not much more you will need. A three-month bucket, a three-year barrel, and a lifetime lake to grow.

We have a plan!

5

A new dawn

It's a new dawn, it's a new day,
It's a new life for me
And I'm feeling good

Nina Simone

The foundational sections have given us some good background. Now, buckle up because we really start our journey. The Excel simulator is our friend and we will make good use of it for various topics which are at the core of your future financial independence. You may find some surprising truths whilst I sure hope I keep you entertained.

Step 36: in employment

Want it or not, banks like to lower their risks when lending. It means that people in stable and good employment are more likely to get loans with the best possible conditions. People who have no job, or unstable and low revenue jobs, are unlikely to get a good deal, or any deal at all. Therefore, our starting point requires a stable and good paying job.

As your income depends on your ability to produce in a market, if you can acquire valuable skills and be highly productive in a rewarding market, you can hopefully earn way more than you need to spend and start saving in good proportion. However, working in a market which delivers low value is likely to constrain you to save less.

As a consequence, if you are in low skilled, low paid employment, I am afraid you will have to resolve this first or be Pi times more stringent on your spending. With low pay, banks may be too difficult to deal with, and we need them to leverage. I cannot resolve the employment step for you. My only advice is as follows: avoid putting yourself in competition against low-skill local people. Instead, compete against high-skill global ones. For this, surf on an irresistible global growth trend and make sure that directly or indirectly, you serve global clients (not local ones). As much as possible, your goal shall be to tick one of these criteria[38]:

- work for a company serving global clients.
- work for a global company.
- work as a freelance serving global companies or global clients.

I admit it: this advice is easier to implement when you have acquired high skills in demand. But ultimately, skills in demand today may not be as valuable in five years. Therefore, the most important factor is your attitude. If you are driven to learn and win despite failure, you will end up winning and climbing up the chain. How you respond

---

[38] There is also a long list of good local jobs such as doctor, notary, plumber, etc... which are not covered by these criteria.

to life's struggles is what will make the difference. Not just the skills you learned ten years ago.

That being said, I will now give you the picture of a near perfect career spanning over 40 years. You will start by earning one unit of money (per year, month or week, as you wish, it will not change the reasoning). You will change job 4 times, each change rewarding you with a 15% salary increase. When in same job, your salary is reviewed yearly at a ratio over twice inflation in first job, around 1.5 times in second job, then around or below inflation during your later career.

The table below shows the years in the header, then in first line is the evolution of your earnings from salary since your first day in job, and in third line is the year on year percentage increase of your salary.

Year	1	2	3	4	5	6	7	8	9	10
Salary	1.06	1.12	1.19	1.26	1.33	1.39	1.46	1.68	1.76	1.85
y-o-y%	6%	6%	6%	6%	5%	5%	5%	15%	5%	5%

Year	11	12	13	14	15	16	17	18	19	20
Salary	1.93	2.00	2.08	2.40	2.47	2.54	2.62	2.70	2.78	2.86
y-o-y %	4%	4%	4%	15%	3%	3%	3%	3%	3%	3%

Year	21	22	23	24	25	26	27	28	29	30
Salary	2.95	3.39	3.49	3.60	3.70	3.82	3.93	4.05	4.17	4.79
y-o-y %	3%	15%	3%	3%	3%	3%	3%	3%	3%	15%

Year	31	32	33	34	35	36	37	38	39	40
Salary	4.89	4.99	5.09	5.19	5.29	5.40	5.51	5.62	5.73	5.84
y-o-y %	2%	2%	2%	2%	2%	2%	2%	2%	2%	2%

Table 36.1 Mapping a 40 years long perfect career

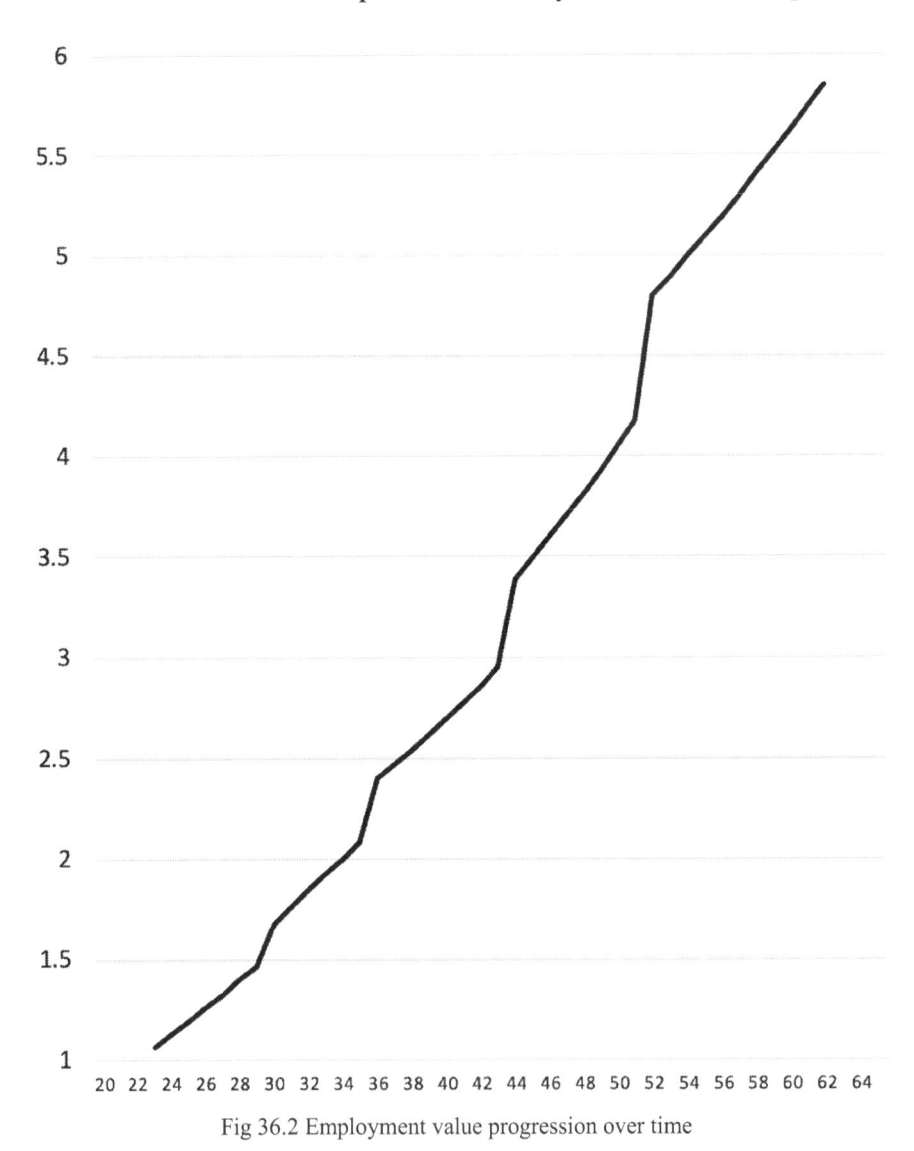

And here is the financial performance of your nice career in picture.

Fig 36.2 Employment value progression over time

If you were earning $10 per hour when you started at 23 years old, you would then earn over $58.4 per hour... forty years later.

Similarly, if you started at £30K per year, you end your career at £175K per year. Or start at $50K and finish at $292K. Seems a very good deal!

Only one problem... this was a sales pitch!

For a start, your career may not be as good as this perfect one. You may take a few years off, you may have to raise your kids, you may have to work part time, or god knows what. It does not matter that much, because I am not here to praise this perfect career and sell it as the Holy Grail of financial freedom. On the contrary, I am here to warn you that being in a secure and well-paid employment may not be enough for reaching financial independence before retirement age. And that's the real concern we have to deal with.

Now, let's assume for a moment that you have this wonderful career progression without much of a blip. As we now know, we can only see clearly when looking at the data on a log scale and rebased after CPI inflation. For good measure, we will take a CPI at 2.8% per year over the 40 years (I am being nice, not even a mild Pi factor in there!)

Look at your new career progression in the light of inflation:

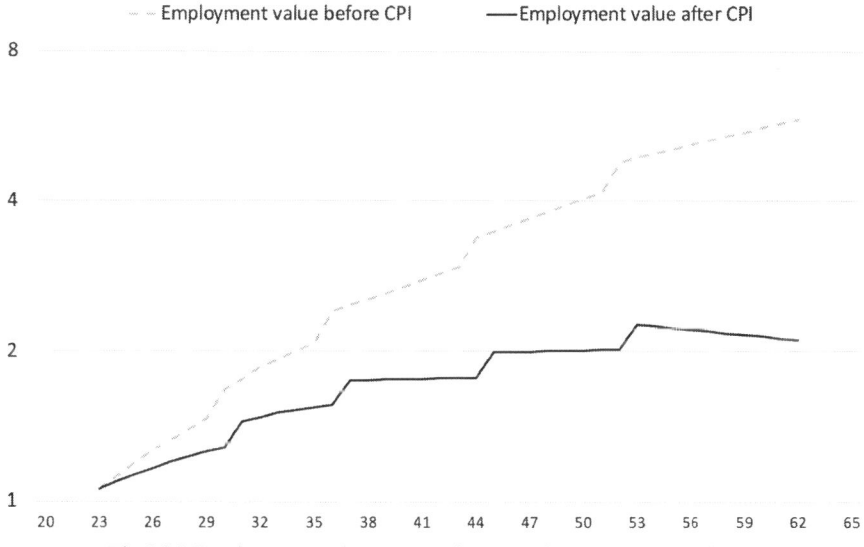

Fig 36.3 Employment value progression over time, not a sales pitch!

The interesting part is obviously the lower line, which reflects the value of your income from employment, after inflation has worked its magic in reverse. In reality, after inflation, the perfect employment career only allowed you to double your earning power over 40 years.

And that's gross salary. If we add the tax, it is obviously worse, as the taxman takes more from those who earn more. Next is a rough simulation of your future income, taking into account inflation and tax.

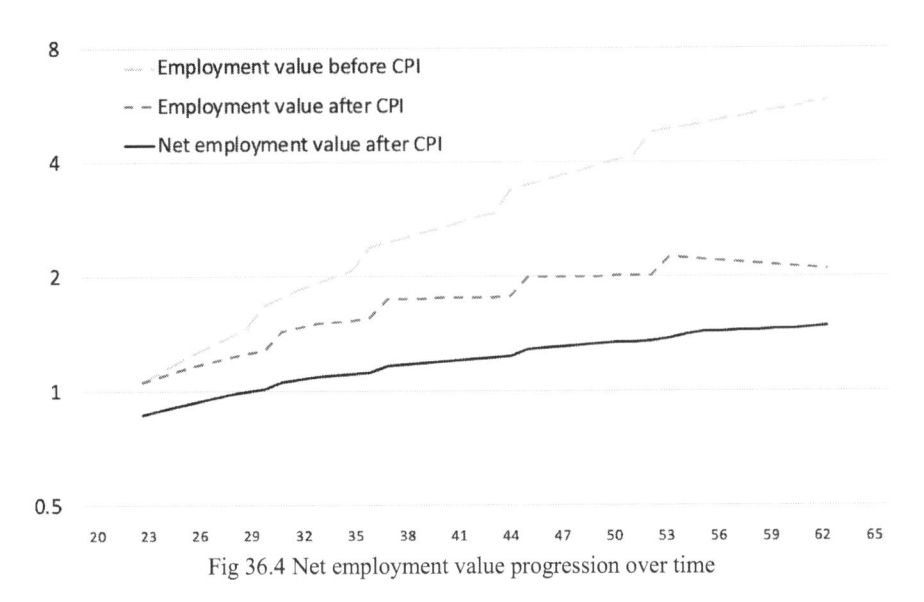

Fig 36.4 Net employment value progression over time

I know, you cannot predict politicians, even less so over 40 years! This graph is only a simulation of the impact of tax according to a chosen tax model[39]. In this model, your first salary at career start is taxed at 18%, your end of career at 29.8%, and your highest point at 38.9% which occurs briefly at peak employment value after CPI.

Yes, it's a pretty depressing perfect career plan... Far apart from the sales pitch! If you want to know, for a starting salary, at 23 years old, net of tax and rebased[40] at 100, the net of tax and inflation rebased career average value is at 140 and the max is at 170. As we can assume that your spending around mid-life is going to be at least double that of your early life, the 40% after-tax average gain is unlikely to bring much extra.

---

[39] After CPI salary is cumulatively taxed in bands (0-0.25 at 0%, 0.25-0.80 at 15%, 0.80-1.20 at 12.5%, 1.20-1.60 at 10%, 1.60-2.00 at 7.5%, over 2.00 at 5%). Max tax is 50%. This model also devalues the band by 1% per year (tax bands tend to not follow inflation over time).
[40] The first gross salary is at 1 (or 100%). After tax it becomes 0.87. We need to rebase this 0.87 to 100% to be able to compare correctly the other net of tax values.

In other words, the revenue stream you gain from your job is unlikely to make you financially independent by the end of your imperfect, or even perfect career. Any way you look at it, you need to plan for more revenue streams, and better hope they kick-in before you reach 60 or more.

I have much anger to vent at full-time employment. The biggest one is that it will never be a good idea to exchange the largest part of your valuable time for money. Money gets taxed and eroded by inflation, while quality time gets crushed and stolen away. And you can never get it back!

But do not get me wrong. I have stayed in employment all my adult life so far. The key is the benefit of a regular revenue stream, as you build other less demanding steady income streams, and the ability to leverage your employment through bank loans. Only get rid of your employment when you are financially independent, multiplied by Pi, or if you have managed to get a better long-term deal (part-employed, self-employed or other).

Step 37: a rainbow of money

Welcome to a colourful world of money!

Earlier, we differentiated two types of money: real money and credit. It is very clear to me that it is a lot easier to raise $1,000,000 of credit via a mortgage, than to earn $1,000,000 from employment. But in the end, one million dollars is one million dollars...

If one is easier to raise than the other is to earn, could we define further graduation of money in terms of their difficulty to acquire and their desirability? Let's try!

You go to a flea market, and you want to buy a genuine Russian bond note from 1910 to decorate your toilet. What will give you the best bargaining power? Cash or credit/debit card? Pretty sure it's cash. Cash is more valuable to the seller.

Also, at least in certain parts of the world, cash is used to buy without having to pay VAT on certain local goods or services. Suddenly, cash could be in the region of 20% more valuable[41]! Cash is probably more difficult to earn, at least in large quantities, but more desirable.

Let's make a list of types of transactions which could legitimately happen:

- Debt
    - Credit from mortgage (the good debt).
    - Credit from loan (the bad debt).
- Income
    - Cash from sale.[42]
    - Salary from employment.
    - Bonus from employment.
    - Perks from employment (restaurant, car, vouchers, etc...).

---

[41] A very average price of VAT, which is good enough for our example.
[42] Selling anything you own and don't need anymore.

- Interest from bank account.
- Dividend from stock.
- Rent from tenant.[43]
- Capital gain from sale.[44]
- Income from subscriptions you offer (youtube, blog, internet marketing, eBay sale, etc…).

• Savings

- Saving into a private pension.
- Employer paying into pension.

• Luck

- Inheritance money.
- Gift from whomever.
- Lotto money.

• Benefits

- Benefits from social security.
- Benefits from unemployment.
- Benefits from long term disabilities.
- Benefits from child support.
- Benefits from Grandma.
- Benefits from more…

You may find more, but already it's a good list. They all have their respective desirability and hardship to acquire. The money we receive from these transactions seem equal when adding up the lines in your account, but in terms of desirability and your sweat, they are not equal.

Note that from this point, we will not consider the income from benefits in our analysis, as it would be very strange and very unethical to attain financial freedom through leveraging benefits. I have also removed receiving income from your pension on purpose, as it defeats the goal of being financially free before receiving any pension income.

---

[43] Although I will use the term "Rent from tenant" throughout, the real meaning is "profit from rental activity" as we must deduct the cost (mortgage interest and others) from the rent.
[44] Could be from selling a property or shares.

With this in mind, we can start building visual pictures of the various attributes we can generally associate with all these transactions.

For example, let's start with frequency. Some of these transactions may happen very regularly, such as a monthly pay cheque, whereas others are rare or even very improbable.

The following graph depicts a possible ranking of the frequency of these transactions, starting with the reference at 100% being a monthly recurring transaction.

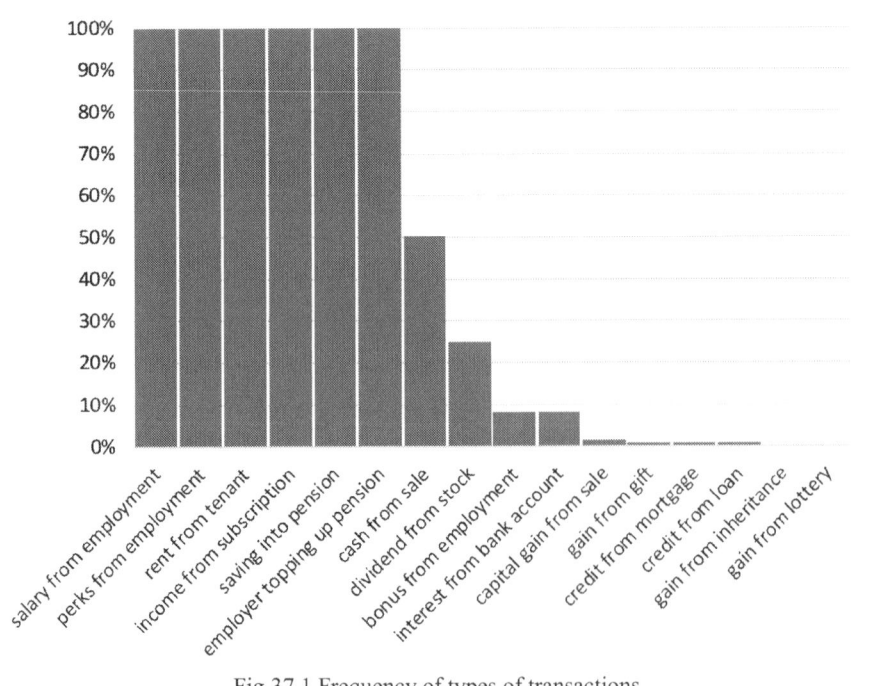

Fig 37.1 Frequency of types of transactions

Of course, some of these values are arbitrary, but we have to start somewhere that is as much as possible a good reflexion of the reality. The next table lists all values for transactions not occurring monthly.

Type of transaction	Frequency
Cash from sale	Once every 2 months
Dividend from stock	Once per quarter
Bonus from employment	Once per year
Interest from bank account	Once per year
Capital gain from sale	Once every 5 years
Gain from gift	Once every 7 years
Credit from mortgage	Once every 10 years
Credit from loan	Once every 10 years
Gain from inheritance	Once every 40 years
Gain from lottery	Once every 50,000 years

Table 37.2 Detailed frequency of transactions not occurring monthly

For each of these transactions, we can also assign, at the indicated frequency, a likely amount value relative to a gross monthly salary from employment.

For example, if a gross monthly salary has a value of 1, then we could possibly have a value of mortgage at 84 (7 years of salary) happening once every 10 years, perks from employment at around 4% of salary happening monthly, and so on.

Again, my choice of values is arbitrary and your personal situation might be slightly different. However, on the whole, the values listed below should not be so bad that they misrepresent the reality by an order of magnitude or more.

Thereafter is the table of financial gains which are planned to occur at the frequency defined in the above table.

Type of transaction	Amount
Gain from lottery	40 years of salary
Credit from mortgage	7 years of salary
Gain from inheritance	1.5 years of salary
Credit from loan	6 months of salary
Capital gain from sale	3 months of salary
Bonus from employment	1.5 months of salary
Gain from gift	1 month of salary
Rent from tenant	7 days of salary
Cash from sale	3 days of salary
Dividend from stock	2 days of salary
Saving into pension	1 day of salary
Employer topping up pension	1 day of salary
Perks from employment	1 day of salary
Income from subscription	4 hours of salary
Interest from bank account	2 hours of salary

Table 37.3 Reasonable amount to expect per type of transaction (at defined frequency)

We can represent these data on a graph, by largest to smallest amount.

Fig 37.4 Typical amount by type of transactions

Note that the variability of the values is very high, spanning over 5 orders of magnitude. Interest paid yearly on a bank account is light years away from winning the lottery in terms of financial benefit...

But for all the hype that the lottery ticket represents, we can sense that such a huge transaction never ever happening is unlikely to provide us with more security than a steady recurring one, such as salary from employment. It also seems intuitive that a small transaction occurring yearly is less desirable than a larger one occurring monthly.

Therefore, the frequency of transactions and their typical amount are contributing, probably not solely but significantly, to the desirability of such transaction. For the moment, let's define this desirability factor as follows:

```
desirability = amount x sqrt (frequency)
```
[45]

That leads us to the following graph which represents the desirability of money by type of transaction.

---

[45] The reason for the square root (the sqrt function) is to flatten the relative values a bit and avoid lone peaks, a bit like the logarithmic scale was useful to dampen the high growth effect.

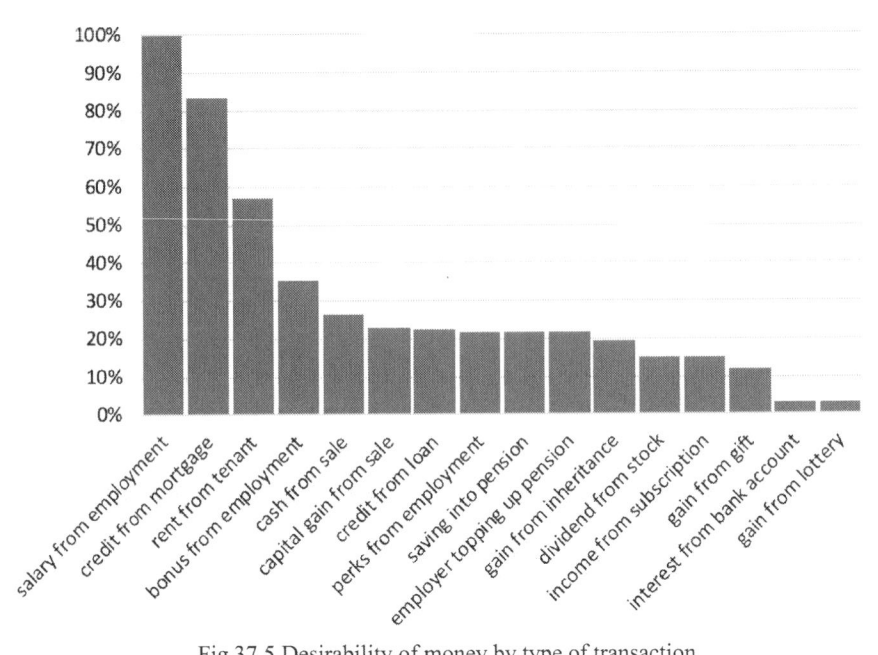

Fig 37.5 Desirability of money by type of transaction

According to this model, salary from employment and credit from mortgage are the most desirable types of transactions. Next is rent from tenant. Then we find the pension (adding employer and employee contribution would rank at 44% on the graph), followed by bonus from employment, cash from sale, and capital gain on sale of assets, which could also be seen as trading the stock market.

It is also striking that interest from bank is fighting the least desirable spot with gain from lottery. So much for leaving money idle on a bank account!

However, this desirability should be tampered a bit by tax. As we know, different types of transactions are subject to different types of tax. A credit from mortgage is not taxed when you receive it. We could argue that a bonus is taxed slightly more than salary because it is likely to tip you in a higher tax band. Similarly, the profit from rental activity is taxed a bit less than salary because of specific allowable deductions (although not guaranteed forever).

The following graph depicts the types of transaction sorted by tax rate.

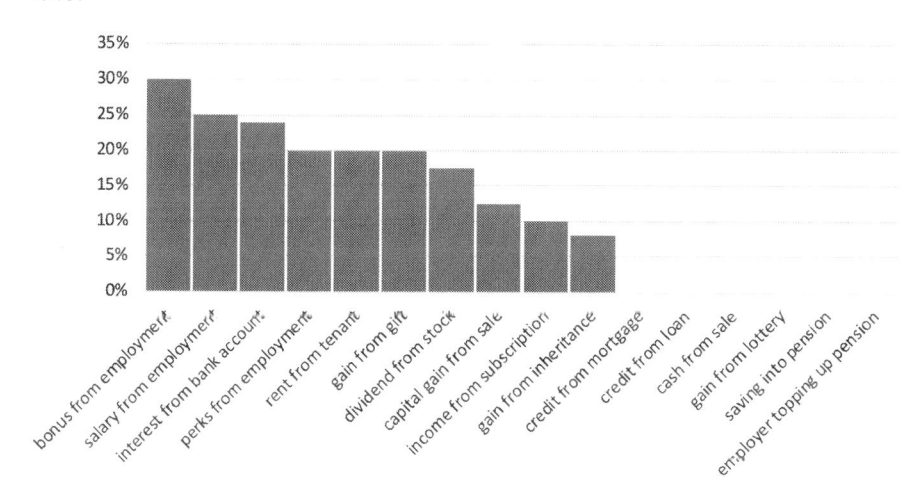

Fig 37.6 Typical tax rate by type of transaction

I do not pretend that all my chosen tax values, are a perfect representation of all situations but on the whole, they feel reasonable[46].

Note that unsurprisingly, all transactions listed as income are on the tax side, except from "cash from sale" which could possibly avoid taxation for smaller amounts. It also highlights pretty well the policies of most governments, favouring saving into pension, taking on debt, and... gambling!

Let's now introduce the concept of net desirability, which will level the playing field of competing transactions net of taxes. To make the highly taxed income less desirable, we define the following formula.

```
net desirability = desirability x (1 - tax rate%).
```

The next graph is rebased at 100% for ease of reading, and the two pensions contributions (employer and employee) got merged to reflect the desirability of the private pension in one bar.

---

[46] I mostly based my tax values on the U.K. tax system, with some necessary interpretations.

128 A new dawn

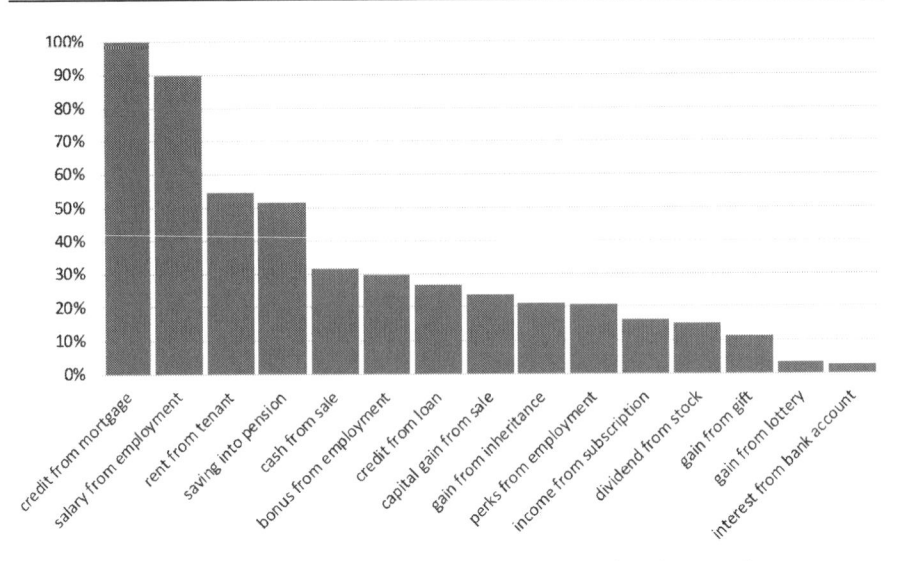

Fig 37.7 Net desirability by type of transaction (rebased at 100%)

The striking bit is that interest from bank account has now definitely won the least desirable medal, thanks in part to generous gambling policies. Jokes aside, the new situation is that a mortgage is slightly more desirable than a salary. Rent from tenant stays in third, but the value of a pension is getting closer. Then, cash is now slightly more desirable than a bonus!

The top five cover two thirds of the desirability spectrum. Add the next one (bonus from employment) for good measure, and you now nearly cover three quarters.

Here is a table of the relative desirability strength for the top five.

Type of transaction	Relative strength	Cumulated strength
Credit from mortgage	20.07%	20.07%
Salary from employment	17.99%	38.06%
Rent from tenant	10.95%	49.01%
Saving into pension	10.35%	59.36%
Cash from sale	6.34%	65.69%

Table 37.8 Top 5 net desirable types of transactions

And here is another visual representation of the same data:

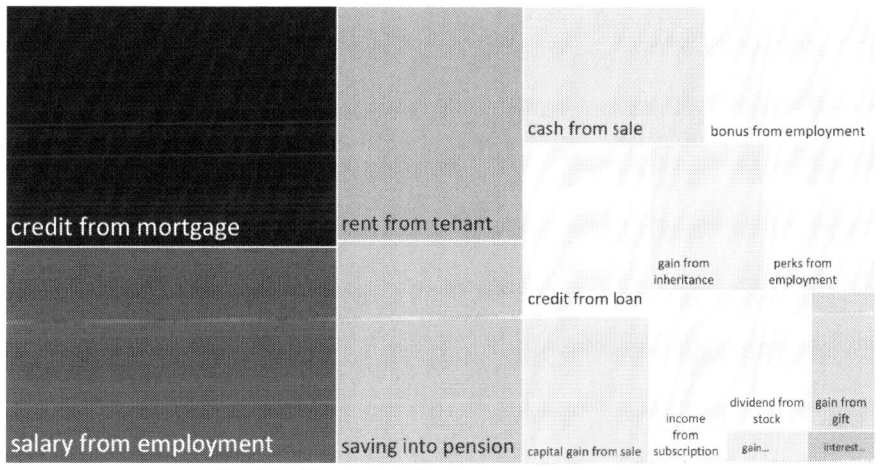

Fig 37.9 Net desirability by type of transaction

When seeing this, we should wonder…

Why bother with the rest beyond the top 5? Credit money, a salary, rent from multiple tenants, topping up a private pension, and cash on occasions.

You can become financially independent focusing on this mix.

Step 38: income vs freedom

The dilemma of income vs freedom is generally at the centre of the quest for achieving financial independence. We want to be financially independent for the freedom it procures. But we know that freedom without income does not last long, or at the very least comes at the cost of our lifestyle.

If we focus a moment on the income part of the financial transactions we identified earlier, we can associate a time intensity to each of them. For example:

- Earning salary from employment is very time intensive, to the tune of, in general, a minimum of 8 hours a day, 5 days a week.
- Rent from tenant may take you up to half an hour a day every day of the month (tenants do tend to need care and attention!).
- Earning interest from a bank account will probably take you only a few minutes a month (login to your bank account, check the value of interest in cents or pennies, move on).
- And gain from inheritance may set you off by 10 hours a week or more[47].

The following table lists all types of income and luck transactions and defines a realistic time intensity (in hours spent per month)[48].

Type of income (or luck)	Time intensity
Salary from employment	172 hours
Bonus from employment	172 hours
Perks from employment	172 hours
Income from subscription	22 hours
Rent from tenant	15 hours
Gain from inheritance	10 hours

---

[47] Did you really think that inheritance just happens without seeing Grandma regularly?
[48] Hours spent per month to obtain the typical amount of income as defined in previous tables.

Gain from gift	5 hours
Cash from sale	3 hours
Capital gain from sale	2 hours
Dividend from stock	2 hours
Gain from lottery	1 hour
Interest from bank account	15 minutes

Table 38.1 Time intensity of income

You did not need me to sense that freedom has an inverse relation to time intensity for generating income. For the freedom it procures, we are more likely to love an income stream that did not incur much effort to fatten our bank account.

As when previously faced with several order of magnitude in difference, we will use a square root to flatten the impact. Let's say that the freedom procured by a type of income is the inverse square root of its time intensity:

```
Freedom from income = 1 / sqrt (time intensity)
```

The next chart shows such a representation of the relative freedom procured by each type of income stream.

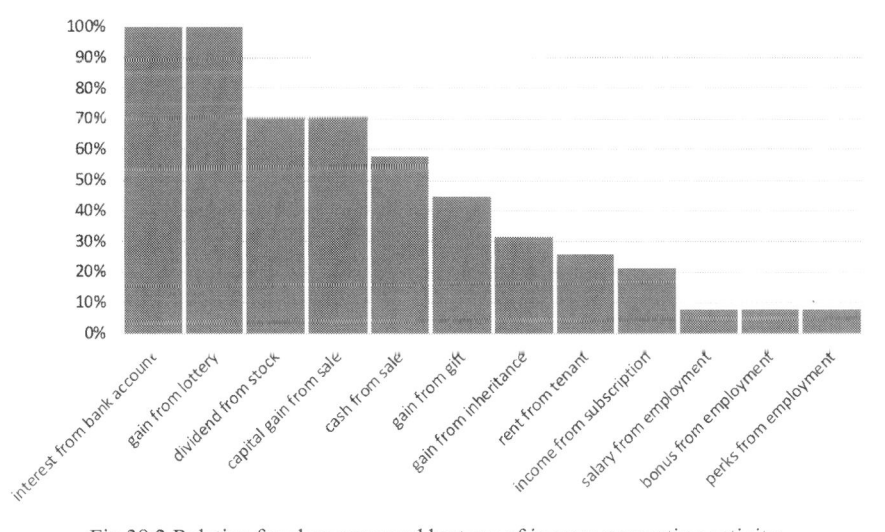

Fig 38.2 Relative freedom procured by type of income generating activity

As expected, we have a reverse order of the time intensity, with a flattened curve[49].

Earlier, we saw the net desirability of money transactions in their various forms. If we now focus on income alone, it seems clear to me that an income stream will be even more desirable if I have to work less for it. Hence, there must be a net desirability of income for those who would rather not spend much time working. Let's call it the net desirability of income for lazy people[50].

Surprise, surprise... here it is!

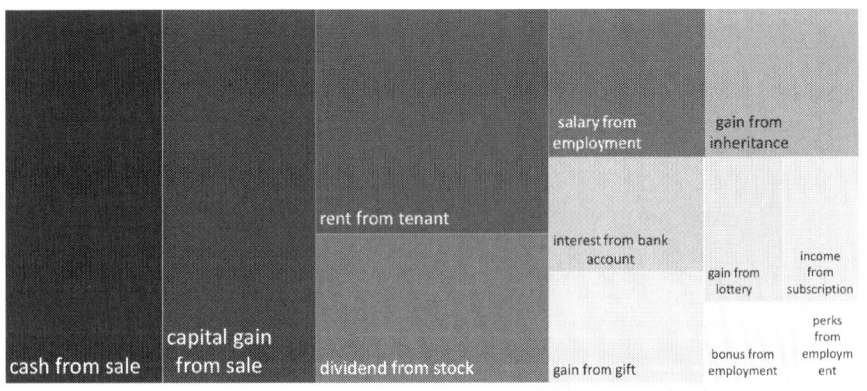

Fig 38.3 Net desirability for lazy people (all activities generating income)

Well, lazy people prefer to sell everything they have...

Sell goods for cash and sell stocks and property for gain.

Why are we surprised?

---

[49] Interest from bank account is off the chart at 200%.
[50] Net desirability for lazy people = net desirability rebased at 100% times relative freedom rebased at 100%.

Thereafter is a table listing the top five for lazy people, all relative to the top 1.

Type of income	Net desirability for lazy people
Cash from sale	100%
Capital gain from sale	92%
Rent from tenant	77%
Dividend from stock	58%
Salary from employment	38%

Table 38.4 Top five net desirability for rich and lazy people

If we refrain from selling the goose eggs, the goose, and the land with the goose poo, which is unlikely to be a good strategy, we have found a natural and weighted order of what should appeal to someone who seeks to maximise income but at the same time, not at the expense of becoming a slave to the employer.

The US taxman (IRS) has categorised these three income streams separately, and it really fits our model. Rent from tenant is seen as passive income, dividend from stock as portfolio income, and salary from employment as earned income. Each of these categories generally bears a different tax regime, and as you would guess, the more heavily taxed is the earned income category[51].

You should realise that the relative proportion of each income stream category in your household is somehow likely to represent how far away you are from a totally secure state of financial independence.

This next table shows the previous figures, now rebased at 100% for clarity of reading, for the three IRS categories of income. We will call it the net desirability of income categories for rich and lazy people.

---

[51] It has the largest base of taxable people and the employer collects the tax, reducing fraud.

Category of income	Net desirability for rich and lazy people
Passive income	44.6%
Portfolio income	33.7%
Earned income	21.7%

Table 38.5 Net desirability of income categories for rich and lazy people

And the next pie chart is the graphic representation of the same income categories according to our net desirability for rich and lazy people.

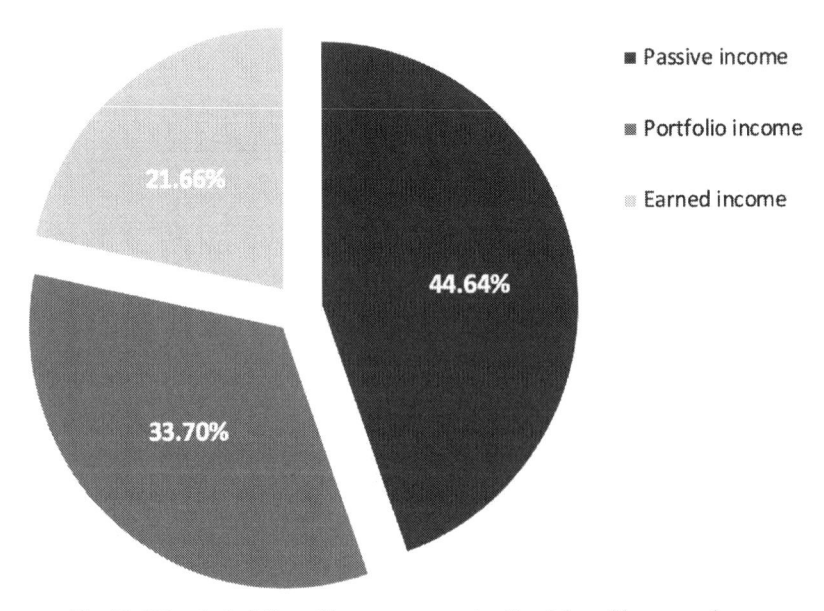

Fig 38.6 Net desirability of income categories for rich and lazy people

It is very tempting to see this as a blueprint for allocation of income by those blessed by financial freedom. Note that according to the model, nearly 80% of income should be earned outside of employment[52].

How would you like it if your income from employment was just a fifth of your total income?

---

[52] For the avoidance of doubt, this split of income streams does not imply that the underlying capital generating the passive and portfolio income have to follow the same ratio.

Step 39: Debt free fallacy

> "My ultimate goal is to repay my mortgage and be debt free as quickly as possible"

How many times have I heard this one? How many times have I thought it was the key that would unlock my financial independence?

But it's wrong.

Will your financial needs stop when your mortgage is repaid? Will you suddenly stop eating, travelling, heating your home, and more? In truth, paying back your mortgage early is only removing one cost among many others. If and when you repay your mortgage, will you then say this?

> "I will stop heating the house in winter for the next 20 years because electricity and gas are expensive"

It looks stupid when put this way.

We are often tempted to associate paying back the capital (truly owning the house) with freedom. But as we saw earlier, financial freedom is less about capital and more about income. It comes with a regular net passive income in excess of your financial needs. Nothing more. Owning your home outright will only be a side effect of you coming closer to financial independence, but should not be the goal, or you will miss many other opportunities.

To put this in perspective let's do another virtual investment exercise. Here is the situation: in a small French village where a local peasant bought a farm 100 years ago, you face the following choice[53] to find a home for your family:

- rent a house for €950 per month.
- buy a similar house for €322,500, which includes 7.5% of tax and fees (house at €300,000, taxes and fees at €22,500).

---

[53] This semi-fictional example is based on true figures from the market in 2018.

Another important piece of information: as long as you are in good and stable employment, the bank will allow an 85% loan to value, and thanks to the European Central Bank buying all assets over Euroland, the interest rate on the loan is 1.4% fixed for 20 years[54].

It's a no brainer…

You do your utmost to buy the house. Scrape every cent you have together and buy it! As long as there is no extra condition to obtain it, I would go for an interest only mortgage, where the capital has to be repaid at the end, with a flexibility to repay 10% of the capital per year without penalty. That is quite standard in the industry.

Now, our no brainer choice looks like this:

- Rent a house for €950 per month to a private landlord, with a risk of having to move elsewhere at the end of the contract, and a risk of inflation on the rent at the contract anniversary or whenever the landlord gets itchy palms.

Or…

- Buy the house (requires a €67,500 capital input for 15% of house value plus all taxes and fees), and then pay €297.50 of monthly "rent" (interest) to the bank for the next 20 years[55] with no risk of eviction (so long as you pay) and no rent increase.

Let's put the repayment of the loan aside for a moment. Let's push it even further and consider that the amount of €67,500 paid partly for capital, partly for taxes and fees, was in fact for securing two distinct contract options with the bank as follows:

- a 20 years lease where the rent is fixed at €297.50 (less than a third than market value).
- an option to buy the house in 20 years at €255,000 (the repayment of the loan).

---

[54] This is not a typo, banks in France offered this fixed rate for their best clients as of mid-2018.
[55] 300K * 85% = 255K ; 255K * 1.4% per year = 3,570 ; 3,570 / 12 = 297.50.

With a very modest 1.75% rent inflation per year (again, it is good practise to be conservative), we can quickly visualise the likely minimum gain from the 20 years lease.

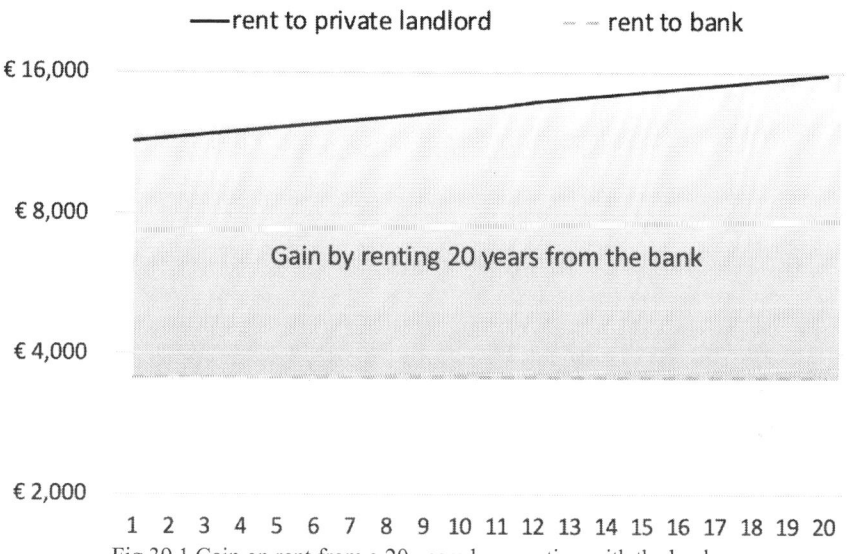

Fig 39.1 Gain on rent from a 20 years lease option with the bank

Over 20 years, the cumulated rent paid to the private landlord would be just over €270,000, or close to the cost of the house in the first place. We have to be careful with this number as this is a value made of cumulated rents over 20 years, therefore with a bit of inflation at work.

On the other hand, the rent (interest) paid to the bank is €71,400. Here again, a slight warning because the €297.50 monthly rent paid in 20 years has less current value than the one paid in year one.

Overall, it balances enough to show a near €200,000 difference. Therefore, we can conclude that the €67,500 option gives us good confidence of a €200,000 cost saving over 20 years.

If we take the same very conservative 1.75% annual inflation for the house itself, the €300,000 house of today will be worth over €417,000 in 20 years. Bear in mind that assigning a house inflation at the same rate as the CPI over two decades is a big discount gift (a big risk mitigation) because it just cancels any effect that our invisible man is supposed to leverage over the long run.

Consequently, the overall picture is that on top of the €200,000 gift from the bank, which in itself would already be worth the deposit investment, we have the option in 20 years, to buy our €417,000 house for the remaining €255,000 loan value. That is buying the house at around 60% of its value, and this time with no tax and no fees, as they were already paid on the initial purchase, at a lower house value.

Our back of the envelope review on this opportunity is €360,000 of value creation over 20 years, in exchange for a €67,500 spend now. How good is that?

But there is an additional good twist that we can play.

The €200,000 gift from the bank could become more than just cost saving. Indeed, this could be an opportunity to setup an automatic tax-free saving system, which is worth around €650 a month in year one, and over €1,000 a month in the last year. This is nearly as good as another source of income. And you can save this money in a view to fund another investment.

Just this saving on its own is enough to constitute a deposit for three other investments, respectively in year 8, 14 and 20.

Year #	8	14	20
Deposit saved	€68,426	€60,683	€69,690

Table 39.2 deposit saved from a 20 years lease option with bank

It is striking that the savings you made by not renting and not paying back the capital quickly are nearly enough on their own to help make three similar investments. By the time you make investment one, if it is correctly planned and financed, it will generate also a profit, and accelerate the day when investment two can be made, maybe at year 12 instead of 14. It's a kind of virtuous circle, slowly but steady.

Now, back you our debt free gremlin:

```
"how do you pay back the house loan in 20 years?"
```

Do we have a crystal ball which shows that you will be living in the same house in 20 years' time? It is frankly as likely that you will be forced to move (job opportunity), or will want to move (to another house), than you will stay put.

The situation is more like this:

```
"when time comes, I will have to re-finance this
                        house."
```

In the scenario that you cannot finance the loan repayment, you will sell the house and pocket the €360,000 profit, thank you. Notwithstanding the fact that you will have avoided moving home many times in 20 years and lowered a factor of stress in doing so. In the best-case scenario, you will keep it.

Now, let's be clear, you invest for life, not for selling 5, 10, or 20 years later. A re-financing problem shall not happen. We will find the ways so that it does not happen. Furthermore, your home of today could well become one of your best rental investments of tomorrow. If it's a good home, do not sell it. Keep it, and when the time comes, re-finance.

Do not forget this. Debt is leverage. Becoming debt free is removing the leverage that the bank gave you.

That would not be a good idea.

Step 40: From human to financial capital

Until this point, I have been quite clear that income, in all its various forms and origins, is what matters. But income does not grow on trees. As we saw already, it comes from capital. Two types of capital to be more precise: human capital and financial capital. As both will vary in value during your lifetime, we may want to understand their relationship and how to maximise them.

Let's start with your human capital.

As mentioned earlier, the market will put a value on your ability to perform a job. Your skills, knowledge, creativity, past experiences, core values, and more, are weighted by such organisation or company in need for them, and translate into a temporary financial compensation (salary, bonus, perks, etc…). I insist on the temporary aspect, because what is in demand today may not be so valuable in five or ten years. You have to stay relevant in your market. Anyway, your human capital is the future economic value of all these factors that ultimately convert into your earned income[56].

Financial capital on the other hand is basically your net assets (assets minus liabilities). The game is to grow the financial capital as the human capital gets depleted, and then replace progressively the income from human capital by an income from financial capital.

We will now continue from our perfect career plan. As we left it, it looked like it would not be good enough on its own to lead you to financial independence long enough before standard retirement day. Let's first have a feel for the human capital value of this perfect career over time. Your human capital seen as of this moment in time, is the sum of all your future revenues, as per the net employment value after CPI inflation, as already described earlier.

To visualise this, let's focus on average Joe and picture his perfect career. We will assume the following:

---

[56] To learn more on human capital, read documents published by Joshua Corrigan, such as https://www.actuaries.org.uk/documents/holistic-framework-life-cycle-financial-planning.

- Inflation is at 2.8% as per our previous model.
- Joe's career starts at £30,000 (at 23 years old).
- on retirement year (at 63 years old in our case), Joe will continue to generate some income from work, albeit worth only 1 month of his past year of activity.
- Every subsequent year in retirement, Joe's work income diminishes by 15%.

The graph below shows Joe's human capital. The starting point CPI indexed value is around £1,490,000. In other words, the 23-year-old Joe has nearly £1,500,000 of future net income[57] to sustain his lifestyle until death.

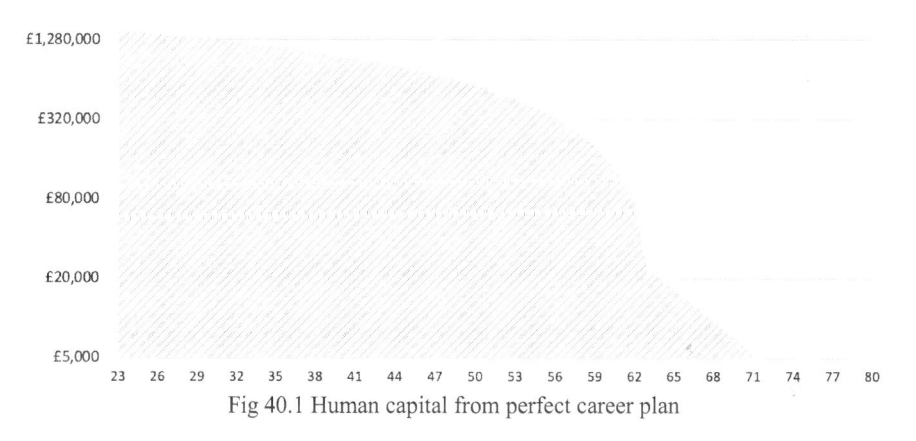

Fig 40.1 Human capital from perfect career plan

Note that due to the logarithmic scale, as well as the effect of CPI and tax, the four 15% increase in salary barely appear on the graph. In fact, this perfect career human capital is very similar to a human capital modelled at 4.75% increase per annum throughout the entire 40 years career with same post-retirement income conditions.

To understand better the challenges facing Average Joe turned Perfect Joe, we will make a few additional assumptions. I try to make these assumptions as realistic as possible[58]. We will first assume that

---

[57] Value as of today discounting future inflation.
[58] These assumptions may not match your personal situation, but they give us a starting point for understanding the challenge of converting human capital into financial capital.

Joe will stay single and will not actively seek financial independence through savings and investment.

Here are the assumptions:

- Throughout his working life, Joe will pay 30% of net income towards either rent or capital repayment. First 10 years renting, next 30 years repaying mortgage capital and interest.
- Joe will save 5% of net income throughout his career, and invest it at 4% interest per annum.
- The remaining income is spent on lifestyle
- On retirement day, Joe reduces his lifestyle needs by a third, and it will stay the same until death (initially more lifestyle amusements, later more healthcare).
- On retirement day, Joe has an additional state pension worth £165 per week[59].
- Inflation still the same at 2.8% per annum.

With this plan, the perfect career of a perfectly normal single person, saving consistently 5% of net income over 40 years and placing it at 4% in a 2.8% inflationary world…will run out of money by age 72 despite having a full state pension!

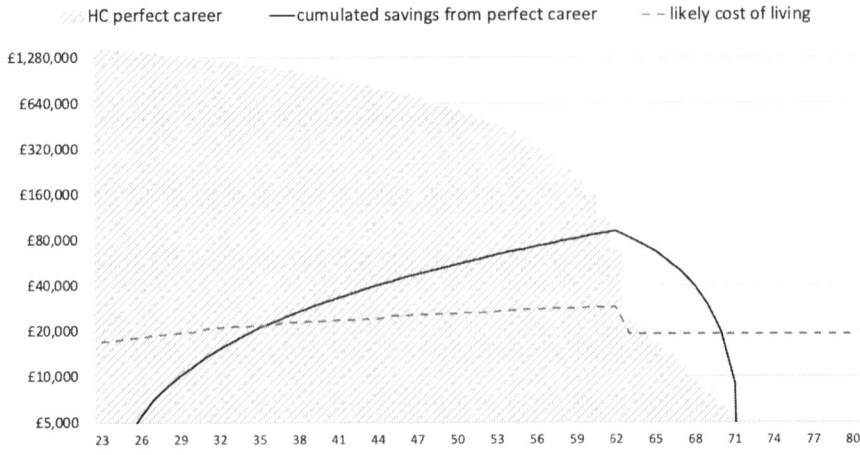

Fig 40.2 Joe's perfect human capital, cost of living, and saving 5% of income at 4% interest

---

[59] Actual maximum state pension in U.K. in 2018.

Joe will then rely only on state pension and/or family. As can be simulated, the state pension will give Joe a shortfall of around 50% of required expense, which again, later in life are heavily weighted by healthcare needs. The likely option for Perfect Joe, who does not want to burden others but is slowly turning into Assisted Joe, is to release equity from his home, or sell his home and downsize, spending the capital gain on retirement lifestyle and healthcare. Anyway, there is not much financial capital left at the end of his life! And let us remind ourselves that it was a life of work until Joe could not do it anymore.

How could Joe get out of this unpleasant forecast?

If Joe gets married but his partner does not have much of a human capital, it will put even more strain on both of them, and the financial capital may run out even earlier, by the time they go into retirement. Love is blind, but better when financially secure…

If Joe now places the savings at 7% per annum, all other conditions unchanged, we have this better picture.

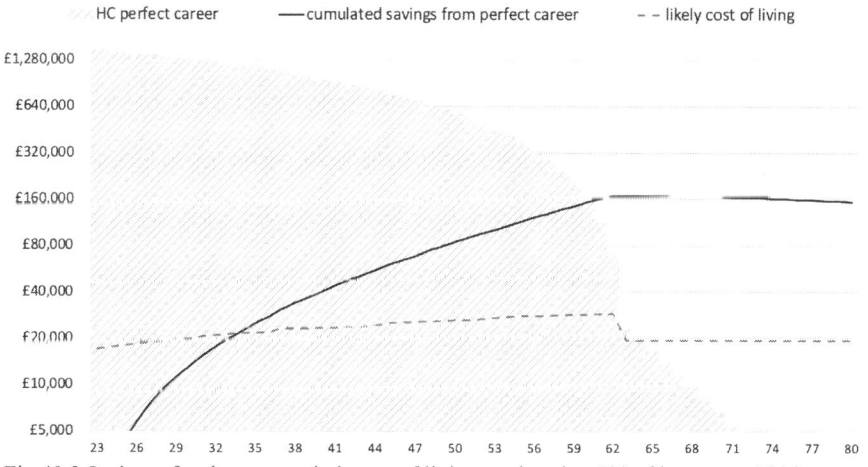

Fig 40.3 Joe's perfect human capital, cost of living, and saving 5% of income at 7% interest

Looks like it's a good plan for securing Joe's future, although we are still at the mercy of a Pi factor surprise somewhere, way into the future. Still, what we see is that saving constantly 5% of net income, throughout 40 years of a perfect career, and investing it at 7% per annum is enough to secure old age, but not enough to have an early exit of the rat race.

For a married couple, we could simulate the same. We would have a couple's human capital which is the sum of both individual human capitals, and the rest follows the same logic, although possibly with slightly different parameters (lower proportional cost of housing, higher cost of living until all children are grown up, etc...).

Let's push the simulation a bit further. Now, Joe will cut on a chunk of his lifestyle expenses and maintain only a minimum of dripping out of the holey bucket. By doing so, Joe can now save 10% of net income, still invested at 7%, all other conditions unchanged. Here is the new picture of the financial situation.

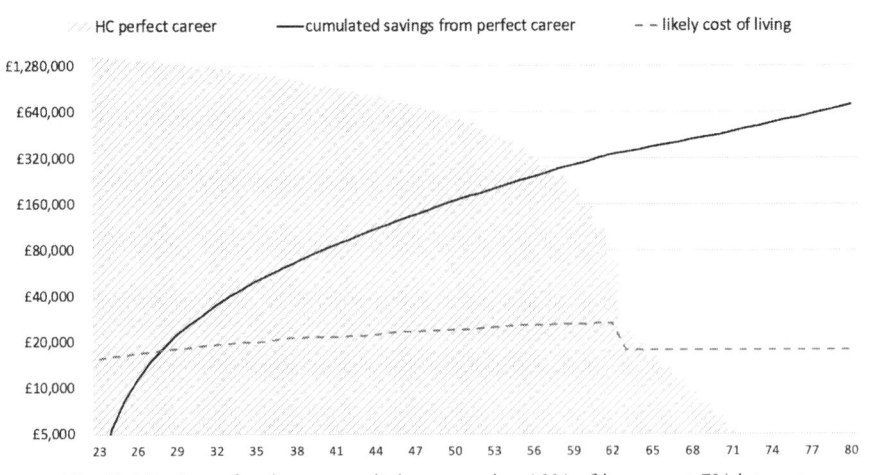

Fig 40.4 Joe's perfect human capital, now saving 10% of income at 7% interest

So long as his investments return a minimum of 7% interest, it looks like Joe's entire life is financially secure. He could even outlive normal life expectations and would not feel any risk. We could factor and simulate an adverse Pi factor in this model, but it is unlikely that it will threaten its stability by much. This is a fairly secure plan. Finally, what would be required for Joe to be financially independent at 55?

This following picture gives us a hint.

Fig 40.5 Joe's early retirement plan, saving 10% of income at 7% interest

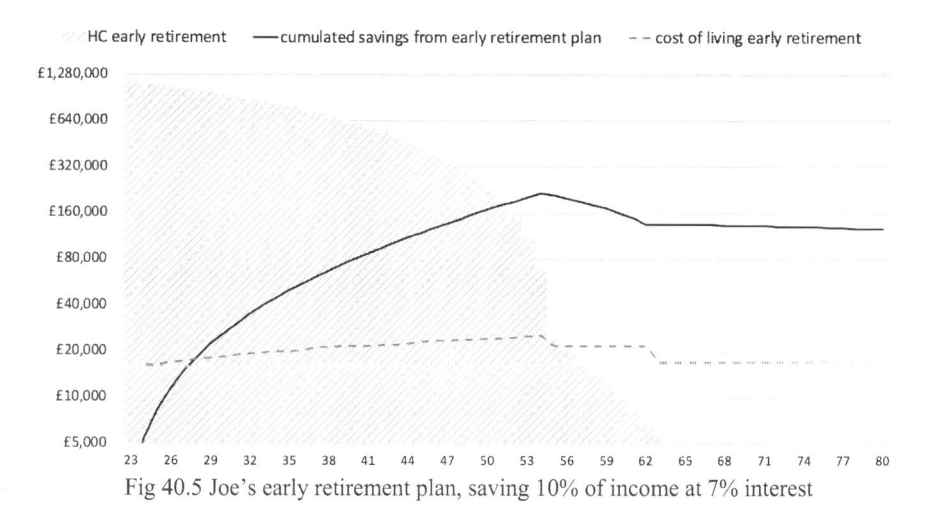

In this model, Joe acquires his home 3 years earlier and repays within 25 instead of 30 years. When turning 55, he fully owns his home and reduces his lifestyle by 15%. All other conditions stay the same, as well as the unknown risk (same unknown Pi factor not integrated here).

What we saw here is that it is possible to build models and use them to simulate our financial situation way into the future. It is very important to realise that our first fictional Perfect Joe, who worked all his life, saved 5% every month and invested all his savings (albeit at a lower rate of return of 4%) has nevertheless managed to land himself in financial trouble and will not have enough to cover his living expenses in old age.

If it proves something, it is that financial planning will require more than just working a lifetime, putting aside some money, and hoping it will be enough!

I want to finish by giving you the ability to quickly calculate your own estimated human capital to get a feel for where you are. You have to take it with a pinch of salt, because this model will not fit everybody's personal situation, but playing with it is a good start to learning and asking the right questions. As seen earlier, the "perfect career" model we used is close to a more generic one which would assume that you will be in employment for 40 years with around 4.75% salary increase per year[60].

Let's say you are 45 years old and you started at $40,000 (22 years ago), then according to this model you should earn $40,000 x 3.39 = around $135,000 pa today[61]. I suppose you could accept a range of +/- 3 years which means in this case a salary in the range $111,000–148,000. Verify first that the model fits your conditions, and that your current salary is indeed close enough to the projected one from your starting point. If the model seems to fit your situation, you are able to calculate an approximation of your human capital (or your household human capital) with the following tables. The first table contains the age in the header, and the remaining capital in the first line.

23	25	30	35	40
100%	96.45%	86.78%	75.99%	64.32%

45	50	55	60	65
52.04%	38.83%	25.04%	10.47%	1.11%

Table 40.6 Pro-rated human capital left at important stages of your life, according to model

The next table contains in the header the starting salary at 23 years old and in the first line the value of the human capital at 65 years old.

15,000	20,000	25,000	30,000	35,000
743,739	991,652	1,239,565	1,434,638	1,735,391

40,000	45,000	50,000	55,000	60,000
1,983,304	2,231,217	2,479,130	2,727,043	2,974,956

Table 40.7 Human capital at 23 years old for various starting salaries, according to model

---

[60] If you plan a 15 years career, or huge salary variations, the model will not fit well...
[61] The 3.39 value is taken from the perfect career table provided earlier, at year 22 (23 year old + 22 = 45 year old).

In our case of a 45-year-old fitting the model with a starting salary of $40,000, the human capital is $1,983,304 * 52.04% = $1,032,111. But that's the value as seen by the 23-year-old back in time. We need to reflate it by 22 years of inflation[62], so in our case the final human capital is $1,032.111 * (1+0.028)^22 = $1,894,850.

Note that to help calculate your human capital, I also provide simulators on the website www.intheRatRace.com.

What use do you have with this human capital value?

It is a starting point for assessing your future wealth potential. It does not mean that you will be as rich or as poor as predicted. Independently of your human capital value, you may still spend all of your income or more on lifestyle. But it gives us an idea of your potential and the leverage that you can play with. Typically, I would see that if you have enough working years left to take up a home residence mortgage (say 20 years), then you have a quick estimation of how much you could borrow. While explaining the assumptions behind this model, I earlier provided a guidance of 30% of cost towards home rental or mortgage repayment. A very rough 30% of human capital gives an indication of maximum mortgage. In our case of the 45-year-old, the maximum mortgage would probably be around[63] $550,000 and there is urgency to take it, as waiting another 5 years may not be acceptable to the banks[64].

In conclusion, want it or not, you carry a human capital value. It's better if you know what it is, and on which model it operates. By visualising your human capital, expenses, savings, and investments on a graph, it brings reality to your financial situation, now and into the future, and your many options to improve it. By reviewing some input conditions, you can identify ways to convert this net human capital, first into savings (our 3-year barrel), and then into investments (our

---

[62] Still at 2.8% in our model.
[63] $1,894,850 * 30% = $568,455 which we round down to $550,000.
[64] Banks prefer to see the end of mortgage repayments on or before your 65th birthday.

pond growing into a lake), so that at some point, you do not become dependent on your employment income.

I encourage you to play with this simulator, understand your human capital value, and form an idea of how you will convert it progressively into financial capital, maybe first via a home purchase.

Step 41: Risk on capital

Losing hard-earned after-tax savings will give you one of the worst feelings, a level of emotion far in excess of the pleasure you feel from making a profit. We want to avoid losses, but if or when we are in the pit, we need to keep learning valuable lessons, and avoid repeating the same mistakes.

As we talk about risk on capital, we may as well first review the risk on human capital. If you have the highest salary of your household and you have dependents, at some point you may want to buy life insurance to protect your family. Your human capital value is close to the amount you would need to insure, as it is the most realistic projection of all your future income. You will decide if you take the insurance or not, but at least you know that in front of the risk, there is a way to cover it adequately.

Regarding financial assets, we will review the risks associated with some common asset classes.

In financial markets, there is this concept of volatility which allows us to gauge the risk of an investment. To make it simple, the volatility is a measure of the potential price variation of an asset over a certain period of time. The volatility is therefore representative of the risk incurred by holding the asset over time.

For an asset valued at $100, a volatility of 10% means that a price move (gain or loss) not exceeding $10 is expected in 68% of the time. Of course, $10 is not the maximum loss you would ever have, as in truth, if the world collapses, you could lose the entire capital of $100. The volatility model only defines the probability of the price move to be within a range, based on the fact that it behaved similarly in a previous period of time. In our case of a 10% volatility on an asset of $100, if you want to cover price moves happening 95% of the time, you have to extend the range to +/- $20. And for +/- $30 you cover 99.7% of the time. The 0.3% not covered indicates that some really bad things, typically in this case a loss of over 30% of our initial capital, could happen in very rare occasions, often referred to as "Black Swans".

With this in mind, we can associate volatility to many asset classes. This is what I provided in the graph below. I accept that the volatility values I used are subjective[65]. For example, real estate may be less or more volatile in your region than my 10% arbitrary value. You may also find many stocks less volatile than the 25% average I have chosen, but many others are also way more volatile. In the end, the data can always be tuned to your situation. However, it is the process of evaluating risk which is more important and that you need to acquire.

Here is the list of potential investment assets associated with a reasonable volatility over a year.

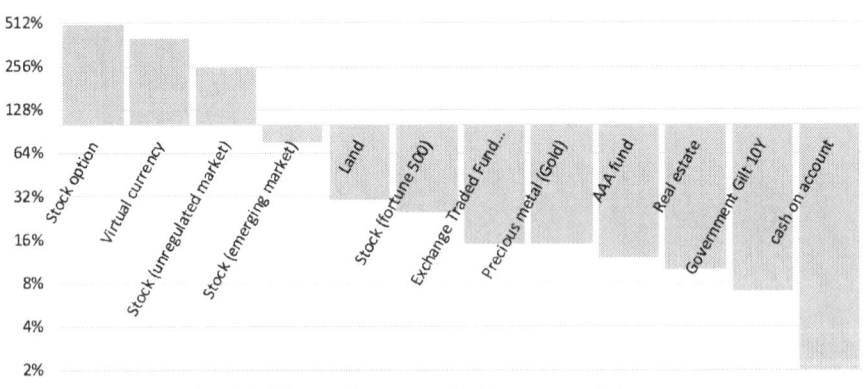

Fig 41.1 Approximative volatility per asset classes

You will note that each line of the graph's vertical scale corresponds to a doubling of the risk. That makes for a very wide spectrum of variability in risk.

I would be tempted to see all those above 100% of volatility as either gambling or just depreciating assets (like your car) rather than assets to invest in for decades. For this reason, we won't let them

---

[65] I do not pretend to have the most accurate value of volatility for each asset class, but the chosen values should not be off by an order of magnitude, which is good enough for our purpose.

paddle in our investment pond, or at the very least, not in large quantities and not before financial freedom is reached.

In the list of investment assets, I have also included land, as it is a proper asset class, but it is the most illiquid one by far[66]. You may invest in land when you start building wealth for the next generation, but not for your pressing need of financial independence. As a consequence, we will not keep this one either.

Let's continue with the remaining asset classes and get a feel for the risk vs reward. The next table shows a typical return per annum for selected asset classes. Again, these numbers are indicative only[67].

Asset	Typical expected return per annum
Cash on account	1.5%
Government Gilt 10Y	3%
AAA Fund	4%
Exchange Traded Fund (SPY)	7.5%
Stock (Fortune 500)	7%
Stock (Emerging market)	16%
Real estate (capital + rent)	7% (3.5 + 3.5)
Precious metal (Gold)	2.5%

Table 41.2 Typical return per asset classes

What we'd like to know is how much of our capital is at risk when investing in certain asset classes. Based on this expected return on investment and the volatility, we can define a confidence index:

```
confidence = (capital + max loss[68]) / capital.
```

---

[66] You can buy more land in an afternoon that you can get rid of in a lifetime!
[67] Typical return on investment for various asset classes.
[68] The maximum loss is obtained by taking the loss at two standard deviations, or 95% of the time, and adding the loss to the expected return of the asset class.

By applying this formula, cash on account gives us a 99.5% confidence level, which should be about right, so long as it's in a mainstream bank. Stock from emerging market suddenly gets a 0% confidence level, and we have to play with the rest.

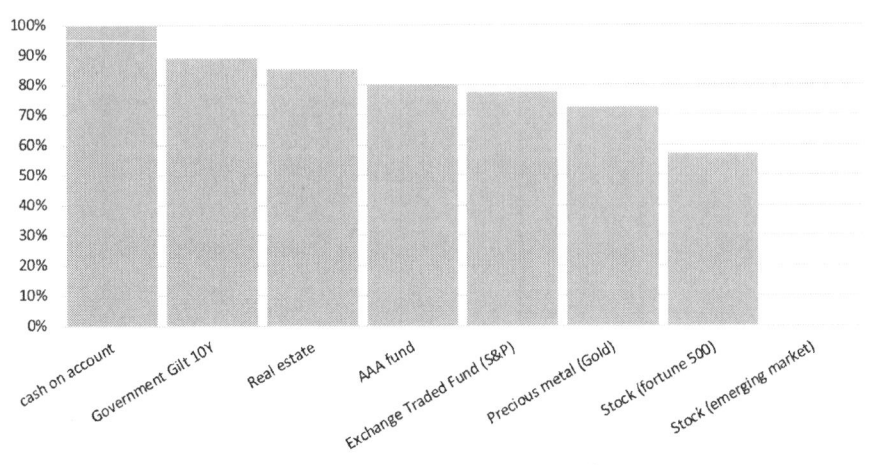

Fig 41.3 Confidence level per asset class

On the face of it, it looks like the difference between Gilt, real estate, AAA funds, an S&P ETF, and gold is not so significant considering that the loss of confidence is compensated by a gain in expected return. So long as we stick to these asset classes only, our risk is not overly bad.

Asset class	Confidence level
Government Gilt 10 years	89%
Real Estate	85%
AAA Fund	80%
ETF S&P	77.5%
Gold	72.5%
Stock (Fortune 500)	57%

Table 41.4 Confidence level per asset class

Now we have to be clear. Investing in a property in a poor location, at the wrong time, with bad finances, and bad management, is on par with investing in a company stock from an unregulated market (which we discarded at the very beginning of our risk review): the risk goes through the roof. Here, we are talking about real estate with a 10% volatility risk, which in my world is good properties in locations of high demand.

In conclusion, if you want to both put your savings to work and sleep at night, you should restrict your investment choices to only the top five asset classes: Government Gilt, real estate, AAA funds, top secure ETFs (typically mirroring the S&P), and gold. Moving out of these is already accepting more risk and having to spend more time to manage, properly or badly, this extra risk.

Now that we have a good grip on our risks, we are faced with our main challenge: discipline. It is easy to say that you should only invest in top quality elements of top confidence asset classes, but what do you do when the next fad arrives? Internet stocks, Healthcare 2.0 labs, Bitcoins, ICOs, and more…

There is more risk on us blowing our capital by lack of discipline, than by making a consciously well thought through and well-prepared investment.

Discipline is key.

Step 42: a first investment plan

It is now time to make use of all we learned so far. We are going to find the best way to fill up the investment pond, considering our ability to save, the asset classes we can invest in, and limiting some risk.

First, let's see a model using Gilt, S&P ETF, and real estate. We will vary the asset classes allocation in our saving pond using three different strategies:

- The first strategy is to fill it with an even spread between Gilt, S&P, and real estate.
- The second strategy allocates the split according to the confidence level seen previously (more Gilt than real estate, and more real estate than S&P).
- The third strategy is to allocate the split according to the lazy rich seen earlier, and then within the portfolio income part, split again according to confidence level

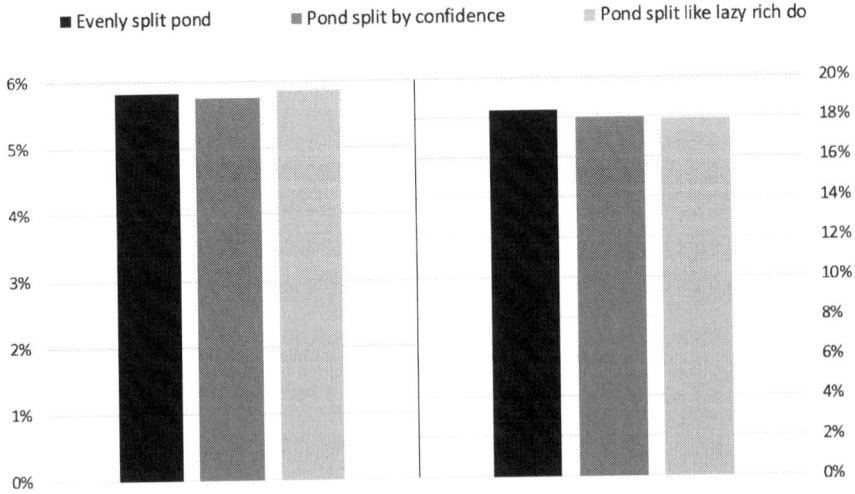

Fig 42.1 Return on investment (left) vs risk at 95% (right)

The least we can say is that it does not have much of an impact. I am not sure if you can see the needle in the haystack.

- We have a 0.45% variation in our risk level. That is very close to admitting they are all equal!
- And we have a 0.12% difference on return on investment. One more transaction generating one more fee one side or the other, and it's swallowed.

We will continue our search for the best strategy by selecting the split according to the lazy rich, which gives by a tiny margin the best return (5.86%) and the lowest risk (17.88%). The exact split allocation inside this portfolio was Gilt at 32%, ETF at 28%, and real estate at 40%.

Now, let's compare this portfolio with two strategies:
- Invest in real estate only
- Invested in an S&P index only

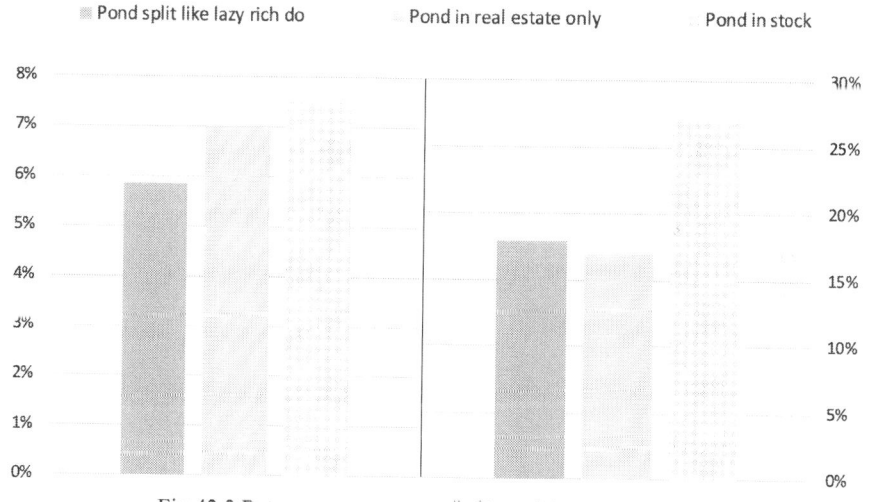

Fig 42.2 Return on investment (left) vs risk at 95% (right)

According to our model, both new strategies deliver a slightly improved return compared to the "Lazy Rich" portfolio. The real estate can provide it mostly thanks to its leverage. As for the S&P ETF this is just an average over several decades. In terms of risk, real estate appears on par (even if slightly lower) with the "Lazy Rich" portfolio, whereas the ETF is seen as over 50% riskier.

Of course, some real estate investment may carry a bit more risk than the data I have provided, and you may find slightly less volatile ETFs. But in the end, there is a bigger elephant that will sway our decision.

First, how fast and how much can we save, in a view to invest the savings in the pond? For this, we need to make a few more assumptions. We will make the investment in real estate as small as possible in value, with a view to invest as soon as possible: investment of £120,000, fees of 10%, loan at 85% LTV[69]. That will mean a deposit of £30,000 to make this first deal. Now we can compare on the next picture the "Lazy Rich" (left) and the real estate (right) strategies which both received strictly the same real estate investment.

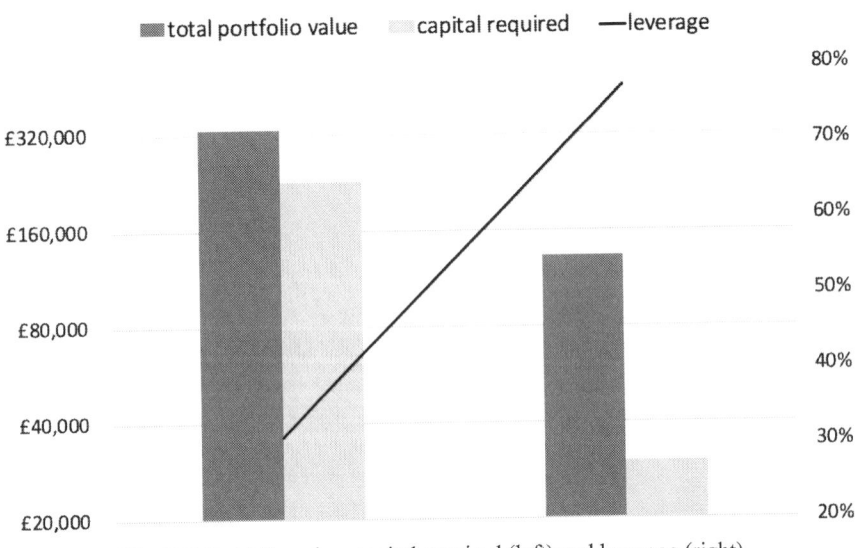

Fig 42.3 Portfolio value, capital required (left) and leverage (right)

Requiring close to £228,000 of capital[70] to start with, the "Lazy Rich" strategy cannot be funded easily. It is likely that one would first start with ETF only or a mix Guild / ETF before investing in real estate and rebalance the mix of allocation. It will take a long time to get to

---

[69] Loan to Value – in this case it means we can borrow 85% of £120,000 = £102,000.
[70] £320,000 investment minus £102,000 borrowing plus £10,000 fees = £228,000.

this balanced portfolio and each new real estate investment, either anticipated or delayed, could severely unbalance it.

However, investing in real estate alone will require the deposit only, in our case £30,000. We can also see on the chart the advantage of leveraging the bank's money. Here we are leveraged at 77%, which is not available for those who invest in the stock market.

Second, if we compare the real estate strategy with the ETF one, there is an advantage with the ETF on the short term, but a disadvantage in the long run. What the ETF provides that the real estate does not, is the ability to invest small amounts in regular and frequent recurrent periods, such as monthly. You can start building your nest earlier. What it does not provide however, is the leverage. And with the leverage, if used properly, comes the long-term power, as your debt gets slowly eroded by inflation and your asset, bought in large part with money you did not have in the first place, gets slowly more valuable beyond inflation.

I am personally not in favour of parking my savings in the stock market if they are to be invested in real estate later on. This approach is too risky. Savings are for going into the Barrel at zero risk until they are invested. When I decide to invest, I make an investment for a very long time to avoid any unnecessary fees and short-term fluctuations in value. In the best cases, this very long time is for life. Any investment in an ETF or the stock market should also be made for the long term and not be an attempt to trade for quick gains.

The following table is a personal snapshot comparison of the positives and negatives associated with investing in stocks (including ETFs).

In favour of stocks	All those negative side effects
You can start with a minimal investment size, such as $1000	You cannot leverage[71] (at least you should not!)
You can invest as regularly as per your savings plan (each start of month for example)	You will have a hard time if your capital gets eroded by adverse market conditions
	You will be tempted to invest in the latest fad
You can invest and forget if you invest in an ETF only, freeing you of much time for other activities	You will be tempted to trade instead of investing (see later)
Past inflation adjusted average return on investment of 7% over the long term	Have we already discussed the fees?
	It will take a lot of capital to generate sufficient income to cover for your lifestyle after independence-day

Table 42.4 Pros and cons of investing in the stock market

If you have found me a tiny bit biased in this section, I encourage you to read on, as I have more surprises for you later.

However, in the end, here is what investing in Buy to Let properties gives me that investing in stock does not:

- I can leverage my saving to around 75% (£30,000 of savings is enough for a £120,000 investment).
- If I invest carefully, I can control my investment risk better.

---

[71] As an advanced sophisticated investor, you can leverage big time, but that is beyond what can be done successfully over a long time by most people, me included.

- I have a fairly stable and regular monthly income allowing me to plan for the future.
- When the property increases in value, I can leverage it again and release equity, to invest elsewhere, thereby accelerating the growth of my passive revenue stream.
- Only four deals (my home and three rental properties[72]) will get me close to financial independence.

Before wrapping-up on this first investment plan, I want to review how we can finance it.

In the perfect career plan, and the perfect human capital chart, we saw that Joe required a lot of discipline and effort to save around 10% of income and be set on the right progression path. There is a little silver lining[73] which was not included in the perfect career plan. Perfect Joe may from time to time get an end of year bonus. In this case, there are no two ways about it: at least 90% of the bonus net income has to go straight into savings.

Let's review the perfect start of the perfect career with this in mind.

If Joe can get an end of year net bonus worth 7.5% of yearly net income (that means four weeks of salary, or slightly less than a month), and at the same time save 10% of his perfect career income, he will have saved around £30,000 by the end of year 6. I remind you that Joe started year 1 on £30,000 per annum gross salary.

	Year 1	Year 2	Year 3	Year 4	Year 5	Year 6
Net savings	£2,609	£2,785	£2,970	£3,165	£3,371	£3,566
90% of bonus	£1,761	£2,006	£2,058	£2,110	£2,165	£2,205
Cumulated	£4,370	£8,960	£13,782	£18,847	£24,166	£29,716

Table 42.5 Cumulated savings over 6 years (10% of net income + 90% of net bonus)

---

[72] We will see the detail of this strategy later on.
[73] It is always a good strategy to keep a few good news for later (under-promise, over-deliver as my American friends would say)!

This is a credible plan to realise a first investment of £120,000, or four times starting gross salary, within 6 years, before Joe turns 30. If this investment is carefully planned and executed, the profit will start a new stream of income and will accelerate Joe's capacity to save for the next investment.

Now, your situation may not be that of perfect Joe. If you are already on a better path, all good, carry on. If not, you need to find a way to get there. Maybe you do not earn as much, maybe you do not have any hope of a bonus, but maybe you have a partner who can save as much as you do, and the savings combined put you on the right path. Don't convince yourself you cannot save. You can save. Pretend it is tax and save it. Maybe it will take 8 years instead of 6 to make your first investment. It is still very good. The next one will come faster.

You need the first lump sum, the first £30,000, or maybe in different circumstances only the first £15,000, or whatever it takes to find a bank to lend you enough money under good conditions.

Work on building a credible credit profile over a year, through a track record of proven regular income, proven spending within your means, and a minimum deposit. Yes, we have a plan, but it is not going to be of any use if your profile appears too risky to the bank. Remember, they want and need to lend as much money as they possibly can. It's how they are built. They only require you to satisfy a few risk criteria. Make sure you tick their boxes. Work on your profile.

That's it:
- Work on your credit profile.
- Build your savings nest.
- Identify a profitable investment and make it happen.
- Accelerate your income by adding another income stream.
- Rinse and repeat!

6

Enter the Property game

I get up, and nothin' gets me down

Van Halen

So we all have to turn into landlords here?

Well, it looks like a lot of landlords and landladies out there have started by accident. I surely did. But then, if it works and delivers the goods, why not? I don't like it when a tenant calls for a problem, but I do like it when multiple tenants pay me every month...

Let's see what this is all about and if we can be good at it. Bring it on!

Step 43: anatomy of a good deal

This is where we enter the Buy to Let property game. This is where we stress-test opportunities to find the pearl. This is where we define a mechanical and repeatable winning process.

Buying into real estate is not just about the house and the price. There is way more than that. I have a check-list made up of four categories. The first three are the most important ones, as the fourth one is kind of embedded in the financial review, but it's good to be aware of it independently. Here are the highlights of the deal.

1. What you buy.
   - Property location.
   - Future value not yet apparent or realised.
   - Ability to attract tenants in a niche market.

2. How you finance.
   - Fully loaded property cost.
   - Financing.
   - Leverage.

3. Operational ratios.
   - Gross income yield.
   - Net profit yield.
   - Cash on cash.
   - Debt ratios.

4. General market conditions.
   - Buyer or seller's market?
   - How far from the last recession?

We will review all of these in detail.

Step 44: what you buy

Let's focus a moment on the property itself, and not on the financial aspects (price and financing), which we will review next.

In the real estate business, the mantra is "location, location, location". I view this repetition as three different location purposes.

The first location is the most important one. It means a place where future land value will grow way beyond inflation. It happens generally around mega-cities or places where high-skilled jobs abound. Sometimes, micro locations suddenly spin out of nowhere, thanks to generous public and/or private money spent massively on infrastructure, shopping centres, leisure centres, etc... In general, these are very good locations to invest in. My experience is that it does not matter much if you did not invest very early, as the inertia of value creation will likely carry on for at least a decade or two.

The second location means close to where you live. If you are buying your home, there is nothing more to say. If you buy a property as an investment, I see it as fairly critical that it is close to your home (or alternatively your place of work) in order to save on costs for properly managing your investment. Investing far away from home means having to rely on other people to manage at least part of your rental business, therefore adding fees, risk, management, all of this adding up to more stress, diminishing income, and worse financial ratios. You are more likely to want getting rid of your investment when a big problem arises if it is far away from your home. That does not align well with a strategy of investing for life.

The third location has to do with convenience. Is the location convenient enough (transport, shopping, school, etc...) to ensure that you will never run out of potential tenants? You may personally be willing to accept a few sacrifices and deal with some inconveniences for the place you call home, but your tenants won't necessarily accept the same.

Location is the most important criteria of the property you are about to buy. Buying in less desirable locations (obvious example: a house in the middle of nowhere in the countryside; less obvious: a flat in a city but 30min walk to main transportation systems – tube or train) is likely to become a burden over your lifetime. This is very important, so let's make it very clear. We are not in "the property business" in general. No, we are very specifically in the business of buying and operating properties in strategic locations of present and future high demand. Ah, that's damn important, so I will repeat!

> "The business of buying and operating properties in strategic locations of present and future high demand"

Bear in mind that the location, condition, and overall convenience of the property will determine the type of tenant you will get. In turn, this will impact the risk and involvement required that you will face when operating it as a business.

My second criteria in evaluating an opportunity is the ability to add future value. Before we get into more detail, the following sums up the combination of location and adding value very well:

> "Buy the worst house in the best street"

If we buy a property which is perfectly fine, without much possibility to add value, we will not have any extra leverage. Paying market price for generating market income is by definition very average. We are not in the business of chasing average deals.

My best friend for adding value is the property floorplan. When evaluating a property, I look at the location, then one or two images to get a feel of what we are talking about, and if both are in the acceptable range, I spend time on the floorplan. I mentally alter the floorplan searching for little modifications that could have a big impact, until I can convince myself that good value can be added to the property. If I am not convinced, I simply discard the deal. If I see hidden value, then I move on to Excel and financial ratios. I go through this floorplan alteration compulsory step because I know for a start that I will not make enough return on investment if I do not improve a property. The financial ratios will just not stack up. And the reason is: my ratios only blink green on 1% of deals out there.

Another way of adding value is to buy a property for the potential of its land. Regulations change over years, and they tend to favour building more on smaller and smaller plots.

We will have to go back to my family experience here. When my grand-parents retired, their eldest son took over the little farm, and they moved to a small one-bedroom house in a village. The house plot was not big but enough to grow vegetables and have a few chickens, thus providing occupation and food. They stayed there around 25 years. After they died, the family of 6 children, now also close to their own retirement, decided to sell the little house. A little house on a little plot in a little village, not much more than this. It got sold... I came back to see the house a few years later. Nostalgia turned very quickly into shock and disbelief. Same plot, but now three houses! Whoever bought it managed to partition the plot, squeeze on two more houses, build them, sell them, and probably ended up with the initial house for free.

Take that for a lesson!

There are other ways to add value beyond improving the house or splitting the land. Changing the purpose of a house, which may require a few alterations, is a good way to add value. For example, buying a 3-bed family house, repartitioning inside, and making it a 5-bed house to rent in multiple occupancy. Or turning a conveniently located flat into a holiday let.

By finding the right niche (students, elderly, holiday makers, etc...) and repurposing the property to fit the needs of the new target market, you can get a leverage on an otherwise average return on your investment.

You see, we look for leverage everywhere. Not just in financing, but right from the start in the type of property we buy, its location, its floorplan, its adaptability to several niche markets, and more...

No leverage, no interest!

Step 45: how you finance

The fully loaded cost of acquiring the property and how you finance this cost is as important as what you buy. The exact same property can either be a good deal (a good value deal with good finances in place) or a very bad deal (a bad value deal with bad finances in place).

It is likely, but not compulsory, that your first property purchase will be your home. It makes sense for many reasons:

- Having a new home, you will stop paying rent.
- You get more long-term visibility, more stability, and normally less recurring stress and cost (granted, it depends what you buy…).
- You generally get a lower interest rate on a home mortgage than on a Buy to Let or a second residence mortgage.
- You generally get an easier approbation from the bank than when asking for funds to operate as a business (Buy to Let, renovation, etc…).

When looking to buy your home, after having zoomed-in on the best locations you feel you can afford, after having screened homes available in these locations where the full value is not yet realised, and after having reduced the list further to those matching your short-term needs and a budget bracket, you will get a list of candidate properties. Now, it's up to how you finance it.

I view the financing part of the deal as follows:

- We want the highest possible Loan to Value (80% is a minimum, maybe we can get more). We need leverage, and we would prefer the smallest deposit as possible. As long as it does not come with too many penalties (too high interest rate), go for the highest possible LTV.
- We prefer an interest-only deal with flexibility to repay 10% of the outstanding amount every year. With an interest only mortgage, we can ask for the longest possible mortgage duration, such as 25 or even 30 years. We want to give

ourselves enough time to re-finance once, twice, or even more, within the lifetime of the mortgage. If offset mortgages exist in your country (Australia, U.K.), try as much as possible to get one, as this is a very efficient way to make use of your savings without having to do anything.

- Regarding interest, it is easier to compare deals in some countries (France, Germany) where the norm is a 15 or 20 year fixed rate mortgage, but more difficult in others (U.K. in particular) where there is very little choice to fix the rate beyond 5 years, making the balancing of options more complex, from lifetime variable to short term fixed. If it is possible to fix the interest rate over the duration of the mortgage, at a good low rate, then you shall take this option. If not, you will have to simulate the pros and cons of having to renew your mortgage every few years vs having a lifetime variable one at a fixed rate above the variable interest set by the Central Bank. Every 0.1% pa of interest you can save counts over the years of repayment. Get at least three offers, from three different banks. Play them against each other, argue, haggle, get your 0.1% discount, and then another one!

- Ideally, the mortgage should come with extra flexibility, such as:

    o ability to port the mortgage onto another home.
    o ability to re-mortgage, for a low extra fee, to at least the same LTV once your house value has increased.
    o as already mentioned, the important ability to repay part of the capital in advance without penalty (typically 10% per annum).
    o even better (but rare), ability to get a lower interest rate if the bank delivers a better offer.

- It would not make a good financial sense to invest if the monthly interest (including pro-rated fees) you pay the bank are similar or higher than a rent you would pay a private landlord.

Your first acquisition does not need to be the best deal of your life, but it has to be a robust deal (what you buy and how you finance it) because the rest of your investments are somehow leveraged on this deal. This deal should make you financially better off from day one, like the example we saw in the "Debt free Fallacy", so that your next investment can be made sooner and with more confidence.

At this stage, if you cannot find good financing conditions, I am afraid that the purchase stops here, even if it seemed a good property to acquire at screening time. However, if the financing conditions seem acceptable, then it's time to move on to the next phase. As we have practised many times now, we will use simulators to evaluate in detail the financial impact of the deal.

In our world, the financial simulator always has the final word.

Step 46: operational ratios

Buying is a one-off event. Buying a good property (location, ability to add value) with good financing is a good start. But it's only the start. Either this is your home, or a rental property, the most important is to operate profitably and to its maximum potential. We want to simulate this before the acquisition. Only if and when we are satisfied with the ratios, should we proceed to making an offer.

Here is an example of simulating the acquisition of a new property, starting with the cost of acquisition. We will first assume that this house becomes your home.

Cost of property	£216,500
Stamp duty	£3,248
Notary fees	£1,000
Mortgage fees	£695
Conveyancing	£200
Survey	0
First refurbishment	£7,000
Total cost of acquisition	£228,643

Table 46.1 Synopsis of first home acquisition

A good financing of this property could look like this.

Mortgage LTV	85%
Mortgage value	£184,025
Mortgage interest	3.50%
Initial deposit	£44,618
Current debt	£184,025

Table 46.2 How the home acquisition is financed

We now want to have a feel for the benefits of this acquisition. Would this really be a positive move?

If you buy this property as your home, the rent you end up not paying to a private landlord (in this example £1,250 per month) becomes your pseudo-income.

	Year 1	Year 2	Year 3	Year 4
Pseudo-income (rent avoided)	£1,250	£1,284	£1,320	£1,356
Cost (interest from mortgage)	£537	£537	£537	£537
Cost (repairs, maintenance)	£30	£31	£32	£33
Cost (operational)	£67	£69	£71	£73
Gross profit (income – cost)	**£616**	**£648**	**£681**	**£714**

Table 46.3 Monthly operational profit of your home, assuming increase every 12 months

As this table indicates, buying this home vs renting a similar one generates a monthly saving, which we will assume we can really save.

In addition, there are benefits in having an offset mortgage in place. The cumulated savings listed above are offset daily against the value of the mortgage, so that you pay the interest only on the residual mortgage value. This lowers your monthly interest payments, lowers your debt ratio, and accelerates your savings pot at the same time.

In terms of financial ratios for a home, we will focus on tracking the savings vs renting to a private landlord, the monthly mortgage interest payment, and the debt ratio. In the next table, we track the value occurring at the end of the first month, for each period.

	Year 1	Year 2	Year 3	Year 4
Cost of interest	£537	£515	£492	£466
Savings vs landlord	49.3%	52.1%	55.0%	57.8%
Debt ratio	85.0 %	78.4%	72.0%	65.6%

Table 46.4 Operational ratios from a home with an offset mortgage

Using an offset mortgage reduces the debt at the start of year 2 to £176,630. This in turn reduces the monthly mortgage interest to £515 instead of the expected £537 if you had no savings and no offset. And each year, it accelerates.

We can see from these previous tables that buying this house under the defined financial conditions and inflation[74] would allow you to save, from day one, nearly half the rent[75] that you would otherwise pay to a private landlord. Other the years, as you can avoid rent increases, you will save even more.

Let's look at the debt ratio over the long term. Our mortgage is interest only (no capital repayment), but when combined with an offset account, it becomes a lot more favourable. Despite holding an interest only 25 or 30 year mortgage, you can still repay it within 15 years.

See on the next chart the dramatic effect of simply keeping on the offset account all savings made by not renting to a private landlord. Minimal effort, maximal return!

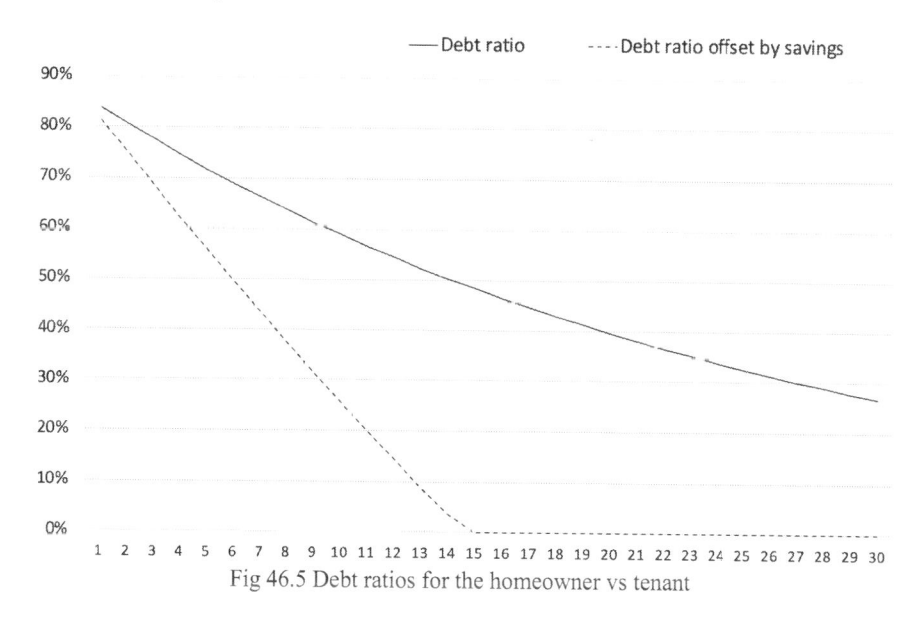

Fig 46.5 Debt ratios for the homeowner vs tenant

---

[74] Rent inflation = 2.75% pa ; house inflation = 4% pa ; CPI inflation = 2.5% pa ; tax = 27.5%.
[75] 49.3% in year one is the pro-rated gain between actual rent to the bank vs rent to a landlord, here £616 / £1,250.

We can also notice that if all goes according to plan, at year 6 or 7 of the investment, your offset debt ratio is trending below 50%, allowing you to review the opportunity of re-mortgaging at a higher Loan to Value, and generate automatically a deposit for another investment. Typically, in our case, you could raise a deposit of around £70,000 without touching any of your savings, just by re-mortgaging from 50% to 75% LTV.

Paying rent (in our case, the interest to the bank) equivalent to half market rate for the next 20 years, building a saving nest worth a deposit for another investment, and hammering down your debt ratio year after year... Isn't that good?

Let's now review the exact same opportunity, but as a Buy to Let investment, instead of a main home.

As a Buy to Let investment, your operational income are a bit different. As already mentioned, you should try to repurpose the house (typically from single to multiple occupancy) to generate slightly more rent income (£1,500 per month) than if renting the same house from a private landlord (£1,250 per month) for the need of a family. In the table below, all other operational costs were kept identical, but I have now added tax on operations and net profit of the activity.

	Year 1	Year 2	Year 3	Year 4
Income (rent received)	£1,500	£1,541	£1,584	£1,627
Cost (financial)	£537	£537	£537	£537
Cost (repairs, maintenance)	£30	£31	£32	£33
Cost (legal)	-	-	-	-
Cost (operational)	£67	£69	£71	£73
Gross profit (income – cost)	**£866**	**£905**	**£944**	**£985**
Tax (on profit of activity)	£238	£249	£260	£271
Net profit	**£628**	**£656**	**£685**	**£714**

Table 46.6 Monthly operational profit of a Buy to Let activity

The ratios we will track as an investment are quite different from the home ratios, as they are geared towards assessing the profitability of the activity. Again, the data in the next table is taken at the end of the first month of each period.

As you explore the next table, I have to make clear again that income is more important than capital, and therefore income is more important than debt. If you have debt but you can service this debt easily and you have capped your risk of a fluctuating interest on the debt, then all is good. Therefore, the most important ratio from this table is the expense coverage ratio. At 230-250%, it shows that there is plenty of margin to cover the cost with the income. Starting at 85%, the debt ratio is high, but as we will see later, it is not a problem when projecting into the future because we have a good expense coverage ratio.

	Year 1	Year 2	Year 3	Year 4
Gross income yield	7.87%	8.09%	8.31%	8.54%
Gross profit yield	4.55%	4.75%	4.96%	5.17%
Net profit yield	3.30%	3.44%	3.59%	3.75%
Net cash on cash invested	16.9%	17.6%	18.4%	19.2%
Cost of financing	35.8%	34.8%	33.9%	33.0%
Expense coverage ratio	237%	242%	248%	253%
Debt ratio	85.0%	81.7%	78.6%	75.6%

Table 46.7 Operational ratios (taken at year end) of a Buy to Let activity

At this stage, we start to have a mechanical way to evaluate opportunities, which makes it easier to compare deals and filter out all those not financially rewarding. But we are not totally finished, as we have left aside two important considerations: we have not yet factored CPI inflation, and we have not yet factored any risk. This is still a happy path simulation.

For an investment, it is important that when assessing the profit of activity and its associated ratios over a very long period, we rebase the figures according to CPI inflation, so that we see them as of today's value. As we saw earlier, even a low inflation can have a large influence when projecting over 25 years or more. The table below shows the inflation rebased net profit, alongside two ratios: net profit yield and net cash on cash yield. As you can see, current CPI inflation does not damage too much our investment performance.

	Year 1	Year 2	Year 3	Year 4
Net profit	£628	£640	£651	£662
Net profit yield	3.30%	3.36%	3.42%	3.47%
Net cash on cash invested	16.9%	17.2%	17.5%	17.8%

Table 46.8 Inflation rebased profit from activity (first month of each period)

The cash on cash ratio is an interesting one to follow. Basically, it says here that for £100 invested, you get back £16.9 in the first year, and as years go by, you get continuously more. In this scenario, it only takes 6 years to get back your initial deposit. The graph below shows the inflation-rebased net profit yield ratio over a 30 years period.

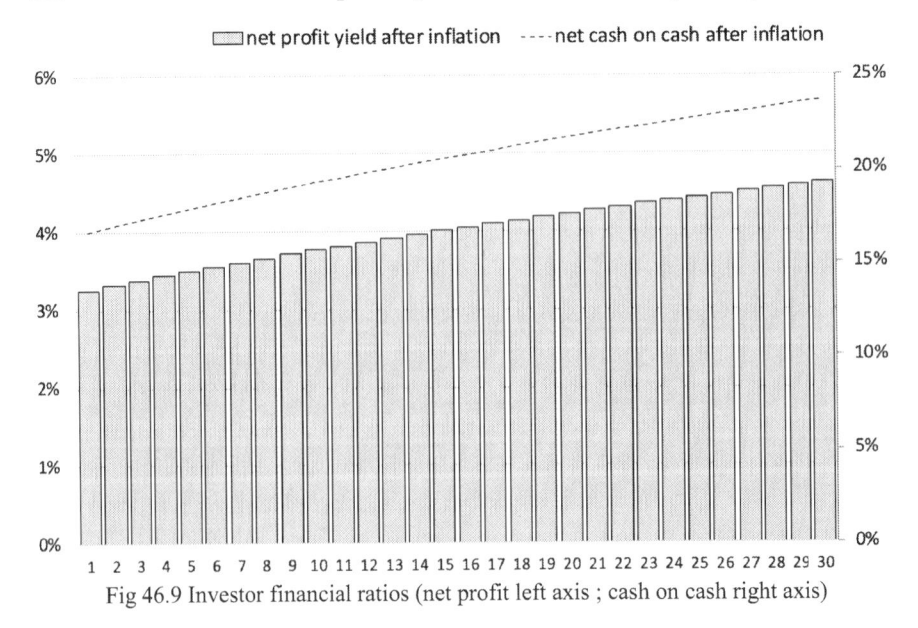

Fig 46.9 Investor financial ratios (net profit left axis ; cash on cash right axis)

Now regarding the risk, as this is a Buy to Let investment, we need an adverse conditions scenario, which for example would assume a 31.40% decrease in rent and a 61.8% increase in interest payment (this last one is applicable only if we are on a variable rate)[76]. Here is what the adverse scenario would look like.

	Year 1	Year 2	Year 3	Year 4
Income (rent received)	£1,029	£1,057	£1,086	£1,116
Cost (cumulated)	£965	£968	£971	£974
Gross profit (income – cost)	£64	£89	£116	£143
Tax	£17	£25	£32	£39
Net profit	£46	£65	£84	£103
Net profit yield	0.24%	0.34%	0.44%	0.54%
Expense coverage ratio	107%	109%	112%	115%
Net cash on cash invested	1.2%	1.7%	2.2%	2.8%

Table 46.10 Adverse scenario (monthly income and cost)

The interesting part here is to find that even in the adverse scenario, this deal is still marginally profitable. Fluctuating around 110%, the expense coverage ratio is not great, but hey, in this distressed case, the cost of operating the business is still covered by the income. In other words, if the market goes under massive stress, I shall not feel much of the stress, and I shall not have to put money in. All my simulators are telling me this is a good deal to make[77].

Finally, we can look at the value created by this investment opportunity. For this, we compare, over 30 years, the value created by the income and the capital increase of the property vs the remaining debt. For a good base of comparison, we will keep the debt flat over the period (no capital repayment and no CPI inflation impact).

---

[76] I hope you recognised the Pi and Phi helpers.
[77] To tell the truth, the assumptions are very similar to those of a true investment I have made.

Under the conditions of this simulation, it takes around 10 years to generate a value equal to the debt (half from capital gain, and half from net cash generated by the operations). Note also that the cumulated cash generated by operations and the capital appreciation of the property follow fairly similar patterns over time.

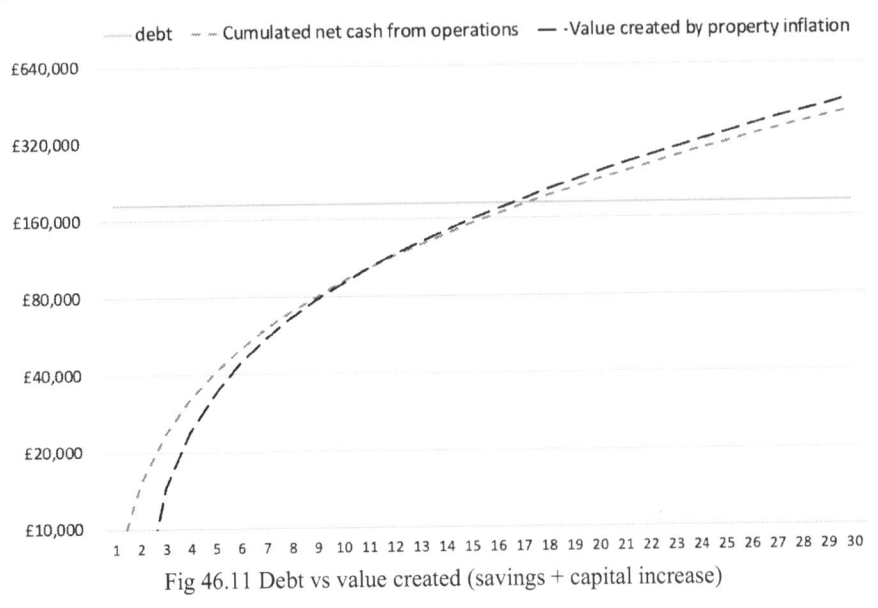

Fig 46.11 Debt vs value created (savings + capital increase)

Either you buy a property for a home or an investment, you now have an easy process to check if the investment is financially sound. You can set the minimum ratios you feel comfortable with. A few minutes of evaluation (less than 10 data entries per deal) will filter out most opportunities.

For a home investment, I am looking mostly at the savings vs landlord. In our example, we got a 50% saving vs private landlord. The deal needs to generate substantial savings from day one, otherwise why invest if the deal is not as clear as daylight to your advantage?

Then, in my investment market (properties in Greater London for Buy to Let), I want the following minimum criteria at investment time:

- Gross income yield at 7.5% (I do not even look further if it gets below 6%).
- Expense coverage ratio above 200% and growing.
- Net cash on cash of at least 15% and growing.

Basing your target on these three ratios only is enough to drive the rest of the financial plan into place, including your mortgage value, mortgage interest, Loan to Value, and others.

Now, it may not look too stringent to you if you do not know this local market well, but I can tell you that there are years (many years in fact) where I just cannot find one property in the market, with financial projections that can meet the criteria. It is as stringent as this. A handful of opportunities a year at most can pass these criteria. I do not need dozens or hundreds of deals, and I am certainly not going to pile on unnecessary risk. As we will see later, I need only 4 good deals and I am done. And I also need to sleep at night. In case of adverse market conditions, 95% of landlords out there could be wiped out before I feel the pain. That's how stringent your deal planning has to be in order for you to be able to sleep well at night.

Any deal we pursue has to pass the non-financial and financial criteria. And with our criteria, the bar is set very high.

Step 47: property market slumps

In early 2007, Gordon Brown, the U.K. Finance Minister, declared in several very public speeches:

```
"No more boom and bust cycles in the property
                    market!"
```

He had invented the recipe for a smooth perpetual growth. We all know we should not put much trust in politicians, and even less when they take the attitude of a salesman. Of course, the market went bust a year later, as you can see on the graph below, which shows the 12 months percentage change in U.K. property prices.

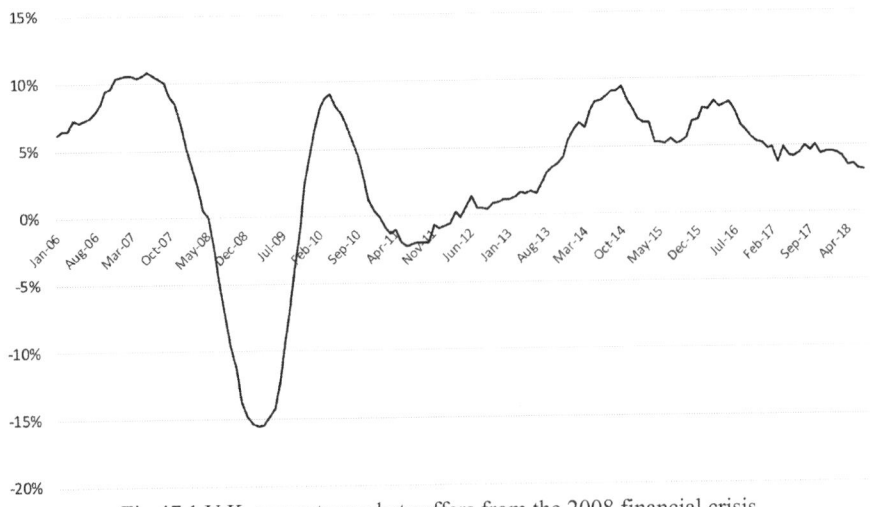

Fig 47.1 U.K. property market suffers from the 2008 financial crisis

It was not the first bust, and it will not be the last. All markets progress in cycles of "boom and bust". Property is no different. There are three lessons to learn from this:

1. Boom and Bust cycles are an integral part of every financial market.
2. Avoid buying at the top of a cycle.
3. It does not matter that much in the long run.

If you use stringent ratios such as those we defined a few moments ago, it is less likely that you will buy at the top of cycles, because stringent ratios simply do not allow you to do this. As I said, there are years I cannot find a suitable property investment with my criteria in place. It tells me something:

> "Let the tide come and go, do not invest!"

Nevertheless, in a very worst-case scenario, if you have the courage, the determination, and put much effort into it, you still can and should survive the ordeal of a deep recession. Let's review the recent U.K. market slump, but now with a house price index reset at 100 on 1st Jan 2006.

The black line and left scale are exactly the same information as in the previous graph, depicting the dramatic dip of the bust effect.

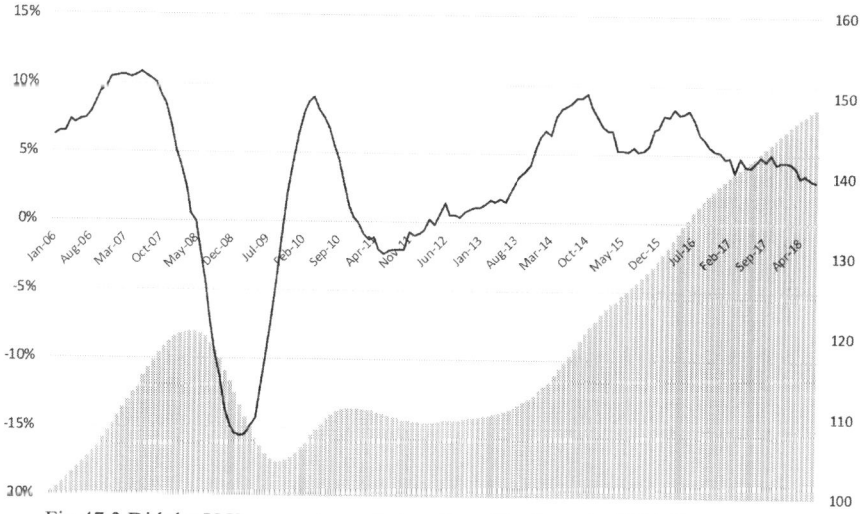

Fig 47.2 Did the U.K. property market really suffer from the 2008 financial crisis?

The grey bars are indexed on the right-hand side scale[78] and show the value, rebased at 100 on 1st Jan 2006, of a typical median U.K. property over 12 years, starting a year before a very nasty recession.

---

[78] Sorry it's not a log scale as it was too flat to notice any bump, which is really the point we are making here.

A few things are striking:
- Had you bought around a year before the start of the recession, you would be around 48% better off[79] twelve years later.
- At no point was there a lower cost to buy than a year before the recession started, which seems very close to the top of the bubble.
- If you bought at the very worst time, you would still be 24% better off ten years later.

As we see on the chart, even the effects of a nasty recession get diluted over time. Do not worry too much about buying at the right time. As we buy with a stringent process and criteria, we are more likely to see a "buy opportunity" at the bottom of the market than at the top. Anyway, over the long run, it will even-out as the invisible man works its magic of house price inflation beyond reason (and beyond CPI inflation). The long-term trend of properties in locations of high demand is 'up'. And this long-term trend is way more 'up' than we can imagine.

Therefore, we shall approach a recession as a very good window of opportunity to load up properties in excellent locations at lower prices and more affordable financing.

Now, let's talk about this next gremlin: affordability.

My great-grand-parents who bought the little farm in rural France probably did it thanks to a few years of savings, and did not use credit, which at the time, was not that widespread. With credit money came the risk of not repaying the mortgage, and therefore commercial banks had to define their own ratios to evaluate the risk. Their main metric is affordability. Simply put, they ask this question:

```
"Will you be able to afford the repayment of the
interest and capital over the term of the mortgage?"
```

---

[79] For this fictional median U.K. house.

Affordability is vague and up to certain limits, subject to interpretations. You may not have the same affordability ratio in U.K., France, Japan, or Sweden. Not the same ratio either in 1912, 1990, or 2018… But what we see for sure is that around good locations in high demand, affordability gets worse over time. Look at how the unaffordability ratio[80] has more than tripled over the last 20 years in one of the poorer boroughs of London, from 3.40 to 10.70.

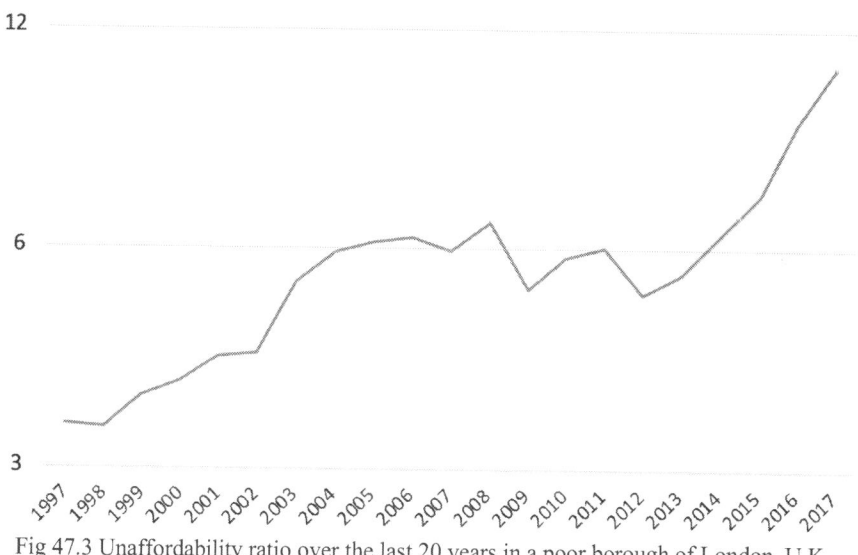

Fig 47.3 Unaffordability ratio over the last 20 years in a poor borough of London, U.K.

Should I add that in the same period, in the richer borough of London, the ratio went from 11.80 in 1997, to 40.70 in 2017. Yes, more than 40 years of an average local guy's gross salary[81] just to buy an average house in the borough.

To cope with this ever-decreasing affordability of housing, commercial banks bend the rules by extending the life of their mortgage offers. Like many, I have experienced directly this unaffordability chart, first by moving to suburbs and accepting the law of two hours commute on a good day, and second by extending my mortgage duration. My first home (in 1995, in the suburb of Paris,

---

[80] The ratio of the median price paid for a residential property to the median workplace-based gross annual full-time earnings.
[81] Before tax, before basic necessities, before eating, before breathing…

France) was bought with a 10-year mortgage, and I was earning nothing like in more recent times. Then, I moved to the UK and bought a house (2001, in the suburb of London) with a 20-year mortgage. Today, the norm is more around 25-30 years.

In Japan, the normal mortgage duration is 35 years. An entire working life to pay for a house. In certain places, they accept to push it to 50 years. We start talking mortgaging yourself and your children too… But why stop here? In 2016, the Swedish financial regulator has introduced legal restrictions to limit the mortgage term to 105 years "only". There is nothing to be laughed at, because apparently, the average term was reported to be too extortionate, at 140 years!

I do not have a crystal ball, but I can see the tricks and the trends. In locations of high demand, mortgage durations are not going to return to 10 years in a song. On the contrary, mortgage duration will very likely continue to extend, until such point where we find it normal that a house in a very desirable location would either need to be bought over two or three generations or will be forever unaffordable.

It is paramount to integrate this as it underpins our whole strategy, which I will summarize very simply:

- Screen opportunities through stringent profitability criteria.
    - Buy the worst house in the best location.
    - Buy with leverage.
- Operate the property as a business.
    - Profitable from day one.
    - Track operations via a financial dashboard.
- Never sell!

Step 48: operating as a business

This may look like the scary part, as it requires taking action and getting your hands dirty. We will leave the world of financial simulators and financial dashboards for a moment. If we want to convert opportunities into deals, and then operate profitably, we have to go through this.

You are not going to do it all alone, but what you can do yourself, at least at the beginning, you should do yourself. Remember the fees? Let's look at what we need in order to operate:

- Lawyer: OK, we need a lawyer to buy a property, and we will not improvise on our own. The good thing is that with internet, a lot of lawyers can now work remotely and that can help in pushing the cost down a little bit. You need someone whose competence is proportional to the complexity of your purchase. Easy purchase, basic lawyer. More complex deal, spend the money on a good lawyer. Very complex deal, find that rare person out there!

- Broker: you may or may not need a broker to get a mortgage. I am baffled that in the internet age we still have to go through brokers, but my experience is that, as incredible as it is, a good broker will both earn a fee on the mortgage he finds you, and at the same time lower the cost of the mortgage for you. Have a look if you can find a good broker, it will save you time, and possibly also fees and interest over the years.

- Agent: you are very likely to interact with an estate agent rather than the owner of the property you wish to buy. Make sure you give the estate agent the best impression, even if the agent is half your age and only driven by commissions. Making friends with the estate agent could give you a lot of insight on the deal. We will review this in detail in a moment, so for now just have in mind that the estate agent needs to be in your pocket.

That's it for what you can delegate. The rest, I am afraid, is for you to deal with directly. If not, although it is still possible, you are less likely to hit our performance indicators. If not, you make a deliberate choice from the onset to make the deal more risky. Your choice!

The last two roles are:

- Finance: the one who makes sure this deal stacks up, and who has a working plan considering all risks. It also includes planning for income, tax, and any financial considerations (improvements to make or postpone). Hopefully, this book will help you to approach this role with more confidence.
- Landlord / landlady: the person making it work when the deal is done. What follows focuses on this role.

The landlord / landlady will probably have to spend a few (or more than a few!) hours a week on this part of the business. It is a commitment for sure. Let's see what the duties can entail:

- Marketing for recruiting tenants (adverts). If you go through agents, you will impact your financial ratios, so there is a new expression to learn here: Do it Yourself!
- Showing prospective tenants around. Another good reason to have the rental property close to your place of work or home (preferably home).
- Vetting tenants. You'd better make sure they can afford the rent.
- Negotiating final conditions and contracting with tenants. With real world experiences, your contract will become better and better, but it's a good idea to start from a good model (your new friend the estate agent has one, or via a landlord association).
- Dealing with tenants. There can be a long list in here. I have one golden rule: for each new problem you encounter, define a process to deal with it more effectively the next time, so that you always improve the efficiency of your business. For example: the tenant called you at 2am because he lost his

keys? Write in the next contract that a new set of key has a cost of £50, and changing the lock is £150 (again, it's just an example), and emergency calls to the landlord after 10pm have a cost of £20. Do they continue to forget their keys? Put a duplicate in a box with a code next to the house (or find a better solution, but do not leave it at the mercy of becoming a repeat problem without a simpler solution). Be proactive. Each of those repeat problems should take you less and less time to deal with.

- Dealing with late payments. Despite your and their best efforts, it will probably happen. Be ready for it. Have a process. Be clear what they should expect from you.

- Tracking cost and income. This part is different from the financial plans we have been reviewing so far. You need to track the actual activity, income and expenses, of each property separately. You should account for it in a good enough manner, so that the taxman will not be able to complain or start an inquiry, which would be the beginning of new troubles.

- Be aware of the law and regulation. That's not an easy one, but for sure if you slowly become a professional landlord / landlady, you need to understand as many of the property rental laws and regulations as possible, because you will be exposed to it anyway (requesting an HMO[82] license to a council, passing inspection from a governing body, etc...). Again, being part of a landlord association may help.

Clearly, this can be overwhelming and put you off already. But let's take baby steps. First, you do not have to do it and learn it all in a few hours or days. This is all progressive and ramping up as your rental activity and income is ramping up too. Second, the level of constraints you will experience depends on the type of operation you run. Student

---

[82] House of Multiple Occupation: a property rented out by at least 3 people who are not from one household but share facilities like the bathroom or kitchen.

lets will force you to manage the tenants a bit closer than other more mature ones would require, and will likely trigger a new batch of tenants each year (understand more marketing, visits, contracts, etc…). Holiday lets will require to deal with a lot more tenants for short periods of time and to have a team that you can trust for managing the cleaning and also possibly check-in / check-out. Renting to families could be a lot more hands off, less demanding, less stressful, but possibly at the cost of lowering the profitability a bit. You can tune your risk and the number of hours you have to put in by selecting the niche market that is more adapted to your personality and availability. Finally, replicate what works well for you. If you have the processes and team in place to operate in a specific niche, the second rental property will be a breeze to manage!

Of course, you could also delegate and find an estate agent to do most of these duties. If you do so, I have some doubts that you will hit our stringent profitability ratios to implement our final financial independence plan. It is not going to come without effort. But look at it this way: the efforts you have to put in are only a small proportion of the 8, 10 or more hours you put in your daily job. Ultimately, you will be rewarded with an extra income stream for as long as you keep operating this activity, and with time, it will become easier and easier to manage.

Do not subcontract the duties of the landlord / landlady, or at the very least, keep most of them close to you.

Step 49: practise, jump, and improve

Practise is free. Granted, it takes a bit of your time but anyway, if you are after financial freedom, you are already committed to investing time in your financial education.

With the Internet and some appropriate property search portals, you can easily scan opportunities within a set of criteria (location, number of bedrooms, price). Out of those you found, take the two or three most promising ones (matching at least a good part of our non-financial criteria), and put them to the simulator test. You need to get a feel for how you will set your financial criteria. If a property looks half decent, check out the estate agent and go visit them. Meet them in person, get a feel for how they work, ask general questions (how long have you been working in this branch?), specific questions (is this property currently rented? Ah yes? Why does the landlord want to sell?). You can spend weeks or months of free practise, there is no problem with that.

I am sure you understand that the estate agent is the archetypal salesman. It means that any advice they have for you is probably not a real advice, just a means to conclude the sale. However, as we saw in the "two brains" section, the hyper positive and hyper motivated agent is likely to let valuable information slip, and neglect some best practises and processes, if you ask the right questions. Granted, this is not guaranteed, as you can have an agent in front of you who is as cold as a North-Sea cod. That will not help. Many of my deals have involved a hyper-excited agent who wants to sell (understand "earn the commission") seemingly more than I want to buy. Having a frank and direct discussion with the agent can give you a better understanding of the dynamic of interest, and mostly what the seller wants, or does not want. Try to get in those situations and get a feel again. Lots of free learning here!

You can even make offers while still learning. There is no offense in making a low offer and see how things go. Making offers force you to be clear in your mind. At the beginning, I used to make simple verbal offers to the agent in a 20 seconds phone call. That was as cold as the cod fish. I now take more time and make sure I write an offer that conveys all the good reasons why they have to accept. I put a lot of reassurance, emotion, energy in there. That does not work well with cod fish agents, as I even wonder if they read the lines, or are only interested in the final figure way down at the bottom of my passionate offer. Who knows, maybe they do not even relay it to the seller. But for super-excited and hyper-motivated agents, they generally make a point to carry my passionate offer to the seller and make it happen.

```
"wait here buddy, I will make sure the seller hears
you well and accepts this very good offer of yours!"
```

Did you see this coming?

```
"OK… I will be your buddy for a day, but then we are
back to you as the salesman and me as the future
landlord-investor in search of a good opportunity…"
```

One main reason why my offers are more motivated and passionate is that I am negotiating lower offers against immediate cash buy. We are going to leave the "how we buy for cash" for a bit later, but this is a very good way to be at an advantage against other competing offers.

As you continue to screen opportunities, do filter them through the financial simulators, go meet agents, make tentative offers. Acting this way is very helpful to refine your understanding and to build more confidence. There will be a moment when the opportunity looks right and you will make an offer that's a bit more like a winning one, and you will get the OK. Your first deal is coming. You have jumped! Congratulations.

At this stage, I have two more pieces of advice for you.

First, make sure that you operate this deal properly, so that you really build a stream of income, not a stream of problems. Life does not stop after you buy, on the contrary it starts a new chapter.

Second… never stop searching, never stop being curious and checking what's on offer. If your financial ratio flashed green, it is likely that other properties around, appearing in the next few months, will also flash green. You have set a benchmark with your first property acquisition. You will clearly see all the important ratios at year one of operations. These are not subject to interpretation or "what if I did it another way" type of mind-wandering. They are here and they do not lie.

Now, your second deal needs to be a better one. Simulate again and get better ratios. If you see that another upcoming opportunity is definitely better than your previous one, you are ready to invest again.

The more you play this game, the more you will find ways to finance a deal when you see a real bargain.

Step 50: Independence in sight at 3+1

You can reach financial independence on auto-pilot, within less than 20 years, by making only four similar deals. Yes, four deals only, made over 12-15 years at most, then financial independence awaits within 5 years.

Coming next is our ultimate wealth building and income generating simulation. We will build this plan on top of everything we have learned so far and push it further than our first investment plan.

There are quite a lot of data to take in as we try to be as thorough as we possibly can when simulating 30 years of income and spending. Let's list all the background assumptions. Here is a set of data that we will keep throughout the simulation. First, some data relating to the tax and inflationary environment.

Type of data	Value	Reason
CPI inflation	2.5%	Above central bank mandate
Property inflation	4.5%	A conservative rate (U.K.)
Interest earned on savings	1.0%	Not much savings anyway
Salary inflation	4.5%	Averaging the perfect career
Tax rate on income	25%	Fixed tax rate across 30 years
Savings on net salary	8.0%	Less aggressive than prior plans

Table 50.1 General assumptions in percentage per annum

Then, some data related to the condition of purchase.

Type of data	Value	Reason
Home mortgage LTV	85%	A reasonably high LTV
Home mortgage interest	2.0%	A median rate for long term
Fees on purchase	6.0%	We take a market average

Table 50.2 Home purchase assumptions

We will not rely on any bonus income in this plan (any bonus would be an accelerator). We will however assume that you are a couple earning £31,250 gross[83] per annum each, and that you have just made the acquisition of your first home for £250,000[84]. This is not a random starting point, as both the home value and the salary are linked via the unaffordability ratio. The home value is four times joint salary, therefore an unaffordability ratio of 4, which is likely to force you in the one-hour commuting belt of a large city. Hopefully, you chose a desirable place with a home full of potential future value additions!

Your starting point after-tax net joint income is therefore £46,875 per annum. One additional parameter is that your full mortgage cost (capital and interest repayment) is normally in the region of 25-35% of net income.

In this plan, you will take an interest only mortgage, and the capital repayment that you are not paying back becomes an extra saving, on top of your normal savings. To be conservative, we take a 25% ratio of full mortgage repayment cost vs net income.

Let's see now the cumulated savings you can expect from this situation after just 4 years.

	Year 1	Year 2	Year 3	Year 4
Normal saving pcm	£313	£327	£341	£357
Capital repayment saved pcm	£602	£602	£602	£602
Total savings pcm	£914	£928	£943	£958
Cumulated savings end of year	£10,969	£22,216	£33,752	£45,588

Table 50.3 Monthly savings from starting point of owning first home

As we can see, thanks to your interest only mortgage, your savings are growing fast. Before you think of investing, the last important

---

[83] You can also take this number in USD, EUR, or pro rata the values to your salary, the model should remain consistent.
[84] As per our model, this required a £40,000 deposit.

point is your minimum living expense. We will consider that in the first year, apart from the savings listed above, the rest of your income is totally spent for your living expense. This crystalises the base of minimum expenses you need to cover your minimum lifestyle. As the savings and expenses are indexed on their respective inflation rates, and as your salary increase is beyond CPI inflation, we will use the difference to cover future discretionary spending. This can cover extra necessities (more children anyone?) or an improved lifestyle.

We have the following summary for your first 4 years:

	Year 1	Year 2	Year 3	Year 4
Home mortgage interest	£375	£375	£375	£375
Other living expenses	£2,617	£2,683	£2,750	£2,818
Total living expenses	£2,992	£3,058	£3,125	£3,193
Discretionary spending	£0	£96	£198	£306

Table 50.4 Monthly spending from starting point of owning first home

Now that we are clear on the starting point, your home as a first investment realised, your income, saving rate, living expenses, and discretionary spending, let's simulate how to invest for an extra stream of income.

Your rental investments will have the following parameters:

Type of data	Value	Reason
B2L mortgage LTV	90%	Maximum leverage as possible
B2L mortgage interest	2.5%	B2L more expensive than home
Fees on purchase	8.0%	More costly than a home purchase

Table 50.5 Buy to Let purchase assumptions

And the business will operate as per the following parameters:

Type of data	Value	Reason
B2L refurb costs	3.5%	One-off improvements 1st year
Operational costs	1.0%	Ongoing yearly costs of operating
First year gross rent yield	8.0%	As per our investment criteria
Savings on net profit	80%	Most of net profit is reinvested

Table 50.6 Assumptions for operating as a rental business

Our target investment properties will be in the same area as the home property. We will try to drive a bigger bargain than for the home property and pay on average 15% less for the investment property. However, as the investment is made in the future, the cost will be inflated by property inflation, as we would expect.

The model defines that the first investment property can be acquired for £276,500 [85] and would require a deposit of £59,500 [86] which can be obtained during year 6.

We shall consider that the investment will be fully realised at start of year 7. This investment will generate a new stream of passive income starting at £822 after-tax net profit per month in the first year. As per our model, it accelerates our ability to save (80% of the net passive income goes straight into savings), and partly funds our discretionary spending (the remaining 20%). You can also see this 20% as an extra Pi and Phi type of risk protection against the unknown future.

The next table shows the impact of this deal on your capital, debt, income, and on a few important ratios.

---

[85] Nominal investment at 15% less than first home = 85% * £250,000 * (house inflation over 6 years) = £212,500 * 1.045^6 = £276,730.
[86] Deposit = investment * (100% - LTV% + fees% + refurb%) = £59,497.

	Year 6	Year 7	Year 8	Year 9
Cumulated value of prop.	£311,545	£602,295	£629,399	£657,722
Cumulated debt	£225,000	£474,057	£474,057	£474,057
Debt vs capital ratio	72.2%	78.7%	75.3%	72.1%
Net total income per month	£4,868	£5,908	£6,192	£6,488
Discretionary spending	£541	£833	£978	£1,132
Passive earnings ratio	0%	13.9%	14.1%	14.4%
Expense coverage ratio	N/A	246%	254%	261%
Freedom ratio	0%	24.1%	25.1%	26.2%

Table 50.7 First 3 years after first Buy to Let investment

It was a lot of numbers and tables, I know! I wanted to make sure you had the entire reasoning behind what we do here. Now, let's see some nice graphs for a change!

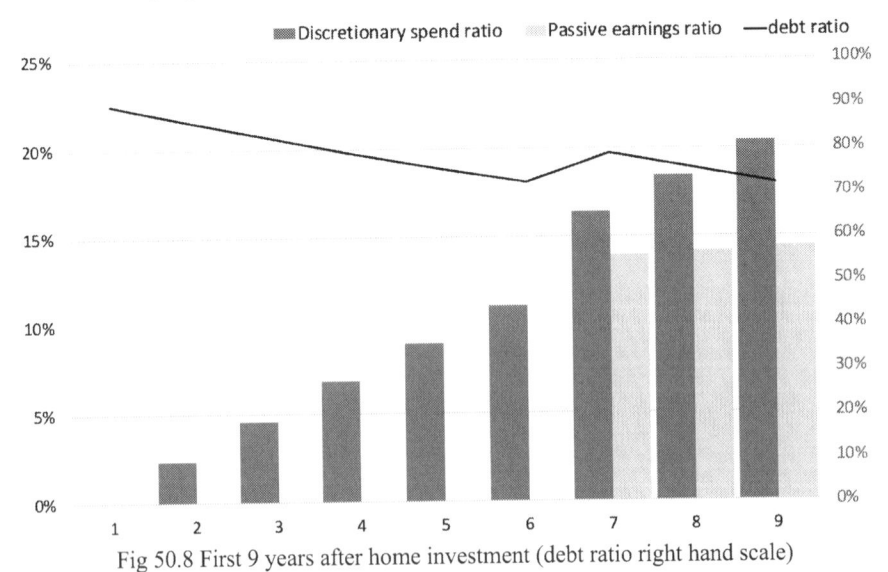

Fig 50.8 First 9 years after home investment (debt ratio right hand scale)

Nine years into it, we are still quite heavily indebted (above 70%) and rely very much on salary to meet end of months. The passive earning stream appears from year 7. Our discretionary spending, which was increasing at salary inflation minus CPI inflation got a boost and reaches 20% of income from employment by year 9. What you do with it is your choice. It may well be that it is swallowed by further life commitments. If that is so, it is welcome anyway.

If it took 6 years to save the deposit for the first rental property investment, it will only take 4 for the second one, and 2 years only for the third one. See for yourself.

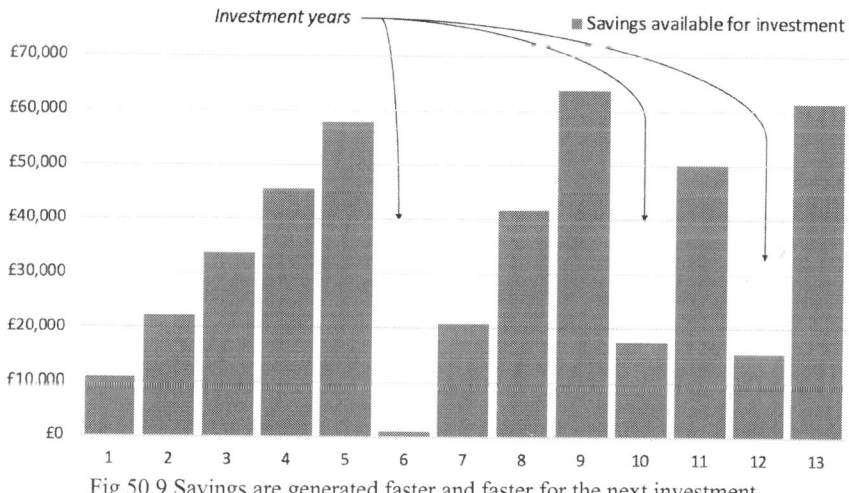

Fig 50.9 Savings are generated faster and faster for the next investment

In our model, the second Buy to Let house will be purchased during year 10 at a value of £330,000 which requires a deposit of £71,000. The third investment is made during year 12 at a value of £360,000 and requiring a deposit of £77,500.

Give or take a few hic-ups in the market or in your personal situation, this plan shows that it is possible to buy 4 houses (1 home and 3 very similar Buy to Let properties) within 12-15 years, for a total cumulated deposit under £250,000, which was funded at around 40% by your passive income, and 60% by your actual savings from employment. Once the investments are made, the rest is only managing the operations such as improving profit and reducing debt, until you reach the point where the freedom ratio blinks consistently green (when it stays well above 100%).

By now, you should know that my most important metric relating to financial independence is how much passive income we generate consistently in relations to our living expenses. But for once, let's succumb first to see the net wealth impact of these 4 deals. Here is what your net wealth position could look like over the 30 years if you start repaying the debt only once the third investment is made and operational.

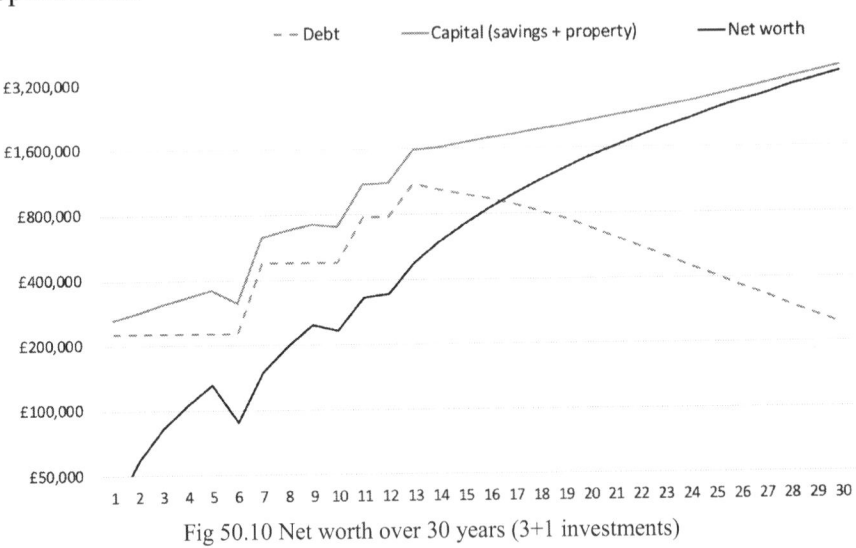

Fig 50.10 Net worth over 30 years (3+1 investments)

From year 13, once your third investment is operational, you will be able to save at least £45,000 per year from salary and passive income. You can start using these savings to repay the debt progressively, but not too aggressively. As we have learned on our journey, our goal should not be to eliminate the debt as fast as possible, because the debt is also a leverage that we want to keep. Following our example, as long as the interest on the debt is at a cost of 2.5% and the income on which it is leveraged is at 7 or 8% and growing, you have no problem with the debt!

As the value of your capital inflates over the years, your debt ratio is getting crushed and your net worth increases naturally. As we can see, in this model, you end up roughly with the same amount of debt 30 years after you started.

But there are also another five huge differences…

- You have multiplied your net worth by 100, starting at £35,000 and ending above £3,500,000.
- You end with after-tax net passive earnings of £120,000 which represents 71% of your last combined net salary.
- You have a debt ratio below 8%, whereas you started at 90%, and the value of the remaining debt has been eaten by 30 years of inflation.
- You reached financial freedom (current lifestyle living expense fully covered by passive income) within 16 years.
- From year 17, you are free to do what you like: either continue in employment, as in this simulation, or refocus your time onto another activity of your choice.

The next graph shows your debt ratio vs freedom ratio over the period. Your debt ratio crosses below 50% at the same time as your freedom ratio goes over 100%, five years after the third investment (at year 17). Debt falling like a stone and freedom ratio beyond 100% forever. It's mechanical and planned!

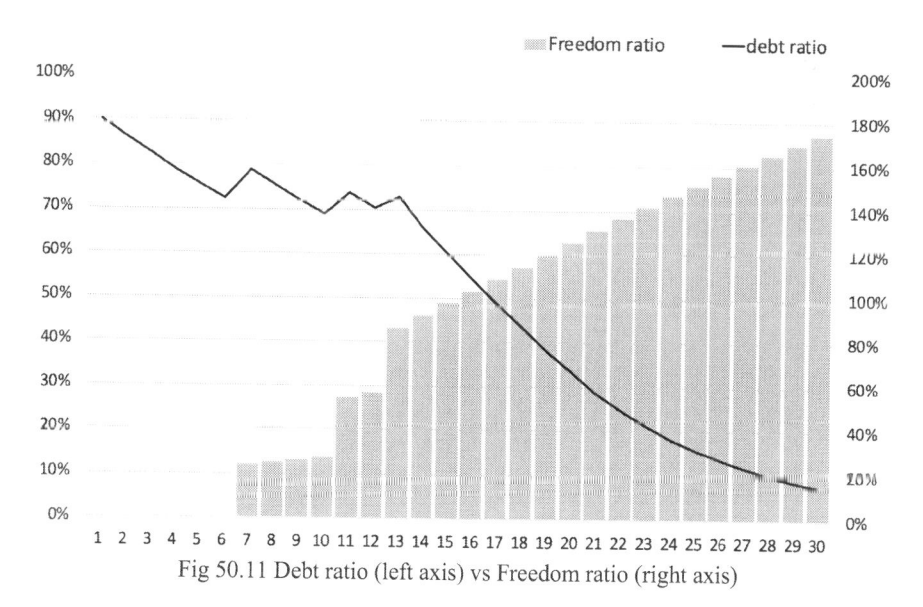

Fig 50.11 Debt ratio (left axis) vs Freedom ratio (right axis)

Let's also reassure ourselves that the all too important expense coverage ratio is good. As we can see on the next graph, not a problem at all! Again, looking at year 17, you have a coverage above 350%, or 2 ½ times more income than cost.

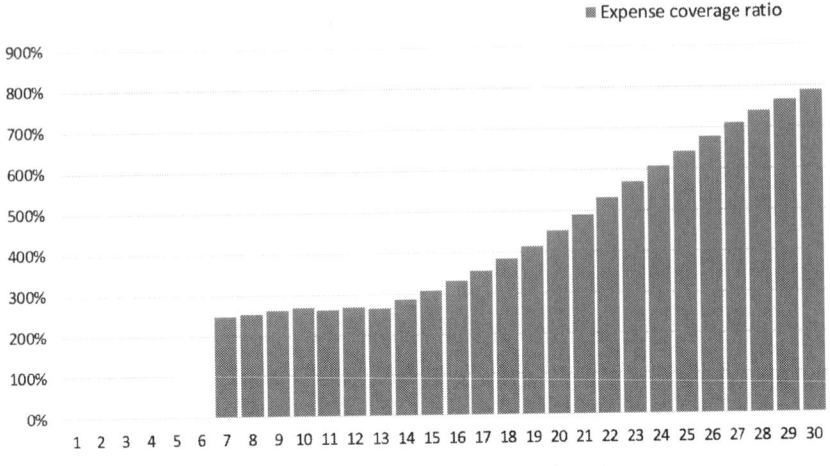

Fig 50.12 Expense coverage ratio

You obviously do not have to stop at 3 rental properties and if you play the game to its maximum, you may find out that the compounding effect of these multiple passive income streams allows you to buy one property a year, and then several a year, with the same process and same logic, keeping the debt ratio between 50-70%.

This is not the path I have chosen for myself, as I preferred to de-risk (as per the situation depicted in the freedom vs debt graph) and also keep the operational management within control and without too many third-party helpers. In the end, a passive income should stay relatively passive!

We finish with an important graph which shows:
- The progression of your passive earnings ratio, which flattens at 37-42% [87] from year 17.
- Your after-tax net operating profit per month, ending at year 30, just below £10,000 per month.

---

[87] The ratio is capped at 42% if you both stay in employment, otherwise if one of you decides to not stay in paid employment, it could reach nearly 60% by year 30.

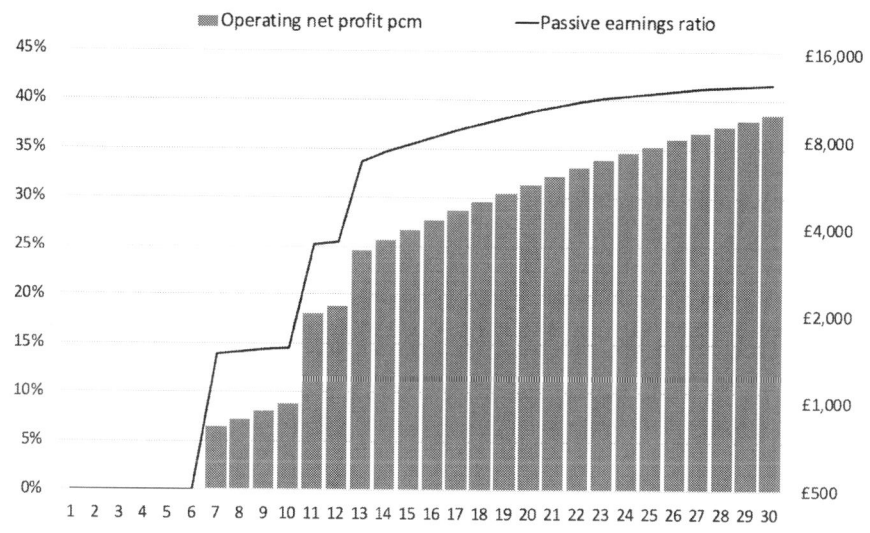

Fig 50.13 Passive earnings ratio (left axis) vs Operating net profit per month (right axis)

From year 15, the net income you receive from your rental activities is greater than the net income you (or your partner) earn from your job[88]. You have definitely built a steady stream of income which can free either you or your partner from your job obligations.

Financial freedom can be engineered. All it takes is regular savings, sound investments, debt, inflation, time, and the invisible man!

---

[88] Rental activities after-tax net income at £3,979 per month ; your net salary at £3,617 per month.

Step 51: no good reason to sell

If you think buying a property is expensive, then what about selling? I must confess that I have sold a few times in my life and I have a long list of good and bad excuses to justify myself as to why I committed this sin.

Bad reasons to sell:
- I would like to sell (that's all it is? Why?).
- I would like to move home (try very hard to keep your first home and buy a new one at the same time).
- The market will tank (you are gambling).
- The rent is not covering my costs (can you find a solution before declaring game over?).

Good reasons:
- This property has given me an intense emotional stress and continuous financial losses over a long enough period of time, and despite all attempts to find a solution I still cannot resolve it.
- I am being forced out by external factors which either force the sale now or will negatively and significantly impact the value of the property in the short term.

I see the sale of a property as a last desperate measure, a sign that there is no better move. I have sold a few properties over time but although I was convinced I had no other choice, I was not inventive or experienced enough to see that I had other choices.

When we can see alternative options, we start seeing the real cost of selling, beyond the initial fees or taxes. On paper, selling a property is generally going to cost you in the region of three to nine percent of the property value. But by far, the biggest cost is this one: you no longer have the property, so you are unable to leverage its growing value over the years to come.

I will explain in more detail later on how I re-mortgaged the same house three times to help finance four additional properties. That's a good leverage I would have lost had I sold at first doubt.

Really, you should only sell if you are desperate beyond desperate. You have worked hard to buy a valuable asset which is generating a passive income and whose value is increasing faster than inflation over the long term.

Do not throw it away at the first hurdle!

Step 52: is your home an asset or a liability?

A property as an investment is not the same as a property as a home. If well structured, the investment is a cash generating asset. Your home, on the other hand, could be at least partly seen as a liability, like your car absolutely is. But how do you tell the difference? When does your home start to be a liability?

We all have to live somewhere, so a good point of reference is to compare the cumulated monthly costs associated with running your home, with the monthly costs of a rental property you would feel happy living in. Now, the hard part is assessing these costs as accurately as possible.

The exhaustive annual cost of running your home should be the cumulative value of:

- All local taxes paid during the year.
- All utility bills paid during the year.
- The annual cost of the "rent to the bank", otherwise known as the interest on the debt.
- The annual cost of the locked capital (your cash deposit plus any mortgage capital repayment made so far), as you would otherwise have put this money to work elsewhere for interest and/or capital appreciation, let's assume at a similar risk ratio.

You can calculate the monthly fully loaded cost of running your home by dividing this annual cost by 12. It is important to note again that part of the cost has nothing to do with the usual running costs of the house, but with how well you managed to secure a low rate of interest on the mortgage, and how much of your capital is locked in your house. As we saw earlier, the house is only half the story, it is the financing that makes it a good deal or a bad one.

But it would not be fair to look only at the running cost and forget one major downside and one major upside.

- Downside: a percentage of the house value for keeping a pot for future maintenance or improvement (say 2% if this is a new build, but 4% if this is an old building)
- Upside: a fair measure of house price appreciation over a year, which I suggest as follows:

```
Annual upside of home[89] =

current home value * 75% of annual house
                inflation[90].
```

Finally, we calculate the net monthly cost of your home as the fully loaded cost of running your home plus the downside minus the upside.

Regarding the rental property alternative, you have to do a bit of research and get an accurate estimate of the local taxes, utility bills, and rent, to come up with your likely fully loaded rental cost.

Let's have a look at a practical example, which is the continuation of the investment case we evaluated earlier. The table below is a reminder of the structure of the deal.

Cost of property	£216,500
Debt	£184,025
Interest on debt	3.5%
Locked capital	£32,475

Table 52.1 Cost of home acquisition

From this starting point, and adding a few assumptions for local taxes and utilities, we can calculate the monthly running cost and net cost.

---

[89] As an obvious consequence, the monthly upside is 1/12th of the annual upside.
[90] The 75% tempers both the cost of converting to cash the value locked in the house (sale) and the risk of overvaluing the house which in turn overvalues the upside.

Cost of local taxes	£100
Cost of utilities	£225
Cost of interest paid to bank	£537
Cost of locked capital (at 4.5%pa)	£122
Monthly running cost of home	**£984**
Cost of future maintenance (at 4% pa)	£722
Monthly upside of home (at 4% pa)	-£541
Net monthly cost of home	**£1,165**

Table 52.2 Monthly running cost of home

Now for the rental equivalent, assuming similar local tax and utility costs.

Cost of local taxes	£100
Cost of utilities	£225
Cost of rent	£1,250
Net monthly cost of rental	**£1,575**

Table 52.3 Monthly running cost of rental house

In this example, it looks clear that we are better off buying this home than renting another house nearby. You could push the simulation further by adding or removing extra cost from the rental if, for example, you would spend or save more on daily transport to work, or any other obvious cost which is impactful. Finally, you could also extrapolate this static simulation to project it in the near future.

Now, if your monthly running cost of home and/or your net monthly cost of home were to exceed your alternative rental cost by a large ratio, say beyond 33%, we could start thinking that you would be better off renting than living in your current home. Of course, it's not always about finance. Emotional aspects come into play. But ultimately, you should live in a house which is in sync with a pleasant albeit affordable lifestyle. If you bought a trophy home, you may well find that instead of being first and foremost an asset, it becomes a liability.

Now, what can you do if your home is becoming more of a liability than an asset? I hope I have been convincing enough that selling is the last option for the desperate. It could be the case that you have to sell for what you see as good reasons. I would just hope that before acting, you use a robust simulation to evaluate sale vs other rental options.

You may have many alternative options to selling. You can again look at repurposing your probably "too big" house and make the most of it. Maybe it's best converted as an HMO, maybe split into flats, maybe rented for short term holiday lets, who knows? You have to do a bit of research and see if there is a profitable business life in this home.

Can you turn this liability into an asset?

Can you convert a cost into a new income stream?

7

Real case study

*It doesn't matter who's wrong or right
Just beat it, beat it!*

Michael Jackson

It was not an easy decision to write so openly about a good part of my personal finances and my long journey to financial freedom. However, I cannot see how another generic and anonymous investment case would bring enough learning experience to you, dear reader. The lessons are in the life we live. Please accept this chapter as the many lessons I progressively learned by actually making these bad and good decisions.

Step 53: in need of a moment of truth

12 July 1998 mid-afternoon. I was walking alone in the fields near the little farm whose ownership changed one hundred years before. It was a moment of deep introspection, a moment of realisation, of insight. You know it cannot continue as before, but so far you've kept going. In a moment I will say:

> "some things need to change"

On this very day, Zidane, Henry, Deschamps and their team mates were going to play the game of their lives in the final of the World Cup. One final moment to put France in the history books for ever. It's never good to compare yourself with stars as I already mentioned, but I couldn't help it.

No, I didn't dream of becoming a footballer overnight, but the now 29-year-old me did not feel particularly well rewarded for all of his struggles so far. I had been working relentlessly at near full capacity for over three years and did not have much to show for all these efforts. Low pay, no life outside of work, a small share of a start-up which did not seem to be worth much to anyone except for me and my fantasies, a life in a remote suburb of Paris which was a lot less appealing than some romantic movie propaganda.

Financially, all was not completely bleak though. By borrowing from five banks at the same time (Mum and Dad, Mum and Dad in-law, and three real banks), we had managed three years earlier to finance the acquisition of a flat in an "up and coming" location, for a cost of €130,000 [91]. I had researched the location extensively and came up with this one where a lot of infrastructure (motorways, regional train, high speed train) were connecting to. The flat was in a good state, in a good building. We could buy and settle straight in [92].

---

[91] Originally at the time 800,000 Francs, or around £80,000 as per the exchange rate back then.
[92] As we now know, buying without a possibility to leverage the floorplan is not optimal.

This moment of realisation led to a few changes, but nothing radical enough to change our lives. It took me two more years to finally accept that for our lives to really change, it required a bigger shock to the system.

Early in 2000, we decided to move to the U.K. and rebuild our lives there. We sold our flat[93] five years after we bought it, for exactly the same price. Remove the fees for buying and selling, and you have the picture: not a good deal at all! We were only forced to repay one loan out of the five, so we suddenly had a bit of savings, although clearly, these savings were debt.

Then, we took the Eurostar from Paris to London together with our two toddlers.

---

[93] Yes, this was a mistake, we all learn. The area changed beyond recognition a few years after we sold. The infrastructure was there, but it needed a bit more time for the properties around to grow fast in value.

Step 54: new beginning

I moved to the U.K. with my family in summer 2000. We rented a small house in the London commuter belt, for £1,250 per month. That was just below half my net pay, which was our family's only income. Lots of changes in perspectives. A big reset of one's own values. At the very least, one thing was sure now: if there ever was a safety net somewhere, it was removed.

After a year, our estate agent let us know that the rent would go up by £50 per month. A 4% increase. In retrospect, it's nothing and was probably to be expected. But at the time, it seemed way too much to swallow. It precipitated a search for a place that we could call home for years to come.

Back in time, I did not have such efficient financial simulators. I would rely more on a few numbers (price, mortgage cost, loan to value, level of debt) and gut feel. Like most people buying a home I suppose...

I toured the area on my bike[94] during most week-ends and went to explore many places and see many houses. After a few failed attempts, we finally bought one. The main criteria? A good location. Close to good schools, close to the train station, close to shops, nice suburb, still no need for a car.

I could not know it at the time, but this house would underpin most of the investments we made later on. For this reason, I will focus next on how this relatively modest investment snowballed into the acquisition of an additional four properties and nearly just by itself, led us on the path to financial independence in less than 17 years.

But for this, we first have to go back to numbers. Here is what the deal looked like...

---

[94] Remember that we did not have nor need a car, that little luxury costing an arm and a leg.

House value	£285,000
Mortgage value	£200,000
Mortgage interest	BOE + 0.75% (initially 4.75%)
Mortgage duration	25 years
Mortgage conditions	Variable offset mortgage (repayment)
LTV	70%
Total fees	Just below £10,000
Monthly payment	£1,235

Table 54.1 Financial condition of first property purchase

As mentioned earlier, this investment was not made with the 15+ years of insight that would follow. It was done on the basis of everything we could find and afford, knowing that a large part of our savings at this stage was already a form of debt. Our application for mortgage was rejected everywhere I went, until a smaller bank that was willing to capture more clients surprisingly said yes. There is a repeat learning point here: you may face many rejections before getting what you want. It's part of this game. You have to knock on doors many times before being granted access. Never ever stop just because someone said "No".

We are going to keep track of the value created through a few interesting ratios and see where this £95,000 investment (£85,000 deposit and £10,000 fees) got us over the next 17 years.

Property value	£285,000
Mortgage	£200,000
Savings	£0
Net wealth	£85,000
Debt ratio	70%

Table 54.2 Important financial ratios

Step 55: the case for selling

By now, we had owned and kept our home for three years. This was already approaching a record of stability!

We were repaying capital monthly and saving as much as we could on the offset. But there was another nice feature of this mortgage, called a Reserve. Basically, the bank agreed that we could draw on the reserve at any time without too many constraints, apart from having to pay interest on the drawn funds. The reserve was initially automatically revalued each year to keep pace with official house inflation.

The small bank got acquired by a mainstream bank, one that rejected our application three years earlier… We managed to renegotiate with the "naysayers", and index the mortgage with reserve on 80% LTV, a higher ratio than originally agreed for the mortgage. We also used our entire three years savings to pay for a loft conversion which consequently increased the value of the house. After this improvement, the house was revalued at £330,000. That was not much of an improved valuation, but with an 80% LTV, it meant that we could now draw down a total debt of £264,000. As the current debt after 3 years of repayment was now £185,000, it meant a possible extra £79,000 from the reserve.

After searching and filtering through many criteria, we found a 3-bed flat which was for sale at £165,000. At the time and for our local area, it was priced much below most 2-bed flats. The type of bargain I was looking for…

We finally bought the flat for £158,000 with a £115,000 additional mortgage (72.5% LTV), and a £50,000 help from the other mortgage's reserve as deposit.

You read correctly, it was financed with zero real money deposit from us.

Out of the Rat Race

The situation was now the following one.

Value of all properties	£488,000
Mortgages	£350,000
Net wealth	£138,000
Savings	£0
Debt ratio	72%

Table 55.1 Important financial ratios at purchase

The following graph shows the net wealth created over time with the outstanding debt (both on the left axis), and the debt ratio (right axis)

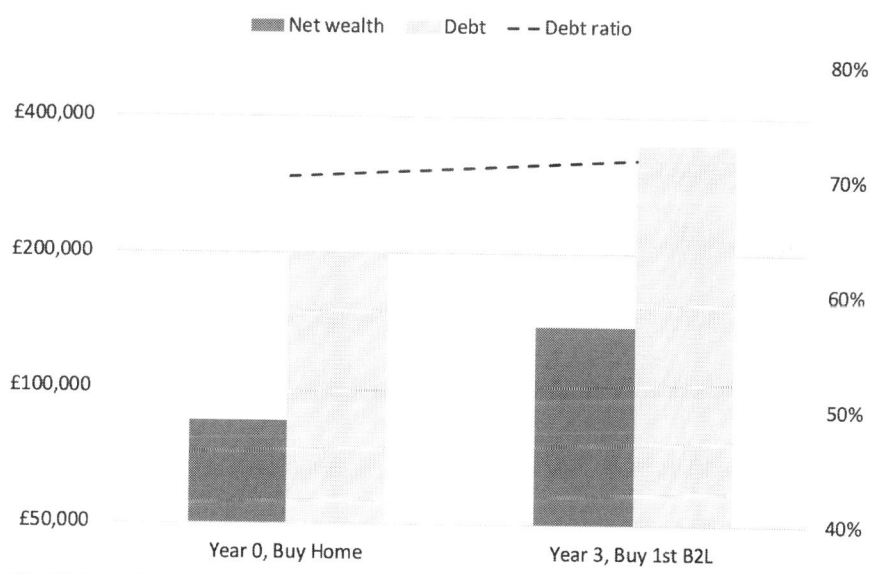

Fig 55.2 Tracking of net wealth, total debt, and debt ratio (right axis) after buying 1st B2L

Now, there is always a good reason for bargains. And they are not just because you may think you are a gifted investor... Time for two new lessons.

First one, is that we did not buy the full ownership of the house, but only an 85-year lease[95]. Well, we knew it at the time of acquisition, but not necessarily all the consequences of not being able to re-mortgage when the lease goes below 70 years, and not to mention dealing with the super landlord who is mostly in the game of juicing his tenants who are after a lease extension.

Second one, well... there was a real reason behind the bargain. A nightmare owner just above. I am not sure how the sale could legally go through with the seller and agent knowing the problems, but hey, the previous owner managed to pass the ordeal onto somebody else. Above our newly acquired flat, we inherited a schizophrenic neighbour who should have been better taken care of by social services. Instead, he lived alone in his flat. This little detail came with occasional flooding of our new investment, a few attempts to set his flat alight, and few other things which are better not mentioning, that a person not able to deal properly with his life would do.

That's what I would call a real case for wanting to sell. I tried many times to buy out the schizophrenic owner's flat, but we were in a legal void. He could own it but not sell it as he was judged mentally ill. His legal representatives would not want to know. Ultimately, after three years of battle and keeping tenants as happy as we possibly could, the flat above got miraculously sold! One would think that I would have seen it as all problems solved, but for some reasons, mainly including those linked with the extortionate super landlord, and the feeling that we had reached a good point in the market and that it was peaking, we decided to sell.

In the meantime, this 3-bed flat with lounge had been converted during week-ends into a 4-bed with a smaller lounge. I think I mentioned already that you need to find leverage everywhere, including in the floorplan! Anyway, as we prepared to sell, it appeared

---

[95] The U.K. is a bit of a feudal place in this respect, as most flats in and around London are bought on lease and revert to a super-landlord at expiration of the lease.

that we had to put back the flat to a 3-bed as the super-landlord did not like the improved leverage...

The flat got sold for £235,000 three and a half years after having bought it. After fees and repaying the mortgage capital leftover, we got £117,000 gross out of this operation, a return of more than 100% on the deposit that we drew down from the mortgage reserve. In a post-tax world, this translated into around £70,000. In terms of cash on cash return, I just cannot calculate, because again, there was no real cash outlay in the purchase.

And of course, we also collected rent every month!

Now, we were back with one property: our home. The new financial situation looked like this:

Property value	£495,000 [96]
Mortgage	£171,000 [97]
Savings	£85,000 [98]
Net wealth	£409,000
Debt ratio	29% [99]

Table 55.3 Important financial ratios after sale

Despite all the pain, we got out of it in a much-improved financial situation than when we started six years before:

- Our total debt ratio went from over 70% to just below 30%.
- Our net wealth increased by an equivalent 30% per year.
- We now had £85K savings.

Again, as a picture is worth 1,000 words or more, let's have a look!

---

[96] This was my valuation of our home at the time, not an official one.
[97] Remaining mortgage due on our home after 6 years of repayment done.
[98] That is £70,000 from capital gain and £15,000 from rent over three years.
[99] (£495,000 + £85,000) / £171,000 = 29.5%.

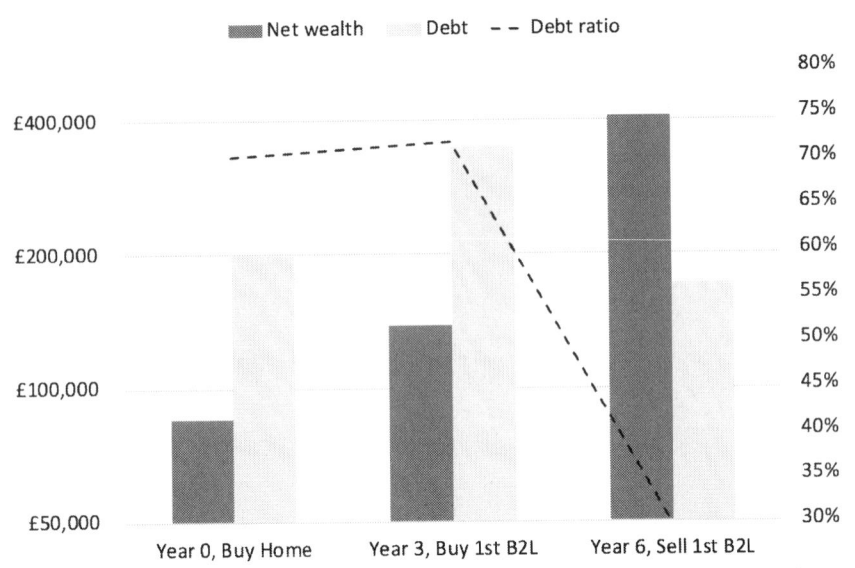

Fig 55.4 Tracking of net wealth, total debt, and debt ratio (right axis) after selling 1st B2L

After such a rollercoaster of pain, stress, and finally nice gains, it's clear you get easily hooked...

Bring on the next one!

Step 56: cash buy from home leverage

Well, take the same and do it again! Let's review our home value, get a mortgage reserve revaluation, find a new property, and make it happen...

Less than six month later, and although this was in a peaking market[100] early 2008, my screening financial simulators were slightly more advanced, and flashed an opportunity on another flat. It must be said again that it flashes its green lights on less than 1% of opportunities out there, so when it does, I have to listen. Even in toppy markets!

This time, we had learned some valuable lessons. We agreed a 999 years lease with the landlord at signature, and the yearly maintenance cost was capped at £100. That's for taming the super-landlord. Checked!

Now, the flat. Same thing really. A 3-bed flat, but this time in a better location. Convenient for train station and local commerce. A better deal than the one we just sold. It was on offer at £210,000. An offer at £205,000 seemed to work for a day (the seller agreed), but then came some competition despite the property having been taken-off the market... We had to align to the asking price. But even then, it was not the end of the competition. The owner decided he preferred the other buyer who was apparently a "professional buyer".

The way we got the sale was as follows. I just said this:

"I will buy at the asking price, and I will buy within a week as I am a cash buyer"

I was not sure it was possible, but I was sure we could try. We got the sale and got the flat a week and some days later. Here's how...

We were now just before the financial crisis and property assets were a bit toppy. Our home was too. We revalued our home and it

---

[100] The financial crisis hit the U.K. hard by end 2008, and by early 2009 nobody wanted to hear about buying houses.

came at £525,000. With an 80% LTV mortgage and reserve, we could get £420,000 of debt, of which £170,000 was already taken. That's £250,000 of new debt ready to be taken up! And then there was the £85,000 savings. We could finance a cash buy and even had enough for some renovation work, which in this case ended up costing £11,000, or just above 5% of the value of the flat.

After the acquisition, the situation looked like this:

Value of all properties	£735,000
Mortgage	£310,000 [101]
Savings	£0
Net wealth	£425,000
Debt ratio	42%

Table 56.1 Important financial ratios after sale

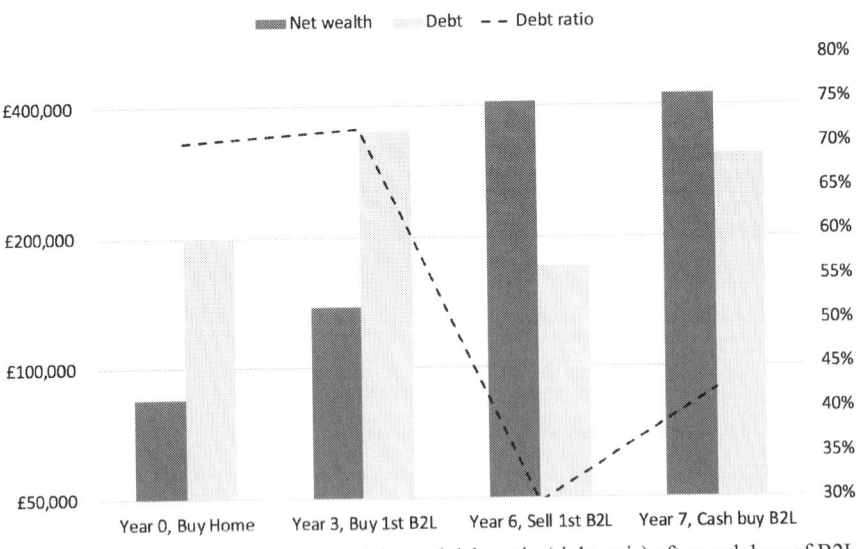

Fig 56.2 Tracking of net wealth, total debt, and debt ratio (right axis) after cash buy of B2L

---

[101] £170,000 of home mortgage plus £140,000 of new debt from reserve (cost of flat after fees and renovation £225,000 minus savings of £85,000).

The overall debt ratio was still on the low risk side and would give us an opportunity for extra leverage later on.

As it focuses mostly on capital, I must confess that this graph does not highlight the improvement this investment brought. But factor a new cash flow positive income stream of over £1,000 a month, of which a large proportion went straight into savings, and you can see the benefits with the right lenses: passive income. I will never repeat it enough times: income is way more important than capital!

The first year, we converted the flat into a 4-bed. But we later discovered it was permitted to leverage the floorplan further and ended up with a 5-bed flat. Of course, the rental yield got a boost after each of these floorplan reviews. To this day, we still own the flat, and despite some ups and downs in the market, and some more restrictive regulations in the U.K. concerning HMO, there is not one good enough reason to sell.

This one proved to be a very good investment case which ticked many good practises' boxes. I list them here, because from now on, and for every new deal, this is the benchmark to achieve or beat.

- It was a better property than the previous one we acquired (better location and better leverage of floorplan).
- We used good leverage by re-mortgaging our home and ended up paying a lower monthly interest than if we had taken a proper Buy to Let mortgage.
- We avoided the fees and complications associated with taking a new mortgage.
- This investment created an instant new positive cash flow passive income stream.
- It allowed for additional future leverage in case of need.
- It was done for the very long term allowing capital growth and rental income to contribute to our future financial independence.

Step 57: home swap from home leverage

This family home had been more than just a house. It allowed the part financing of a first flat alongside with an extra mortgage, and then the complete financing of another flat. This was more than a home where our children played. This was a dynamic financial asset, and it had been put to work pretty well so far.

But for those who cannot stand still, there are always these two questions in the back of the mind.

```
Should I push to repay the family home mortgage fast
               and be debt free?
```

and...

```
Should I climb up the property ladder, sell this
          house and buy another one?
```

I played with the first question quite a lot, because it seemed a very laudable and rewarding milestone to achieve. Around this time, I built sophisticated simulators which proved that I could be debt free on my home (but not on my Buy to Let operations) within two years. Squeeze more savings from your work, load more debt on the rental properties to free the debt on the home, and you could have a debt free home faster than you initially thought it was feasible. We were on the brink of repaying a 25-year mortgage in 7 or 8 years. When you can nearly touch it, you really think that the reward is all worth it.

But this thinking led me down a worse path. I had the opportunity, as everybody in the country had at the time, to change my home mortgage conditions and get an offset mortgage at a rate of Bank of England + 0.40%. It seems incredible that such good offer was on the table, but the banks were competing hard against each other, in a race to win more clients as fast as they possibly could.

I made the wrong call.

My thinking was that the fees incurred by re-mortgaging would not be compensated by the savings from the lower interest. I was trying to pay off the mortgage on our home, so I thought it was better to keep the current mortgage conditions, pay it off as fast as possible, and be done with it. Of course, that was the wrong approach. I finally understood I should not repay so fast. The mortgage still had 18 years of life, so the 0.35% interest difference, which I did not lock-in, lost me many times over the cost of the fees I tried to save. I finally realised, as we saw in the debt free fallacy, that this was not a good end goal.

The real end goal is to generate enough net passive income to live the life you want to live. Not to repay your bloody mortgage!

But as you slowly discard the first question, you quite invariably end up asking the second one:

"should I move up the chain?"

I played quite a lot with this question, its benefits for our family, and its added financial risks placed on my shoulder. So much that I ended up building further dedicated simulators to help me find the answers.

As in the case of the previous cash buy, preparation is crucial if you want to act fast when the opportunity appears. This time, we used a broker. We got our family home revalued again, just six months after the previous valuation, and managed to squeeze an extra £25,000. So we had a home valued £550,000. The mortgage negotiations dragged on for quite some time, with more conditions attached. I wanted to push the 70% LTV to a new 80% LTV and convert the repayment mortgage into an interest only mortgage. Basically, a change in the amount of capital I owed the bank, and also a change in when I would have to pay it back. It was finally agreed that 75% LTV would be interest only, and 5% LTV would be capital repayment. We also got the right to port the mortgage onto another property within six months, at the same 80% LTV conditions. The broker was instrumental in these negotiations.

A year after having bought the second flat, the housing market was in a very bad state. Nobody would dare buying a house. That's exactly when you have to be brave.

As we searched for a new family home, we soon found one which had been bought "subject to contract" a few months earlier at £670,000 but the would-be buyers got scared by the state of the house and called it off. Because of this fast sinking market, the house came back on the market, for sale at only £650,000. It was the perfect candidate. Well, as you may have guessed already, perfect for us meant that not many people out there wanted it, as I will describe shortly...

Let's pause for a moment and see our options to finance this purchase.

We had our home recently valued at £550,000, and for which we had already taken £310,000 of debt. This debt also included the one incurred by the flat we bought cash. Had we sold our home at its valuation price (not completely a given as the market was changing fast), the probable free cash generated would have been around £220,000.

Home value	£550,000
Cost of selling	- £20,000
Repay home mortgage	- £310,000
Free cash after sale	£220,000

Table 57.1 Selling the home

But we also had the possibility of raising a £520,000 mortgage[102] if we bought the new home.

Let's do a quick simulation of the acquisition of this "perfect" new home that nobody wanted.

---

[102] An 80% LTV on the £650,000 new home, after porting the mortgage from current home.

Cost of new home	- £650,000
Cost of buying	- £28,000 [103]
New home mortgage	£520,000
Cash from old home sale	£220,000
Savings after operation	£62,000

Table 57.2 Buying the new home after selling the old home

Our financial situation after selling and buying showed not only that it could be done, but it would have left us £62,000 of savings after the operation, which we could have used at least partly for renovation works.

In this scenario, the new financial situation would look like this.

Value of all properties	£860,000 [104]
Mortgage	£520,000
Savings	£62,000
Net wealth	£402,000
Debt ratio	57%

Table 57.3 Financial situation after buying the new home

In truth, it is likely that more than 95% of home-owners wanting to climb up the property ladder would structure their acquisition this way.

But for sure, this was not what my simulators told me. It made no sense at all at first sight, and I had to triple check it and ponder for many days before coming to accept this: it was financially way better, and not much harder, to buy the new home and keep the old one too.

Let's do this again. We are not going to sell our current home, but we will re-mortgage it with another bank, in a view to rent it later.

---

[103] 4% tax on house purchase (stamp duty in U.K.), plus £2,000 fees.
[104] £210,000 for the flat plus £650,000 for the new home.

Home value	£550,000
Current home old mortgage	£310,000
Current home new mortgage	£310,000

Table 57.4 Not selling the current home

As we can see in the next table, a quick simulation of renting our home[105] showed that we could generate an extra £1,000 per month net of tax, passive income stream for the foreseeable future.

	Year 1	Year 2	Year 3	Year 4
Income (rent received)	£2,200	£2,233	£2,266	£2,300
Cost (financial)	£745	£745	£745	£745
Cost (repairs, maintenance)	£30	£31	£31	£32
Cost (operational)	£135	£137	£140	£142
Gross profit (income – cost)	**£1,290**	**£1,320**	**£1,350**	**£1,381**
Tax (on profit of activity)	£355	£363	£371	£380
Net profit	**£935**	**£957**	**£979**	**£1,001**

Table 57.5 Monthly operational activity of current home turned into rental

Now, the plan for acquiring the new home could be as follows:

Cost of new home	- £650,000
Cost of buying	- £28,000
New home mortgage	£520,000
Required deposit	£158,000

Table 57.6 Attempt at buying the new home and keeping the other one

---

[105] Note that the rental cost had gone through the roof in the 7 years, from £1,300 to £2,200.

We were £158,000 short for this operation. But what would it look like if we managed to negotiate the cost of this new home down?

Cost of new home	- £600,000
Cost of buying	- £26,000
New home mortgage	£480,000
Required deposit	£146,000

Table 57.7 Another attempt at buying the new home and keeping the other one

Could we increase a bit the mortgage LTV on our current home?

Current home value	£550,000
Current home mortgage	£310,000
New 80% LTV mortgage	£440,000
Equity release	£130,000

Table 57.8 Equity release from current home

An 80% LTV on the current home would give us a mortgage of £440,000. In other words, an equity release of £130,000. With this, we would only be £16,000 short to pass this deal.

Let's put this figure in perspective:

- It is in the region of 1.5% of the combined value of both properties, or less than an estate agent fee.
- It is less than a year of future savings from both rental properties secured on the current home mortgage.

But in addition to this I had the following thinking going on:

- The property market is taking a beating. It could go down more still, but at least I am surely not buying at the top, probably more at the bottom. But if I sold my home (to buy the new one), I would more likely sell it at the bottom.

- I was convinced the new house would be worth at least £800,000 after some renovation works[106]
- I was expecting that because of the financial crisis, the interest rates would have to go down. My bet was that they would come down to at most 2% for at least 3 years[107]. We would have to find the extra £16,000 somehow, but the lower interest rates would easily pay for it, as we would end up having a very low cost of servicing the mortgage debt for the first few years.

In the end, after much uncertainty and negotiation, we ended up making the deal as described above.

We bought the property for £600,000, ported the £480,000 mortgage, and most importantly, we kept our previous home, re-mortgaged it, and converted it into a rental investment. The timing of mortgaging the two operations was critical as if both banks had known of the cumulated debt I was committing to, they would probably have added lots of complications to accept what became a jumbo-mortgage.

In addition, despite my risk-averse approach at all times, we had a few days of risk between having re-mortgaged the old home and not having yet exchanged on the new one. I discovered the risk only when it occurred! Sometimes it's best not knowing everything, or you may not jump... Let's review the new financial situation in our usual table.

Value of all properties	£1,360,000
Mortgage	£920,000
Savings	£0
Net wealth	£440,000
Debt ratio	68%

Table 57.9 Financial situation after buying the new home

---

[106] Always check recent and actual sold house prices in the same street, and you get a good feel of what it should be worth.
[107] In reality, U.K. interest rates went quickly to 0.5% and stayed there for around ten years, giving a headache to savers, but giving free money to those with debt indexed on BoE rate.

We have a debt ratio which is slightly less than when we started eight years earlier, an improved net wealth, and a new positive cash flow income stream. We also have a good part of our capital tied to property, which despite the temporary ups and downs, should perform better than CPI inflation. And finally, we have a bet on this new house which with time and repairs, could and should be worth more than what it was bought for at the worst of times, and in the worst of conditions.

The visual situation after 8 years now looks like this.

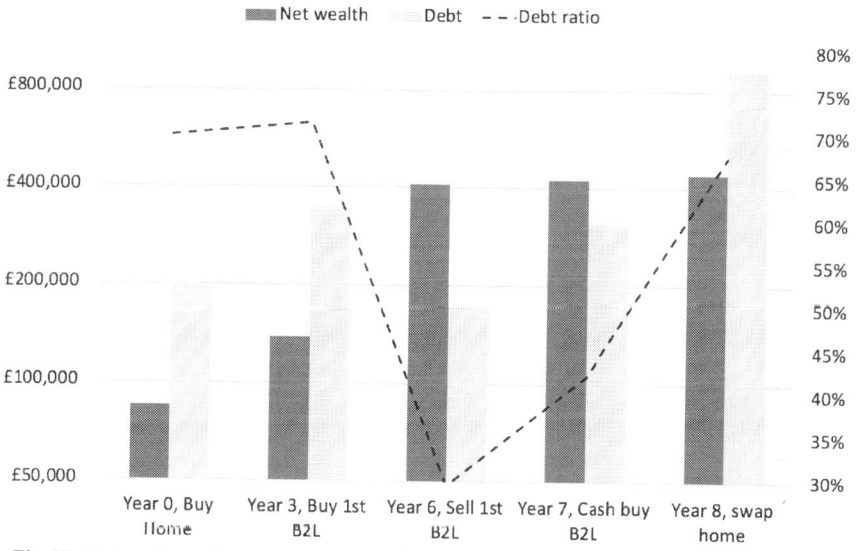

Fig 57.10 Tracking of net wealth, total debt, and debt ratio (right axis) after home swap

Now, to understand the risk vs reward balance we played, you need a little more information about this new family home of ours. Here it is:

- We spent a winter without hot water.
- For many months our kitchen was just made of a sink, a microwave and a fridge.
- We could barely access the garden as it was covered by overgrown vegetation (a jungle).
- The property had been recently underpinned to deal with subsidence problems.

Real case study

I have forgotten most of the other pain points by now, but to sum it up, it was a perfect example of enjoying endless possibilities to add value!

After three years, our two rental properties had paid back the £16,000 advance a few times over, and the interest rate on our new family home mortgage dropped to 1.25%, allowing our "rent our home from the bank" cost to be as low as the cost of renting a single bedroom in an HMO. These generous savings helped us finance some renovation works and make it a very liveable home. Finally, similar houses in the street were now selling for around £900,000, which leads us to the new financial situation.

Value of all properties	£1,660,000
Mortgage	£920,000
Savings	£0
Net wealth	£740,000
Debt ratio	55%

Table 57.11 Financial situation 3 years after buying the new home

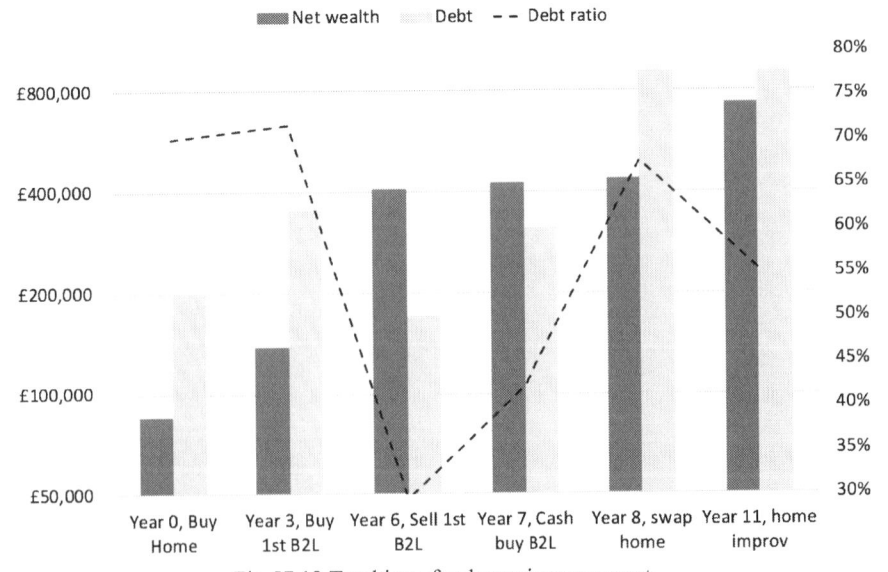

Fig 57.12 Tracking after home improvement

Indeed, after three years, the debt ratio fell to around 55% and the net wealth approached the £750,000 mark.

Our invisible man was starting to work his magic. With the help of the Central Bank alchemists, he gifted us the right to live in a 5-bed detached house with a large garden in a nice suburb, for the cost of renting a single bed bedroom in a shared student house.

Never sell!

Step 58: Dream home from home leverage

15th July 2018 mid-afternoon. It had been 20 years since my important introspection moment. Deschamps was now managing the French football team whose youngsters were once again playing the game of their lives in the World Cup final. A French teenager who was not even born when they last won it, and scored a goal that night, was recently "bought" for €180,000,000. Talk about inflation! As for me, I was sweeping dirty floors of a rundown house in the south of Spain.

As I was sweeping floors and moving shitloads of other people's shit[108], I sensed that I now had all I required to be financially independent. And again, it all came from leveraging my first home.

Mid-2017, we were 16 years after our first home investment. The U.K. property market recovered very well after the 2009 financial crisis, and most properties in or around London gained around 30-45% from the low point. In addition, we used most of our savings from work and rents to partially repay the old home mortgage and moved the remaining debt onto another property[109].

All this had a dramatic impact on our debt ratio which fell below 25%.

Property value	£2,150,000
Mortgage	£475,000
Savings	£0
Net wealth	£1,675,000
Debt ratio	22%

Table 58.1 Financial situation at year 16

---

[108] Sorry, but I cannot find better words for describing what was happening...
[109] This table shows the debt associated with the properties we track, those linked with the first home acquisition, not my entire portfolio of properties and debt, which is structured in a similar way, with equivalent ratio of debt vs equity.

Fig 58.2 Tracking at year 16

This time, I knew that the goal was not to be debt free, so I did not waste months thinking what the next step should be. By now, it was a well-known process. Revalue your home, re-mortgage, invest. The only problem was that the property market was really toppy again, and my simulators had not flashed an opportunity for 3 years... Nothing worth buying!

Well, there was this 4-bed house that I visited. I spent a few hours on the floorplan and found out that it could be really leveraged... to no less than a 7-bed with a larger kitchen to accommodate all those tenants. I visited it twice, and finally made a low but passionate and motivated offer (the "I will buy cash and fast" type of offer). It got rejected as fast I as pressed send.

"There is really nothing out there!"

But maybe next year, there could be an opportunity? May in two years there will be a crash? Who knows? Will I be prepared, or will I say:

"if I had known..."

OK, then let's get prepared now! What would be the cost of refinancing and not using the money? That's the worst that could happen. I refinance, I pay monthly interest, but I am not using the funds. Let's go back to our simulators again...

My current offset mortgage was still grossly unchanged at around £475,000 and was costing Bank of England (BoE) + 0.75%, which at the time was 1.25% per annum. But it was clear that interest rates had more potential up than down. Three more ticks down and they are at zero, whereas with three ticks up, they are not even at their long-term average, and not even at CPI inflation level...

The situation was:

Mortgage on current home	£475,000
Current interest per month	£495
Interest if BoE at 2%	£1,088
Interest if BoE at 3%	£1,484

Table 58.3 Variability of financing the debt on home mortgage

I was risking having to pay double or triple the interest I was actually paying if BoE moved interest rates towards 2% or even 3%.

I asked my bank if they would be OK to refinance my old home which had now been mortgage free for just a few weeks. After much hesitation, the bank said they would consider it. As luck would have it, the property was now worth significantly more than when we first acquired it. A new valuation came up at £800,000. I planned to refinance at 50% LTV, and 2.25% fixed for 5 years.

First home value	£800,000
Mortgage at 50% LTV	£400,000
Cost at 2.25% fixed 5 years	£750 pcm

Table 58.4 Refinancing my first home and associated monthly cost of interest

If I did nothing with this money, it could sit in my account and offset part of the £475,000 debt of the other mortgage. If BoE were to decide to move their rates to 1.5%, then my variable offset mortgage would be at 2.25% which means I pay on one side 2.25% but I save on the other 2.25%. In the next table, we can see the impact of BoE change in interest rate on the cost of my combined mortgages (current offset and potential fixed).

Cost from this operation at BoE 0.5%	- £333 [110]
Neutral operation at BoE 1.5%	£0
Savings from this operation at BoE 2%	£167 [111]
Savings from this operation at BoE 3%	£500 [112]

Table 58.5 Monthly savings from offsetting new debt at 2.25% 5 years fix

If BoE does not move rates over the next 5 years, I have to pay £333 per month for the privilege of having this £400,000 cash ready to be invested. But as soon as they reach 1.5%, it gets balanced, and if they dare push it to 3%, having taken this extra debt at those conditions will save me £500 per month compared to where I am now with around half less debt.

This scenario seemed insane! I would take on twice the debt, and I could get paid £500 per month for it...

When seen this way, it feels that it is worth getting into more debt, because either it will be used for an acquisition which will hopefully create more income and more value, or it will sit on the offset and possibly balance itself over the 5 years fixed term. Worst case, if I have not invested it, I will repay the debt in 5 years and move on.

Looking at this simulation, it is a very good moment to reflect on the risk. I understand that taking on loads of debt can be scary, but as long as the cost to service the debt is low, well below the net profit the assets leveraged on the debt will provide, and the acquired assets are

---

[110] New monthly cost = £750 + £495 − (£400,000 * 1.25%)/12 = £828, or £333 more than normal cost of £495
[111] £750 + £1,088 − (£400,000 * 2.75%)/12 = £921, or £167 less than normal cost of £1,088
[112] £750 + £1,484 − (£400,000 * 3.75%)/12 = £984, or £500 less than normal cost of £1,484

not too volatile, there is nothing to be scared about. This particular kind of debt is an accelerator of your net wealth. Yes, at some point it will have to be repaid, and it may be a very large sum but, at this later stage, the debt may be worth only 20% of your assets, or even less. You will probably be able to re-finance it. Worst case scenario, if at this stage of your life that is what you want or have to do, you will sell 20% of your assets and be debt free.

Back to my story...

I cannot begin to describe how long and painful it was to get this £400,000 mortgage. Yes, in principle the bank was OK, but in detail, they were not. To the point where I ended up asking them if this was a fake offer they were advertising, because the level of cautiousness and de-risking they were asking for was out of this world. Anyway, after around 6 months of sending more proofs of everything and anything, I finally got the go-ahead, and they indeed created a new account for me, where new credit money was deposited: £400,000 minus fees.

Even with the 6 months struggle, that sum was still earned incommensurably more easily than years and years of working for pay cheques! That's another moment when you realise that money really is debt!

A few months before the failed 7-bed conversion opportunity, I had started to show an interest on a house in the Costa del Sol, Spain, which I saw while wandering around on a rare holiday trip. Initially a very casual curiosity, which as time passed transformed into a more persistent interest, to end up with a rather passionate "I want this house" type of stance. The location did not tick all my criteria (mainly we are really not close to home), but as we were now getting very close to financial freedom territory, I took the liberty of being more flexible. Anyway, where "Home" is could change again!

Over the nearly 12 months from the first viewing, I was told 3 times that I had lost the opportunity (somebody else bought it!) for it to reappear "available" again each time. I was so pissed off the first time

I was told I had lost it that it made me realise how much I wanted this project very badly. Then, it reappeared two months later. And it went. And it reappeared. When I finally got a chance of an offer "accepted in principle", I was faced with having to change lawyer three times as none would accept to advise me about buying this property. At last, I found a lawyer who was top class and thought the deal could be done. I'm sure you must wonder what this is about... Wait for it! I had already some experience in buying an unmaintained property (my current home), but here I went to a complete other level.

The property had been uninhabited for around 15 years, it had no water, no electricity, it was in a foreign country, a 3 hours flight away from home, I still do not speak Spanish, and oh yes... the property was illegal! As a consequence, I only bought two juxtaposed but separate parcels of land (only one would have been too easy apparently...) which happened to have a structure made of bricks on top[113]. A nice stretch where the brave meets the stupid. I was totally convinced that I was brave but not stupid.

The £400,000 went into it!

We managed to legalise[114] it within a few months, which de facto meant that the illegal pile of brick became a house, and this house just got a kick in value[115].

We now have a house to rejuvenate and make as splendid as it deserves to be. We would never have dreamt being able to afford such a house in such a location 20 years ago. This was not even part of the most extravagant dream.

After this last deal, my debt level is climbing back above 35%. Guess how it makes me feel...

It is time to pause and reflect again.

---

[113] A very nice structure in fact, but as top-class lawyer number two told me in no uncertain terms: this property does not exist (I said "I visited it!" ; He said again "It does not exist!").
[114] I will just say this: a very good lawyer is priceless.
[115] As it soon gets electricity, water, is renovated and becomes mortgageable, the value will be on par with other houses in the neighborhood, not just on par with other building land.

What made this possible?
- A first investment in a home in a good location.
- A leveraging recipe applied as many times as it was possible.
- A relentless drive to maximise value when the skies open up.
- A few alchemists…
- And an invisible man…

The same invisible man who is slowly but relentlessly pushing up our passive income despite all other adversities thrown at us.

You can ignore this invisible man, or you can be friends with him.

It's entirely your choice!

8

Enjoy your new freedom

Free from the debt
Don't be afraid of your freedom
The Soup Dragons

If you are still with me at this stage, very well done, you have gone through most of what you need to be financially free. But what will you do with this new freedom? We will take a bit of distance from the financial world to explore some facets of your future lifestyle.

Step 59: levels of freedom

My financial simulators have a very simple definition of independence-day. Basically, this is when my net income from all activities outside of my work can cover all my outgoings with a margin of safety, both at current time, but also when projected into the future, so that I can keep my lifestyle for as long as I can foresee. That is when I hit financial freedom.

Now, it is possible that I could be financially independent earlier if I accept to lower my expenses, and therefore my lifestyle. That would be a viable downgraded option. It is also possible that it could happen later if I aspire to enjoy more of what life can offer, or if I want to help others as they either start their adult life, or need more care during their later life, or need funding for their projects, etc... This is an upgraded option. Therefore, we have several levels of financial freedom. For simplicity, we will keep these three levels: default, downgraded, and upgraded. The one you target is your personal choice.

To claim having reached a level is a huge victory in itself. But it's important to not cheat with oneself and avoid later deception. To this effect, let's define what "claiming victory" entails in more detail. For each level of financial freedom, you will need to have fulfilled a list of minimum common requirements:

- You no longer rely on a paid job[116] to cover any cost associated to your lifestyle.
- You have been able to live at this level of freedom for at least a year.
- You are happy with this lifestyle and are able to continue living at this freedom level into the foreseeable future.

And now for each individual level:

---

[116] It does not necessarily mean that you do not have a job, but that at least you do not depend on it financially.

- Downgraded option: you have accepted to downgrade your lifestyle but to a level that does not risk creating any additional stress or health problem.

- Default option: you did not downgrade your lifestyle, and if you happen to have more free time (less work constraint), your passive and financial income still cover the cost of your extra activities.

- Upgraded option: you have upgraded your lifestyle significantly, and you have enough passive or financial income to be generous and regularly help other people without this impacting either your new lifestyle or your future financial security.

As we can see, whatever the level, financial freedom is very much linked to lifestyle. In the end, it's a lot about controlling what's happening in your life instead of being controlled by relentless daily tasks.

I will try to be as analytical as I have been with the financial aspects and get a grip on this elusive lifestyle that we all strive for.

Let's peel the lifestyle onion!

Step 60: lifestyle

Let's forget for a moment the cost of a lifestyle but instead, focus on the key components which contribute to the Quality of Life. A group of experts was recently asked by the European Commission to establish the list of factors contributing to the quality of life[117].

They listed nine, which I have reported here below for reference.

Material living conditions	Income – Consumption – Material conditions
Productive or other main activity	Quantity and quality of employment
Health	Life expectancy – Health status – Healthy and unhealthy behaviour – Access to healthcare
Education	Competence and skills – Lifelong learning – Opportunities for education
Leisure and social interactions	Leisure – Social interactions
Economic security and personal safety	Wealth – Debt – Income insecurity – Physical safety
Governance and basic rights	Institutions – Public service – Active citizenship – Discrimination – Equal opportunities
Natural and living environment	Pollution – Landscape and built environment – Access to green and recreational spaces
Overall experience of life	Life satisfaction – Meaning and purpose of life

Table 60.1 Nine dimensions and sub topics of quality of life

---

[117] https://ec.europa.eu/eurostat/documents/7870049/7960327/KS-FT-17-004-EN-N.pdf

We will have to trust that they did a good job and were thorough. I have spent a very long time looking at this list asking myself a few more questions:

- Where does my newfound financial independence improve my quality of life?
- What could I improve anyway irrespective of my financial situation?

I suggest you ask yourself the same questions for all the categories listed above. Do it in your own time, it will be very valuable.

For example, keeping healthy does not require too much of a financial commitment. Sleeping is free, being on a good diet does not incur much more cost than eating too much of those things we should not eat, and running to keep fit is also free. I can keep healthy without requiring much wealth. And I must, because getting back to good health when not so healthy, that is costly!

As I drilled down into all these indicators of quality of life, I found that I could cover a good part by focusing on a first factor which is mostly facilitated by financial independence, a second one only partly helped by it, and a third and last one unrelated to it.

The first of these three important life improving factors is my place of living. Granted, one could live in a hut and still have the good life. This was not my path and I am not convinced that the demands and pressures of a 21st century western life are compatible with living in total harmony with nature whilst being brutally exposed to the elements. Therefore, as an adopted Brit (19 years and counting), my Home is my Castle! My place of living has the biggest impact on many indicators of quality of life listed above. This home has a direct influence on the physical location where I live (health, environment), its social surroundings (leisure, social interaction, safety), its convenience for opportunities (work, education), and its comfort (material conditions, and life satisfaction at least in part).

The second factor must be the quality of my time spent. Why do we accept all this effort and sacrifice, this endless deferred gratification, if it's not to improve the quality of time we spend in our lives? There is a two-fold approach to this one. The first one is in relation to the freedom offered by our financial independence. The second one is unrelated to it and touches on the third factor.

As for this third factor, I will let you know a bit later… Let's first go deeper in the first two and see how our financial independence could improve them.

Step 61: quality of accommodation

My home is really my castle! It has an impact on my mood, my stress, my social activities, my professional activities, and much more. There is no escape: where I live is a major determinant of my lifestyle.

To better understand what we can do about it, I will be a tiny bit analytical once more... and define 10 levels of "quality of accommodation", from benefactor to billionaire. Bear with me for a moment.

Level 1 – Benefactor: you live on a couch or in a bedroom provided to you by a benefactor. You are not really in the "financial independence" category, but you have to start somewhere. Let's be clear: if you stay in your parents' home, or if they (or someone else including the providential state) provide financial support for your accommodation, even if it is more than a simple bedroom, you are in this category.

Level 2 – HMO: you live in a bedroom that you are paying for, with your own finance. The bathroom and kitchen may be shared with others, but at least you have a separate room for yourself!

Level 3 – Studio: you live in a little studio, where the bedroom, kitchen, bathroom, are just for you. No-one else is pissing on your toilet seat by negligence, unless you invite them in!

Level 4 – Flat: you live in a flat, and you now have either a spare room or a larger lounge, which can be used partly as an office, or to have guests stay over from time to time.

Level 5 – 3-bedroom house: you now live in a 3-bed semi[118]. Your garden is made for gnomes, but at least there's a bit of outside space. If you are lucky, maybe there are two toilets in the house!

Level 6 – Detached house: something is better. Maybe it's now a detached home, or maybe you have one or two more rooms, or most

---

[118] The 3-bed semi is the archetypal suburban home in the U.K. Three bedrooms, lounge, kitchen, bathroom, joined by a party wall to another mirror image home. For most people, it's the end goal.

rooms are larger, or the garden is larger. Anyway, it feels nicer to be in this home than in the previous one.

Level 7 – House with pool: you have something more which most people do not enjoy. It can be a swimming pool, a large cinema room, whatever is your fancy. Rooms are big, and your house shouts to everyone around: "look at me, I'm big!"

Level 8 – House with fairies: same as before, except that now you have managed to get other people do the chores. Someone will do your shopping, another one your garden, clean the pool, or anything you prefer others to do for you. And by the way, you have managed to squeeze in 5 toilets, no less!

Level 9 – Mansion: Not only you have permanent little fairies in your house, but now your house is called a mansion. You have rooms you barely go in within the course of a year. Extravagance!

Level 10 – Billionaire: The billionaire next door has just added another floor to their palace, and you're not going to let them get away with it. They added one floor? You will dig two more basements under your supersized mansion! Screw them!

At this stage, I do not feel a need to describe anything beyond the billionaire status, and I am not totally convinced either that level 9 or 10 are good options for a relaxed state of mind. I believe most people will like to shoot between level 5 and 7. You could probably do with level 4 in case of a downgraded financial freedom, and you can also obviously strive for level 8, although this is really becoming top of the range of upgraded financial freedom.

It's pretty likely that most of us started in life at level 1. Again, level 1 is not being financially independent. Moving out of level 1 must be your goal if you are still stuck there. But you should only make the move when you can afford it. After this, moving up the ladder takes an ever-increasing financial commitment as you progress.

You can argue about every model, but we have to start somewhere. We will assume that it takes 50% more financial resources to climb from level 2 to 3, then 60% from 3 to 4, 70% from 4 to 5, etc...

In short, if your tiny bedroom was costing 100, your studio is at 150, the flat 240, the 3 bed semi 408, the detached 737, the house with a pool sets you back to 1,395, the little fairies come at 2,791, the mansion at 5,861, and the billionaire row, I give you cheap at 12,893 which is still 129 times the cost of the single bedroom...

The table below shows the value of each accommodation level for this model.

benef	HMO	studio	Flat	3bed	detach	pool	fairies	mansion	billion
Lvl 1	Lvl 2	Lvl 3	Lvl 4	Lvl 5	Lvl 6	Lvl 7	Lvl 8	Lvl 9	Lvl 10
0	100	150	240	408	734	1,395	2,791	5,861	12,893

Table 61.1 From benefactor to billionaire, the relative cost of accommodation per level

Of course, you can tune-in these numbers to reflect more what you see out there, but I believe they carry a fairly good representation of the reality. This model also gives us a feel for how difficult it is to move up one level of quality of accommodation. Each jump requires a proportionally bigger effort. Now let's put a real monetary value behind this basic model.

If we define an expected gross yield between rent and property value, we can use the above table to get a feel for rent and value at each level. For example, let's say that around London, U.K., renting a bedroom in a shared accommodation is at £450 per month and we have a 3.5% gross yield. We can directly calculate an expected value of rent and cost of property for this model, as shown below (first line is rent per month, second line is property value in thousands of £).

HMO	studio	Flat	3 bed	detach	pool	fairies	mansion	billion
£450	£675	£1,080	£1,836	£3,305	£6,279	£12,558	£26,372	£58,019
£154	£231	£370	£629	£1,133	£2,152	£4,305	£9,041	£19,892

Table 61.2 Monthly rent value and property value per type of accommodation as per model

Obviously, we can also do the same exercise for other locations on the planet. For example, let's say that in Malaga, south of Spain, the shared bedroom is at €200 and the gross yield at 3%. In this case, we will also add a third line to show the conversion from Euro to Sterling[119] to compare with the London table. We keep the property prices in either thousands of € (line 2), or thousands of £ (line 3).

HMO	studio	Flat	3 bed	detach	pool	fairies	Mansion	billion
€200	€300	€480	€816	€1,469	€2,791	€5,581	€11,721	€25,786
€80	€120	€192	€326	€587	€1,116	€2,232	€4,688	€10,314
£69	£104	£167	£283	£511	£970	£1,941	£4,076	£8,969

Table 61.3 Monthly rent value and property value in Malaga, Spain

We can see quite clearly that for the same money value, one can jump by one quality of accommodation by moving from London, U.K. to Malaga, Spain.

Let's do the same exercise with Cape Town, South Africa, and set the HMO rental to 2,000 Rand and the gross yield to 6,5%, which is more reflective of inflation and yield in this part of the world. The first two lines are in thousands of Rand, and the last line is also the Sterling conversion[120] of the property value, again in thousands of £.

HMO	studio	flat	3 bed	detach	pool	fairies	Mansion	billion
R2.0	R3.0	R4.8	R8.1	R14.7	R27.9	R55.8	R117.2	R257.8
R369	R553	R886	R1,506	R2,711	R5,152	R10,304	R21,638	R47,605
£21	£32	£51	£86	£155	£294	£589	£1,236	£2,720

Table 61.4 Monthly rent value and property value in Cape Town, South Africa

This time, you can jump three levels by switching from London to Cape Town. From a 3-bedroom house in the commuter belt to a detach property with pool and little fairies!

---

[119] Exchange rate taken at 1.15 (November 2018).
[120] Exchange rate taken at 17.5 (December 2018) although this one varies quickly and wildly.

I let you apply the numbers for locations closer to your current home compared to where you aspire to go. What I wanted to demonstrate, although we can very naturally sense it, is twofold.

First, it takes an ever-larger effort to move up one notch, which at some point does not justify the extra pain. It's just not worth the one-time (purchase) cost, and not worth the long-term (running) cost. Indeed, a bigger house is likely to come with bigger expenses (cost of mortgage, insurance, and all these little gadgets that come with the trophy) and one shall not underestimate the pressure to keep up with the Jones (the big-size-house neighbours who keep spending what you'd rather save). We saw earlier that a home can move from being an asset to becoming a liability. It is wise to avoid crossing this line. After all, financial freedom is about freedom, not about showing off!

Second, you can move up by one, two or even three notches on the quality-of-accommodation scale by moving to different locations. It will not necessarily give you the perfect lifestyle, but you can see that once you have secured at least a downgraded financial freedom, you can then secure a better lifestyle by moving from a costly place (where you want to be in your employed life to earn the best salary) to a more relaxed and less costly one (where you may want to be when you have reached financial independence).

Remember that if your home is your castle too, it does not have to stay in the same place forever.

Step 62: quality of time

Einstein discovered that time is relative. In his case, relative to speed and acceleration. I hope you will agree that your time is also relative, to how you enjoy your activities. Waiting, even just for 5 minutes, takes forever, but good time flies.

If you ever doubt this relativity of time, I have a little test for you. Take your mobile phone and set a countdown alarm at 3min. Do not start it yet. Now go to your bathroom and run the shower at the coldest temperature you can. Put your phone away so you do not see the timer, but close enough that you will hear the alarm, start the countdown, and go straight under the shower. Don't get out until you hear the alarm! When you hear the alarm, get out of the shower, take a towel, dry yourself as quickly as you can, and reset the alarm to 3min again. Avoid shivering so much that you mistakenly set it to 33min! Now go to your bedroom, place your phone so that you cannot see the timer once more, start the countdown and plunge under your duvet. You can swear at me as much as you like (that will keep you entertained) but when you hear the alarm, one more swear and you must get out of bed. Out!

Now tell me: did the 3min under the cold shower feel as long or longer than the 3min under the duvet? If you think it's the same and you did not cheat[121], I really think you do not need much more advices from me, because you have an extraordinary tolerance to harm coupled with an extraordinary acceptance of rules. We are in a different category!

Hopefully we now agree that time is relative. I cannot tell you how to spend your time, but I can help you ask the right questions to make your time fly.

Let's see... We all have 24 hours in a day, and by our very human nature, there is an uncompressible amount of time that we have to spend on certain necessities, such as sleeping, eating... and from time

---

[121] Like taking a cold shower on an unbearably hot day, or after a long run...

to time, going to one of those too many toilets of this fairy home of yours.

It looks to me that you are most likely to spend a good amount of time sleeping. Well, I have good news for you! Buy a good mattress, and you can sleep like a billionaire every night. It's not meant to be a joke. Seriously, if like most people you spend 6 to 8 hours in bed every night, it is the easiest activity for which you can simply improve the quality of time spent. Freshen up your bedroom and buy a good mattress!

I could also advise you to buy the nicest toilet rolls, but I will refrain. You have full freedom and accountability on the choice of colour, texture, and perfume.

Unlike the toilet or bathroom where one generally wanders alone, eating touches on the social side of life. Eating alone, or eating with others? Eating to fill your tummy, or eating to enjoy a break in the day?

So far, we did not need to get rich to sleep or pee. And I do not think either that we always need to go to the best restaurants in town to enjoy a lunch break with friends or family. Therefore, after not having spent much money out of the ordinary, we are left with 14 or 15 hours a day, which will either feel like weeks if they are not so enjoyable, or like minutes if they are.

Out of these 15 hours or so, there is no question that at some point in your life, you will need to set aside some routine time to keep physically and mentally fit[122]. When and how you do this is your choice. We all have a choice, but sometimes we are so conditioned with old habits, that we do not see we have choices. Let me give you an example.

I live 26 km / 17 miles away from my usual place of work[123]. I have been living roughly at the same distance to my office for the last 25

---

[122] You may discover it late, but discover it you will, so better know it sooner rather than later.
[123] Well, that was in the old days before I became fully OOTRR!

years. No matter if the office changes location or if I move my home, or even if I change country, this distance stays the same. It's kind of a personal law of physics. It seems it cannot change. For 20+ years, my only option to go to work has been like everyone else around: walk to the station, commute to the capital by train, take the tube, walk to the office. That's one hour when all goes to plan. And then back. As we all know so well, there is no other commuting option. The car is not an option as it would take longer, be less predictable, and you cannot find a parking space anyway. You cannot walk there. So you continue the same commute...

That's until one particular day, where you are way too fed up having missed 2 or 3 trains that you could not board because they were too packed, and then you boarded the next one and you arrived at the office half an hour late sweaty and grumpy. Over the weekend, you say it again:

"Something needs to change!"

You check the travel map again... Wait a minute! You go to a cycle shop, and suddenly your horizon expands. I can cycle to work when it's not raining[124]. It keeps me fit, I have a very predictable commute time, I enjoy most of the ride, I have a shower at work before everybody is in, and after 6 months of this, my bike is paid for with all the savings in train tickets I do not need to buy anymore.

Who knew it could be done? Who knew cycles existed? Who knew it's possible to cycle 26km back and forth? These dreaded old habits have kept me 20 years standing in packed commuter trains when I could have enjoyed two decades of cycle rides, been happier and fitter. In one moment of realisation, I just converted 120-180 minutes of daily pain into the same duration of sport and enjoyment.

Do you have old habits too? Things that you do because there are no other alternatives? Well, maybe there are a few other better options. Just review how you spend your time during a normal day. Which of

---

[124] I guarantee this is still more than half the days, even if like me, you live around London!

these activities feel like they are an awful waste of time? Can you replace them, move them, shake them until they become good moments? Memorable even?

If and when you get to at least a level of downgraded financial freedom, one would hope that you can take the opportunity to free up some time and replace some unpleasant activities by more pleasant ones. In the end, the process looks very similar. Which activity of lower personal value can you replace by another one that brings you more satisfaction?

However, be aware that if financial freedom can give you back some time, it does not automatically mean this will be quality time. This totally depends on you. Financially free or not, as strange as it sounds, you can manufacture the good moments of your life, and you can choose who you allow in.

So I have a few more questions for you.

- Who should get in or out of your close and extended circles?
- Who do you want to spend your time with?
- How often?
- For what purpose?

Step 63: money vs time

Have you ever wondered what the value of your time is?

Because the ultimate currency is not the US Dollar, the Euro, Yen or Sterling. It is time. Time is money and money is time.

Let's think about it for a moment.

- When you work, you exchange your time (8 hours per working day for example) against money.
- When you pay for a service or a product, you exchange some of your working time against the time of the person giving you the service, or against the cumulated time of all those people who contributed to create the product.
- When you take on debt, you exchange money against a promise to repay, which we can see as a promise to give away (a lot of) future time, in order to repay.
- When you save money, you exchange a bit of today's time against an improved quality of time which will happen in the future.
- And when you receive rent from a tenant, it is the consequence of the contractual agreement allowing the tenant to live in your property, against a chunk of the tenant's time.

It looks to me that we could buy and pay with time, both in the present and in the future. We could exchange part of our present time at work against a duration of a certain quality of life in the future. I would hope that adopting this thinking gives you a boost and triggers more important questions, such as the next two.

> "How much of my present life am I willing to sacrifice in the quest of a better future?"

That is an important question. Quality of time now vs sacrifice for a quality of time later. I do not have a ready-made answer for you, it's your life and your choice. You have surely gathered through this book that I have personally favoured my future to the detriment of my present. It does not make it the best strategy, it is what it is. You will have to find the one that works for you. It does not have to be completely black and white either, and it can evolve in time. In fact, when I look back in the mirror, I see that I gave myself a little bit more present time after reaching a few key milestones. The dreaded 40th anniversary was such a turning point. On the 45th, I gave back even more, and as the 50th was approaching, I gave myself a few months to write this book.

But "quality of time now" is not necessarily only compromised by "saving for your future". There is worse. As you work in a more and more demanding job, and earn more and more income, you could well fall in the most common trap. More income will invariably mean more demands on yourself from your work, which as a consequence means less free time. Assuming that you have a family, your priorities could well end up being ordered like this:

1. Exchange part of your salary for a basic quality of life: housing, food, basic health, basic education for kids, basic leisure, etc…
2. Exchange a bit more salary for more fancy stuff: electronics, fancy vacations, subscriptions to clubs, a car, etc…
3. Exchange a lot more salary for more extra fancy stuff: private school, new fancy car, new posh neighbourhood, trips around the world, etc…
4. Time with family and friends.

If your priorities are ordered like this, you are at risk of looping in stage 3 for ever and only visit stage 4 on rare occasions. If your priorities are different and stage 4 is now priority 2, you may find out that to deal well with fancy and extra fancy, you end up sacrificing time with others anyway. You say it is priority 2 but the facts tell you otherwise: time for others has disappeared. And because of the race to provide fancy and extra fancy, time for your future was never in the equation either.

My friend, this is the worst Rat Race you can ever want to run. Not much quality time in your present, and no good plan for quality time in your future either. At least, if you sacrifice your present, do it for your bloody future!

And now to the second question, for which the relevance depends on how much sacrifice of present moments you are ready to make:

```
"How many days of my expected future quality of life
can be financed by a day of my current work effort?"
```

In the perfect career example, Joe was earning around £12.50 per hour at the start. Consequently, at our low range of an 8% saving rate, Joe saves £1 per hour worked. The table below shows how much more this £1 is worth in 30 years' time but in today's money, depending on how much interest Joe will earn on this £1 saved today[125].

	Earned interest	% of initial worked hour
Interest at 3% pa	£0	0%
Interest at 4.5% pa	£1.56	12.5%
Interest at 7.0% pa	£3.24	25.9%
Interest at 9.5% pa	£6.61	52.9%
Interest at 12.0% pa	£13.27	106.1%

Table 63.1 Inflation rebased value of interest on £1 in 30 years in different savings scenario

Over 30 years, the 8% savings on this hour worked in youth will give you back an hour of same value only if you manage to place these savings at 12% interest (in a 3% CPI inflationary world). If placed at only 9.5%, you get back half your hour. At 7%, only a quarter of it. I suppose you remember that the stock market gives you a rate of return averaging 7% over a long period of time.

And if you were thinking of doing it in 10 years, then beware! At 8% savings of net income, 12% interest would not even give you back

---

[125] We assume a CPI inflation of 3% over 30 years. In all the upcoming examples, we also assume that we want to keep the original capital saved (here £1), which is here to generate interest for the future. We never spend the original capital, only the interest generated from it. In case you wonder why... you never know how long you will live, and you need a Pi factor!

a fifth of the initial hour worked. The next table shows that over 10 years, to get back the 100% value of your hour worked, you will need to have a very aggressive 45% savings and a very aggressive 12% interest too. This is becoming border line insane in terms of current lifestyle and interest expectations over a shorter period.

	Earned interest	% of initial worked hour
Interest at 4.5%	£6.53	52.2%
Interest at 7.0%	£8.33	66.6%
Interest at 9.5%	£10.56	84.5%
Interest at 12.0%	£13.32	106.5%

Table 63.2 Inflation rebased interest in 10 years of an hour's work when saving 45% of it

Of course, your future lifestyle will dictate how many past saved hours of work you will require. Maybe one day worked in youth could finance two or three days of a lower lifestyle 10, 20, or 30 years later. How you swap present sacrifices for future quality of life depends too much on many personal choices you make today and in the future. I do not have a ready-made simulation for you.

Instead, I give you this last upcoming table.

For each net income saving rate situation, displayed in the column on the left, from the low 8% to the ultra-aggressive 50%, I have calculated the number of years it will take to get back around 100% of your past worked hour, for each interest rate on your savings, from a low 4.5% to an aggressive 12%. We still keep the 3% CPI inflation assumption.

I will help you read the table. For example, take the net income you earned at work yesterday. You will get back the same amount in the future, earned via interest on your saved capital, with the same purchasing power as today (inflation proof), if you are prepared to save 25% of yesterday's net income, find a way to earn 9.5% per annum tax free on it (that's no small feat) ... and wait 22 years! Or for the same 25% saving but a lower rate of interest of 7% (again, the average stock market return over long periods), then you need to wait 36 years.

Interest return pa Savings rate	4.50%	7%	9.50%	12%
8%	☹	☹	☹	30 years
15%	☹	☹	30 years	22 years
20%	☹	☹	26 years	19 years
25%	☹	36 years	**22 years**	16 years
30%	☹	31 years	19 years	14 years
35%	☹	27 years	17 years	12 years
40%	☹	24 years	15 years	11 years
45%	☹	21 years	13 years	10 years
50%	47 years	18 years	11 years	8 years

Table 63.3 The long wait to get back 100% purchase power of a day worked in the past

Hopefully that puts into perspective how much in proportion of your net earnings you have to save, how you have to find very high rates of return without going too much on the risk side, and how long you have to wait[126].

This is where we find ourselves!

How much of today's earnings are going into your savings? Which investment should you make? How much of today's lifestyle should you sacrifice for your future lifestyle?

We all have the same amount of time: 1,440 minutes per day. We do not earn the same amount per work hour, we do not enjoy the same amount of quality time, but we spend the same time. It would seem

---

[126] It also puts in perspective our slow-but-steady strategy of investing in properties in locations of high demand by financial and floorplan leverage. Over time, it can generate more than 7% return and the new passive earnings can also boost your savings rate significantly.

that work time and quality time are the two faces of the same coin, the time coin. But that's a wrong representation. I give you a hint, and you should read it a few times before moving on.

```
"In the money-time system, anything that is not
       Earning or Enjoying is a loss."
```

Granted, you can enjoy a good sleep, but it is more difficult to enjoy a commute standing pressed against other people in a packed train, or to enjoy spending 10 minutes sitting in one of your many toilets. And we have not yet found how to convert toilet time into earnings. These are dead time!

Now, there is a trick and we are about to unmask it.

It feels at first that the money-time system looks like this picture, where time is scarce and is either spent to earn money or to enjoy life.

But it's a flawed and simplistic representation.

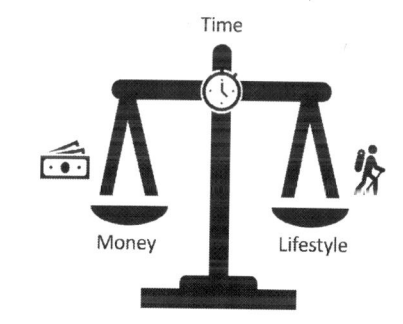

Fig 63.4 Time arbitrates money vs lifestyle

If you have the most enjoyable life of all, making your work so enjoyable that it becomes quality time, not having much of a commute, enjoying every possible otherwise dead time, and even enjoying your daily visits to a magical toilet experience, you would not be able to cram more than 1,440 minutes of enjoyment in your day. Yes, even in this idealistic life, you cannot enjoy more time than the laws of physics grant you.

However, the time that you convert into money, most likely by working, is expandable beyond limit irrespective of whether you are actually working or not. If you have managed to acquire a few streams of passive income and/or portfolio income, you earn work time for free. Let's say that, like Joe at the beginning of his career, you earn £12.50 an hour. If you manage to find a magic formula to stay awake all day, all night, and manage to work 24 hours per day, you will earn £300 per day. Well, as we approach the end of this book, I am sure you will agree that there are ways to end up earning £300, £400, or even £500 per day without working a significant amount of time in relation to this earning.

Let's pause again and make a new sense of this.

We can never enjoy more than 1,440 minutes of quality time per day, and we sense that we should enjoy as much as possible of these minutes. It is the same for everyone, and other people's quality time will never be our quality time. It's theirs, as part of their 1,440 minutes allocation. But other people's time can magically transform into money-time for us. Without limit. One tenant, 10 tenants. One employee, 100 employees. No limit!

Therefore, if time is money but time is limited, the time coin can only be one time: quality of time. It allows me to rewrite our previous statement as follows.

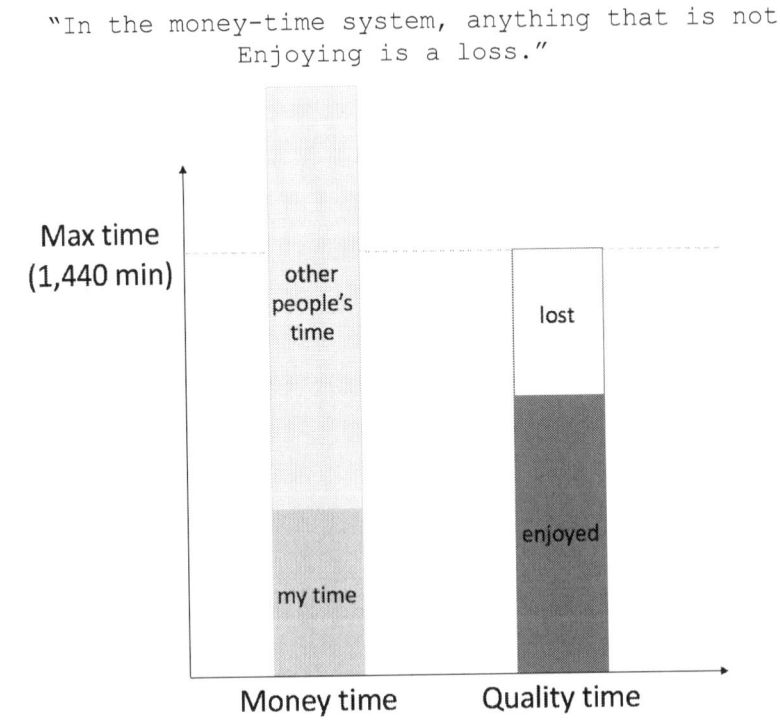

```
"In the money-time system, anything that is not
            Enjoying is a loss."
```

Fig 63.5 Quality of time not enjoyed is lost but money time can be borrowed from others.

How you make the most of your time and how you prioritise your quality time vs work time is entirely your choice. It is not a static choice, and you may rebalance it from time to time as you advance in life. You also have the choice to establish or not a stream of passive income to supplement your earnings. As your passive income grows over time, there will be a moment when it could entirely replace your earned income stream. At this point, you expand your choices: you are free to rebalance your work time, and swap less enjoyable activities with quality ones.

Make the most of other people's time[127].

Make the most of your time[128].

---

[127] Money.
[128] Quality of life.

Step 64: What was this all about?

Every couple of years, my dear wife would remind me of the Greek fisherman story. It goes like this.[129]

A businessman took a short vacation to a small Greek coastal village. Unable to sleep he walked the pier. A small boat with just one fisherman had docked and inside the boat were several large tuna.

"How long did it take you to catch them?" he asked.
"Only a little while" the Greek fisherman replied.
"Why don't you stay out longer and catch more fish?" he asked.
"I have enough to support my family and give a few to friends," the Greek fisherman said as he unloaded them into a basket.
"But …. What do you do with the rest of your time?"
The fisherman looked up and smiled" I sleep late, fish a little, play with my children, take a nap with my wife and stroll into the village, where I sip wine and play guitar with my friends".

The businessman laughed "Sir I am an MBA and can help you. You should fish more, and with the proceeds buy a bigger boat. In no time you could have several boats with the increase haul. Eventually you would have a fleet of fishing boats. Then instead of selling your catch to the middleman, you could sell directly to the consumers. You could control the product, processing, and distribution. You would need to leave this small coastal village and move to the city to run your expanding empire."
The fisherman asked "But, sir, how long will all this take?"
"15- 20 years, 25 tops" said the businessman.
"But what then?" asked the fisherman.

The businessman laughed and said "That's the best part, when the time is right, you would announce an IPO and sell your company stock to the public and become very rich. You would make millions".
"Millions? Then what?" asked the fisherman.

The businessman replied, "Then you could retire and move to a small coastal fishing village, where you could sleep late, fish a little, play with your kids, take a nap with your wife, and stroll to the village in the evenings where you could sip wine and play guitar with your friends."

---

[129] Courtesy of the internet. This story is posted so many times, I am not sure who wrote it first.

It should make you wonder why we are seeking financial independence. It's the eternal story of "living day by day" vs "seeking ever more security". Or "living in the present" vs "living to build your future".

Apart from the unfortunate accidents which can happen in life, and discounting those rare individuals who are seeking to build an empire or a legacy for the next century[130], I see three ways to exit the Rat Race:

- Early for a choice of "lifestyle first" even if insecure.
- Early for a choice of being "financially secure first".
- At end of the race when it's official retirement time.

Fig 64.1 Exiting the Rat Race

To make it simple, I shall consider that those who never entered the race have taken the decision of an early exit, probably a lifestyle one, although it could be a financially secure exit if you were born lucky enough. I suppose it is also possible to exit for lifestyle, become a kind of artist or unique personality in the world, and then become financially secure. But that is like winning the lottery. So basically, you have to choose:

Lifestyle first, Financial Freedom first, or Racing till the end.

---

[130] If this is who you want to be, you are already in a different Rat Race, a race with yourself with zero exit on the horizon.

I am not convinced that those who are mentally focused on exiting early and being financially secure can also seriously contemplate the other two alternatives.

Personally, I could not be the Greek fisherman. I could not even begin to envy him! That's bad but that is probably how you and I are wired if you have been with me until this point. We are built like this. Our mental references are aligned with these relentless needs for achievement. We always need a bigger goal than the last one and we need the exhilaration to prove that we can make it. And we enjoy the challenges. We say "challenges" to give a positive spin, but in reality, these are struggles. Yes, admittedly, it looks like we enjoy some kind of struggles!

I will not go as far as to say that this enjoyment is constantly pure quality time, but it is not just time for earning, and certainly not dead time. And let's say it loud and clear "we live in and for our future". Our ability to sacrifice the present for a better future is immense and that is why we can only exit through one door.

We would feel extremely vulnerable if we were going to exit without being financially secure multiplied by Pi. And we would feel close to depression if we were forced to stay in the same routine loop until a constantly postponed retirement date. We just cannot exit through the lifestyle door first, and we just cannot stay in this race.

This brings me to the third factor for improving the quality of life, the one I kept hidden so far. Well, it was here in plain sight, listed by this group of experts researching the factors contributing to the Quality of Life. And the good news is, it does not need to be related to your financial status, earnings, or other material aspects beyond some basic necessities.

Their last line: Meaning and Purpose of life.

```
"How I can have a meaningful and purposeful life?"
```

I cannot continue more on this path without referring to Ray Dalio. He explains "meaningful relationships" in such powerful words that I do not have much to add[131].

> "The most meaningful relationships are achieved when you and others can speak openly to each other about everything that's important, learn together, and understand the need to hold each other accountable to be as excellent as you can be."

This relates to our close circle. Not only the quality of those people who are in our close circle, but also the quality of our connections to them, transcending time and distance.

And then there is purpose…

I think purpose is meaningfulness to the power of Pi! We want to exit the Rat Race being financially secure because we cannot contemplate staying in it nor exiting without a meaningful achievement. So we find our ways through it and we finally make it, because it was unbearable to stay in there. But in doing so, as we were too focused on achieving, and as we continued our life on auto-pilot, we may not have found our real purpose yet. I'm sure money will help, as money brings a peace of mind and buys time.

But money will not find your purpose.

As part of my many attempts to find a way out, I once went to an internet marketing seminar. It was hosted at a big hotel in London, and the room was packed with probably two or three hundred people. At the break, a small guy walked into the room with two big suitcases. The main speaker announced a change in the plan for the next session and rallied everybody back into the room. This new guy[132] was just coming off a plane from Australia, after a 24-hour journey or so, took the tube, and literally just "landed" in our seminar hotel room. And

---

[131] Tiny extract from the book "Life & Work Principles" by Ray Dalio.
[132] I am very sorry, but I do not remember who this was!

he just lit it up. I mean he put it on fire. Everybody on their feet asking for more.

Totally out of this world!

If you have no idea what purpose is, and what yours should be, go visit a world-renowned motivational speaker. There are good chances that it could change your life.

Freedom acquired yet or not, it could just change your life.

Find your purpose!

9

Other financial games

Vicious games, vicious games
With different names, different names

Yello

Some of these other games were supposed to unlock my financial independence very early. But it did not happen this way. Therefore, I found it fairer to relegate all this financial playground stuff at the end of the book, after independence reached through slower but steadier property investment. It does not make them any less important. They all have a big part to play, but I suppose that I found most of them to be less predictable.

Step 65: wrapping-up real estate

Let's get real. Investing in property and managing tenants is not without a number of risks and pains. I have highlighted a fair number of those throughout the shared simulations and past experiences. There are at least an extra two which I have not covered much.

First, even if your property is an appreciating asset, it is somehow also a decaying one. You have to maintain it. First for the obvious repairs which will announce themselves when you'd rather not spend more (there is never a good moment for spending on maintenance jobs), but second for those forced upon you by changes in regulations. In short, what was acceptable yesterday suddenly becomes outlawed. This can be quite dramatic sometimes, such as having to redo all the electricity wiring because your old installation does not pass inspection anymore, or worse, having a bedroom (an income producing asset) outlawed because new regulations stipulate that it's not large enough, not light enough, not high enough... or just simply not "let's find another reason" enough!

Second, your property cannot move much! I am sure this does not come as a surprise to you, but it also means that the tax authorities struggling to find new sources of income may find it easier to issue new taxation laws against property owners who will find it very hard to convert their property into cash as rapidly as the (generally retroactive) new laws get into place. Therefore, taxation on property and on activities from property (such as rental) can be subject to erratic ups and downs which follow the mood of the times.

Despite all this, investing in property is the only financial game that allows average Joe to use high leverage (3, 4, 5 or more times deposit) and consistently beat the CPI inflation over time, so long as Joe is strict enough in his investment criteria. Therefore, when playing in most other investment games, the comparative disadvantage is the loss of the leverage of other people's money (the bank) and the increased risk on your own capital. That warning being said loud and clear, let's see what other games we could play, in our quest for financial freedom.

Step 66: Mr Market

Let's first tackle the elephant in the room: investing in the stock market. At this very early stage, I want to differentiate investing from trading. Investing is putting money on some financial instrument (bond, stock, fund, etc…) at regular intervals (months or quarters for example) and sleep on it. Not even bothering checking your investment's value each week or month. That's investing.

Worrying about it, checking its value daily, weekly or even monthly, and taking action more frequently (buying, selling, buying again, selling again) is trading.

I personally find it extremely difficult to invest in the market as the constant pressure on your invested assets (Why is it losing value? Should I sell now? Look at this other asset here going ballistic, should I catch the trend?) is pushing me every day closer to trading instead of investing. But making a decent and long term living out of trading is for the 0.1% of us out there: the professional traders. Give it enough time and the remaining 99.9% of all other traders invariably end-up with another nickname: suckers!

The following paragraphs convey my personal experience of trading and are only intended to be semi-educational and entirely recreational…

Some people say that Mr Market has ways of its own to squeeze you out of your hard-earned cash. I think they are very polite. I like to think of trading in another way: trading is like throwing a miniaturised version of you, all cash in hand, in a washing machine. At the beginning, as it spins slowly, you want to play the game…

Who would not want to play this game?

```
"Let's see how much I can win in the washing
                    machine!"
```

You have a few wins, you get confident, you bet a bit more[133]. And then someone engages the real program. You did not know, but as you were playing happily, the washing machine was in rest mode. Like not spinning, only balancing gently. But now we go. Bring on the spinning!

As you start to get dizzy, it sends you water in the face, soap on all sides, and now we get to spin at 100 rpm[134], then 500 rpm. Still hanging in there? Wait a minute, what about 1,000 rpm, or even 1,500 rpm? It continues like this for a few hours (or a few days!). Before it even stops, you want out and feel like vomiting soapy water all day long. As you prepare to step out of the washing machine, your broker is at the door, asking for the fees. You look at what's left in your hand. Not much left... You blew up your betting account (sorry, your trading account), still not fully understanding how it happened.

A few weeks later, as you partly recover from the emotional spin, you look again at your brokerage account, and try to make sense of what happened. Now, let's see the replay.

As you were in the washing machine, another million guys like you were getting soaked too. At 10 rpm, all were keeping their biggest smile and sharing jokes. At 100 rpm, most got dizzy ("is this alcohol? I feel invincible!"), but some were still showing the same happy face. Anyway, a lot less jokes in the humid air...

At 250 rpm, no jokes. Only the sound of the spinning machine, and a long line of people wanting out. But the door is closed until the program finishes. When it was spinning at 1,500 rpm, only a few dozen out of a million were still keeping the head straight as almost all the other million guys had their faces in their asses, washed over, sick, green, and vomiting.

Yeah, I know, it's not pretty to be trading at 1,500 rpm, I can assure you!

---

[133] Yes, betting is the word!
[134] Revolution per Minute: the number of rotations around a fixed axis in one minute.

In the washing machine, if you had paid attention (not easy when vomiting at 1,500 rpm), you would have seen thousands of robots, programmed to withstand even 3,000 rpm. Robots are built with a virtual head but not with a virtual ass. No use for that. As a consequence, they will never end up with their head in their ass as 99.9% of all human traders invariably do. Robots win more than 95% of the time. So when the majority of robots start losing, the entire world is sent into the washing machine and gets its own vomiting experience for a little while.

And then there is the "Crème de la Crème". When you are in the tumbler, you cannot see the outside. But in fact, the most intelligent players and lots of their robot fellows, play just outside the spinning tumbler of the washing machine. You spin, but they don't. When it spins at 1,500 rpm, it throws coins to whoever is there to catch them. A coin here, a coin there. Those professionals and automated algorithms playing outside the spinning tumbler get the privilege to enrich themselves without the risk of getting sick.

Of course, the whole industry is made for you to play inside the washing machine. At the door, you will find experts, advisors of all sorts, gurus, and so-called trader millionaires who want your own good but at the same time will skin you slowly but surely.

By the end of the 17th century, Louis XIV's finance minister, Jean-Baptiste Colbert said this about taxation:

> "the art of taxation consists in so plucking the goose as to obtain the largest possible amount of feathers with the smallest possible amount of hissing"

I think it also applies very well to the industry of financial experts.

For a few thousands of Dollar a year, they will give you the best advice to stay head straight when it starts spinning. Well, maybe you can withstand only 25 rpm alone, and a super ultra-best guru coupled with much learning time and dedication from you, will make you withstand 250 rpm. Beyond 500 rpm, you are alone! At 1,000 rpm, you have no idea where your coins are. Ultimately, the guru will always find the next newbie to train, but when your game-over moment comes, it will be your money, not anyone else's.

So now, dear trader, let me ask you: where would you rather be?
- In the washing machine with your savings firmly in your fist?

Or…
- Far away from the Launderette?

Step 67: Investing

Investing should be the opposite of trading. It should not produce much excitement at all. It has to be a boring, slow, and steady game.

Many top-class fund managers have built and shared models of investments, keeping a pro-rata of invested funds into specific asset classes, such as for example a simple allocation of 65% on stock and 35% on bonds.

As this is my second reference to this person, you will understand that I am personally a great fan of Ray Dalio and I always seek to read and watch his latest books, articles or videos, which always make for great learning[135]. He publicly shared a model of a robust, balanced, all season portfolio[136] to "invest and forget", which is made of 30% US stocks, 15% intermediate US bonds, 40% long term US bonds, 7.5% gold, and 7.5% commodities. There are many low fees fund trackers on pretty much anything you want or need, such as the long list of the Vanguard funds for example. Thanks to these tracker funds, most of us should be able to build a balanced investment portfolio without touching any individual stocks or bonds. The key is to contribute regularly into such low fees funds and not fiddle with it.

As this is a slow game that requires discipline and lacks any form of leverage (such leverage would tip us into the trading game), my simulators fail to convince me that most of us out there can get to financial independence solely by making regular investments, and suddenly wake up one day discovering that all interest and dividends earned can pay for our lifestyle.

Earlier, I shared with you an important table showing how long you have to wait until your compounded savings give you back an equivalent purchasing power in the future.

Invested at a 7% return (a stock market return average) in a world of 3% CPI inflation, it took 36 years to give back the purchasing power

---

[135] You should start with http://www.economicprinciples.org/ and then go with the flow.
[136] From the book "Money Master the Game, by Tony Robbins".

of your hour of work, for an initial saving rate of 25%. That is a massive chunk of savings, therefore a big sacrifice made in the past, and a very long time to wait. For a more reasonable 15% saving rate, all other conditions unchanged, you would have to wait 48 years… In comparison, I remind you that most of my models for investing in property are based on nearly half this value, at a modest 8% saving rate. I hope you understand why I am not convinced…

Anyway, for those who have chosen this path, I give you my 2 cents worth of advice:

Discipline is your most precious asset!

Step 68: retirement accounts

Let's stay in the investing game for a moment. I mean really investing as opposed to trading. As a general observation, governments of this planet try to favour employees who save for their future into pension pots, by removing partially or entirely the tax associated with the origin of savings. Although it varies greatly and depends a lot on the direction of the political winds of the day, it is quite likely that the combination of the tax rebate and the compounded interest on investment is worth the delayed gratification. Anyway, when in doubt, there is always a simulator to help you decide.

We first need to go back to our perfect career and perfect investment (the 3+1 deals for life). If you remember, we started at year one with a £250,000 home investment and a £225,000 debt. We will redo the same exercise, with the same Joe and his partner, but instead of investing their after-tax savings into buy-to-let properties, they will save into a pension pot. This pot is also topped-up generously by their employers at 7.7% gross salary[137] and by the state at 20% tax rebate on employee savings[138]. For clarity, these extra contributions do not exist in the "3+1 deals for life". We keep the same inflation rates (for CPI, salary, and property) as before, and we now assume a lavish 7% pa growth of the pension pot value.

Here below is the situation taken at 5 years intervals, where the pension pot value is on the first line, and the total net worth (home minus debt plus pension) is on the second line.

Year 1	Year 5	Year 10	Year 15	Year 20	Year 25	Year 30
£15,507	£92,943	£232,990	£439,315	£738,556	£1,167,566	£1,777,270
£40,507	£166,072	£379,145	£677,302	£1,090,521	£1,661,569	£2,448,279

Table 68.1 Pension value (first line) and net worth (second line) over time

---

[137] U.K. tax and pension system: a fairly common 5% employer contribution on pension, which is complemented by the savings on National Insurance contribution, making an average of 7.7% of gross salary.
[138] In their tax bracket they are allowed a 20% tax rebate (U.K. tax and pension rules).

It becomes interesting to compare these figures with the net worth we got from the 3 rentals investment plan (3+1 deals for life). Here they are:

Year 1	Year 5	Year 10	Year 15	Year 20	Year 25	Year 30
£35,969	£130,864	£230,668	£712,368	£1,435,273	£2,362,770	£3,541,159

Table 68.2 Net worth of the 3+1 deals investment over time

The graph below shows the compared net worth over 30 years.

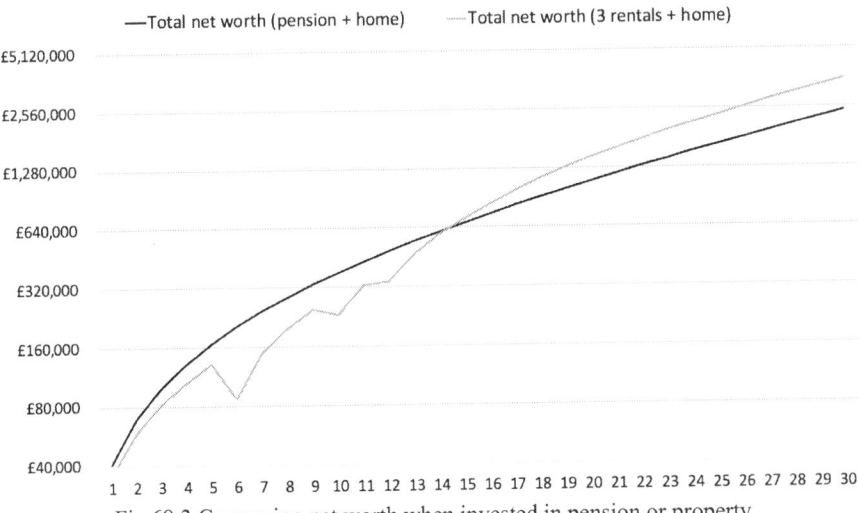

Fig 68.3 Comparing net worth when invested in pension or property

Don't be fooled by this. It looks like the end trends are not that far from each other, but by now, you should really have acquired all the right bullshit detectors to analyse beyond the vague similarities.

- We are in log scale, so the difference between both values at year 30 is significant. As seen from the figures in the tables, the "3 rentals" option represents a 45% increase in net worth value from the "pension" option.
- To get money out of pension, you will have to pay tax, which depends on the generosity (or the lack of it) of the government in place at your future time of need. As I write this, the U.K. for example allows a drawdown of 25% tax free, but after this you pay tax as if it was a salary. Yes, just like this and just

because they can, the state has decided that 75% of the capital that you saved and stored in your pension pot suddenly and magically became income. And therefore, it has to be taxed like income. Ouch!

- The "3 rentals" option ended at year 30 with a debt of £238,636, or a 7.5% debt ratio, which could still be granted to you by the bank in all fairness because you have many real estate assets and a rental business covering this mortgage, until it gets fully repaid. In the case of the "pension" option, we have a debt of £225,000 which is a 9.2% debt ratio on the total assets including pension. But your pension is not as liquid as cash or even property, unless you accept to be taxed in one go on 75% of the pension pot, as mentioned above. So the reality is that you have a 25% debt ratio[139]. However, it is quite unrealistic that the bank will let you have this debt on your main home, still unpaid, 30 years after having taken it. Somehow, you are forced to repay, which means your pension pot will become £225,000 smaller at year 30 at the latest.

- And I kept the most important comparison for last. What really counts is what you get as net income at the end of the period. In the case of the "3 rentals", you have a £9,975 net income per month from all rental activities. In the case of the "pension", after having paid back the debt of your home, and still keeping a flattering gross interest income at 7% per annum, you get a gross income of £9,055. By using the same tax ratio used in the "3 rentals" simulation, this translates into a net of £6,791. What it means is this: the "3 rentals" option gives you an improved 46.9% net income over the "pension" option. In addition, unlike the pension which was locked for the entire 30 years and only really started paying you at end of the locked period, the rentals paid you cash every month. We used this cash to reduce the debt on the 3 rental properties, but

---

[139] That is £225,000 of debt vs £896,000 which is the value of your home in 30 years.

in case of necessity we could have used part of this income to fund any emergency need.

Don't get me "too wrong". In principle, I am all for retirement accounts and the benefit they provide. However, as much as they can be tax efficient for saving, they are not always similarly tax efficient for drawing money out of the account, and they may not be the best long-term option for generating your future inflation-proof income.

I am not here to advise going against this huge fee-hungry pension industry. I just say this: be wise and build simulators. See for yourself.

Maybe topping up a private pension is the way to go…

Maybe there are other options.

Step 69: finding your place in the workspace

I am quite confident that I was crude enough in explaining the difference between investing and trading. So crude in fact, that you shall not mistake one for the other in the future. Well, there are also a few critical distinctions to make concerning the workplace, and I sure hope to make them clear too.

We should not consider "putting food on the table" as a good enough goal when we are in the game to become financially free before normal retirement day. I will therefore leave you with two questions and the following four answers, which for each question, you have to put in order of your personal choice. Here we go.

First question:

"why did you go to work the past month?"

And the second question:

"why would you like to go to work?"

Now for the answers:

1. To improve your career and pay cheque
2. To improve your chances of winning a jackpot
3. To enjoy a good work-life balance
4. To participate in interesting projects with interesting people

Your priority order is: Q1:_____ and Q2: _____

If answering both questions lead to different answers, I hope this will help you reflect on what you try to achieve vs where you are now, and the path you may need to take.

Your choice of priorities drives which type of professional career you have, or you should have, in order to be fulfilled. I will list four categories, for which a different mindset is required.

	Typical career plan	**Priority**
Work for others	You privilege working in medium to large size companies, typically being an employee in the corporate world.	1-4-3-2 1-4-2-3
Work for yourself	You privilege your lifestyle although you could still be earning good money too (typically freelance)	3-1-4-2 3-1-2-4
Share with others	You privilege both lifestyle and social relations, which are likely to happen in a smaller organisation.	3-4-1-2 4-3-1-2
Build with others	You privilege exploring higher risk and higher reward opportunities (typically the start-up game).	4-2-1-3 4-2-3-1 2-4-1-3

Table 69.1 Types of career

I have already touched on the "work for others" choice in the money vs time discussion. Working for others is the choice that will most likely keep you in the Rat Race, having you chase both acquiring more fancy stuff and improving your career. For these reasons, I will not discuss it further.

The "share with others" is one foot away from exiting through the lifestyle first door, or at least experiencing as much as you possibly can of the lifestyle-first way of life. I will not comment about this one either as it does not fall much in our quest to financial freedom first.

That leaves us with the last two, which I will caricature as "freelance" and "start-up". Let's review them next.

Step 70: freelance or small lifestyle company

You will probably consider this option if you want to align your ideals and values with your lifestyle and be more in control of your life. You may have worked in a corporate structure and did not find their values aligned with yours. Or you wondered if you could work as hard for yourself as you do for your boss. Anyway, your ultimate goal is likely to be along those lines:

- freedom to work when you want and for whom you want.
- maximising the return on your time spent working.
- maximising the enjoyment of your time spent working.
- maximising the enjoyment of some newly acquired free time.

I suppose that because freelancers are in general more protective of their lifestyle, the boundary between work and life is made clearer than for employees or frenetic start-up'ers. Indeed, freelancers are very likely to get more lifestyle. But can you still be a freelancer and strive for financial freedom?

When you work as a freelance or a very small company, the value provided by your operations is basically the value of You. But as any good marketer will tell you, there is value and perceived value[140]. The client buys the perceived value. And as a solo guy, to build more perceived value, there is nothing more important than building and maintaining your Reputation. In simple terms: a long list of five stars happy and referenceable clients to the power of Pi!

It is not so different from a larger company which must maintain a good reputation to get new clients, but because you are solo, you are more fragile, and your reputation has way more of an impact on your business.

It is not for me to judge if you can reach early financial independence working as a freelancer. I suppose you can. I would only

---

[140] This is not another salesman story. The marketer paints the picture while the salesman uses all the tricks in his book to sell it.

suggest that you model it carefully and build a few simulators to evaluate your business model over time.

The more perceived value you can create for others, the more you can benefit, either in terms of income or lifestyle, or both. You will need to understand what your maximum perceived value is[141]. I personally have a small formula to help me understand the potential monetary value of "anyone". The simple version goes like this:

```
Maximum Market Value = monetary value-add x size of
                  captive market x frequency
```

For example, if you provide a room cleaning service and do it yourself, your maximum market value is the value of one room cleaned in the specific location where you operate (say $20), times the number of clients you could have at most (say 50), times the number of times you clean for each of them (say once a week), measured over a period, for example one year. Here you have a maximum market value of $20x50x52 = $52,000 pa. In this case, because you deliver a physical service, you cannot go much beyond the laws of physics. When you have cleaned twelve rooms in the day, you collapse in your own and start again the day after (talk about lifestyle!).

However, the magic comes with digital services. Let's say that you provide a website selling a booklet which is a step by step guide for converting any standard toilet room into a magical toilet experience retreat (marketing here we are!). Your maximum value is the perceived value of your booklet (say $2.99) times the captive audience (say 10,000 per year). Here a maximum market value of $29,900 pa. The trick is that you do not need to work proportionally more to sell 10 or 10,000 booklets.

But in this case, you have not made the most of your potential value, because the frequency was kept at one. You sold the booklet once per customer and then nothing more.

---

[141] Here, we are really into a monetary value, relating to the benefits you provide others, not "what are your values?"

Let's say that you can convince your clients that the magical toilet experience is provided by a little wifi visual-musical-olfactory connected device that they will get with your booklet (a bargain at $2.99), but they will have to pay a recharge every week, at $0.99, which they pay quarterly (now $12.87 per quarter) and get delivered for free. Your new maximum market value looks like it's going to be $29.900 + $9,900 x 52 weeks = $544,700. But wait... because the magical toilet experience connected device is now the talk of all diner parties, your target audience suddenly gets exponential... and we are soon talking a few million Dollars[142].

My point is this: if you are a freelancer in search of an early financial freedom, either sell your hours for a very high price / high margin (be a world-renowned guru on whatever subject you can legitimately claim), or be in the business of selling or marketing a recurring digital service that scales to millions without much more additional work. If not in these two categories, what you provide is surely more self satisfying than cleaning rooms, but in terms of scalability of business, the same frustrating laws of physics apply: you are the product and you are the limit.

Last, I will finish with a word of caution. Be careful you don't end up in a worse situation than the employees in their Rat Race. Granted, you may have gotten rid of your boss, but you may discover that you've just inherited a greater number of controlling bosses: your clients.

It is very easy to become enslaved in any job.

Even if you think you are your own boss.[143]

---

[142] Admittedly there is still a little annoyance that the recharge is a physical product, but you did not think I would give you a perfect lifestyle-friendly business model on a silver plate, did you?

[143] You should not get into this thinking, because you cannot deliver good value to others if you take no accountability for your work and delivery. You have bosses and your clients will remind you of this truth every day of the week.

Step 71: money printing via internet-based venture

We touched a bit on the scalability of digital products. Well, internet-based ventures are all about this. Either harnessing the power of website traffic and taking a commission on the sale of other people's goods, or building digital assets for which the cost of production will not vary too much if you sell them 10 or 10 million times. What a good leveraging power!

Internet ventures, those promoting, marketing, or selling digital products, have their own laws of physics. The simplest of those laws is this one:

```
Initial Value = average order value x
       conversion ratio x traffic
```

It means that you start with three main levers to maximize income.

The order value may also be the commission you earned as referral on the sale of the final product. In this case, you may need to find the best balance between a product that is top seller and a commission that is decent.

The conversion ratio is generally a low number such as 1 or 2%. It is worth noting that if you manage to push the ratio from 1% to 2%, you double your final value.

And then there is traffic. Nothing happens without traffic. This is how these internet businesses work: send as many people as possible to your best conversion web-page, and let the magic begin.

To complete this picture, most Internet Marketing gurus will tell you that for each new acquired client, the initial sale is the most costly and the most difficult one. If you stop there, you leave a lot of money on the table. Basically, they have this concept of "lifetime value" of a client. If someone purchases a product from you, make sure they receive within five seconds a thank you email alongside another offer for add-on products at an unbelievable discount valid for only 30 minutes. And then if they buy again, you send them an opportunity to receive another bargain within a week, and so on. There is no other word: Internet Marketers juice opportunities until their last drop!

Without going too much into the nitty-gritty of Internet Marketing, Affiliate Marketing, or other Internet related ventures which can be operated by a single person part-time, the point is that when it works, this is like printing money[144].

The top guys in this industry can make a few thousands Dollar in a few hours just by sending an email to their list[145].

> "Dear Joe, I hope you enjoy your new magical toilet after having applied the principles from my booklet. For an extra $9.99, only if you pay before tonight, I will explain all you need to transform your garage into a rental bedroom earning you an extra $250 per month."

And they print money…

Seriously!

---

[144] Many people will make it look easy but I do not believe this is the case. It requires a lot of dedication and keeping on top of changes in internet tips and tricks.
[145] Such list may contain 50,000 emails, or double that – it really is a numbers game.

Step 72: money printing by growing a start-up

As far as I am concerned, this is the game. But what a challenging one! When realising that the start-up game was going to be a lot more complex and painful, and most importantly that I was having far less control on the outcome than I had initially envisaged, I ended up playing additional games, including the slow but steady property game, as a safety measure. But make no mistake, I have been fully committed to the start-up to IPO hype for over two decades.

This is not a book to teach you how to go from garage to IPO. Here, I will just focus my interest on the leverage offered by being a significant-enough[146] shareholder of a company whose selected Key Performance Indicators grow in a rather exponential trend. These KPIs could be turnover, profit, but also not necessarily pure accounting ones, such as Lifetime Value (here we go again!), Customer Acquisition Cost, Customer Retention Rate, Monthly Active Users, and many others...

To understand this particular game, we first have to understand those who put lots of money in it: the Venture Capital (VC) industry.

First, you have to understand that the VCs manage funds which in most cases are made of other people's money. Typically pension funds, wealthy people, institutions, insurance companies, etc...

Second, their funds have a lifetime, which in general is 5-7 years, after which it closes and the money (less commission, see later) is sent back to the initial investors in the fund. Funds are raised in a cycle of 2-4 years, so a VC always has a fund in activity, sometimes two.

Third, the VC knows by experience that a large percentage of their investments will fail. Yes, they know from the start that they will entirely lose the money they put in on those bets. Depending on VCs, this percentage may vary between 40% for the conservative ones to over 75% for those who take more risks.

---

[146] There is no rule as to what this number should be, as it may shrink after rounds of investments, but I would think that more than 10% after dilution is still significant enough.

Fourth, if a VC got a good return on investment on a past fund (say over 20% per year), they stand a good chance of raising enough for the next fund. But if they did not invest their money (a sleeping 0.1% return) or invested too badly, their chances of raising money for a next fund drop.

Fifth, in most cases, those who manage the VC firm generally have an agreement with their investors that they will retain by way of bonus around 20-25% of the profits generated by the fund. We are talking about a handful of guys who may take home up to a quarter of the profit generated by a fund which had one hundred million dollars, or maybe even a billion dollars, maybe more. Do your maths...

All this has several consequences, which are fairly general across the industry. A typical VC will:

- Try to invest the fund in 15 to 30 companies to spread the risk.
- Know that 10 to 20 of those will fail before the fund expires.
- Know that 3 to 8 of those will survive but muddle through to allow them to painfully get back some part of their initial investment.
- Hope that 1, 2, or god willing 3, could be big winners, delivering into the several hundreds or even thousands percent of return.
- Hope that 1 could transform into a Unicorn (a company valued at more than $1,000,000,000), returning piles and piles of cash.
- Put in place automatic dilution pills in the contracts with start-ups to progressively take over the control of the company, with other VC investors, if the agreed growth does not materialise in time.

Further consequences are that if you had some VC investment and you are in the majority of companies they will allow to fail, you are toast. You can either start again with a harder story to tell, or you find a normal job, or you go on a lifestyle binge to reassess your options...

Again, the VC will look at companies in their portfolio like you look at employees in your company. You may not want to keep your worst sales person in employment beyond the second warning, they may not want to keep what they think is an investment turning too risky either. Nothing personal, it's just business. But from this point, they will not be helpful, and your start-up had better not need money.

You could also be in the larger minority of companies they allowed to continue going, but if all co-founders have the bad luck of losing the majority, either after a new investment round, or after a bad result and a dilution pill had to be swallowed, you may find out that the controlling VC could at some point give the management of your company to someone else, and we are back to the same situation as the previous scenario, except that it's even clearer: you are out, and it's not a "financially free Out"!

Therefore, only a small percentage will make it. For those who make it or those who muddle through, there is one more challenge: converting an illiquid asset (shares in this growing start-up) into cash. And that's no small feat. Just doing this could take years, and each additional year waiting is another leap in the unknown with new pitfalls that past experience could never have foreseen. For me, the wait in the muddle-through-zone has been more than two decades!

I feel sorry I had to paint such a bleak picture, but if you think that an idea, a garage, and a good coffee machine will do it, please take some time to reflect on the risks you are taking, and the reward you are expecting. However, if you are all clear and aligned, then go for it, because it will likely be the most exhilarating experience you could ever wish to participate in.

For those who can make it and convert the illiquid asset into cash, I cannot think of a better money printing machine on earth.

"You said banks are printing money?

Come on, look at my start-up!"

You will probably start with little capital but lots of determination, skill, acumen and many other facets of human capital which are required for this challenge. Let's say that you were 4 co-founders at 25% each. I will not paint the case of a Unicorn. They are in the clouds and we leave them there. Just a very successful start-up will do. We will keep track of the value creation in the following tables.

Value of the company at creation	$10,000
Value of your 25% share	$2,500

Table 72.1 Value of your start-up at creation

After a few months (or a couple of years) you have enough to show a VC that what you have created will definitely change the world for the better. You pitch, they listen, and they decide to invest. They value your company not just for its present state (you lose money and don't even have a sales exec yet), but for its future potential. Another good example of perceived value.

Let's say that the VC values your company at $8,000,000 pre-money and injects $2,000,000. They also give you a little pill in the contract, for which you do not pay much attention. After this operation, you and your three co-founders each have $2,000,000 in paper money.

Value of the company before investment	$8,000,000
VC investment	$2,000,000
Value of the company after investment	$10,000,000
VC share allocation	20%
Your share allocation after dilution	20%
Illiquid valuation of your share	$2,000,000

Table 72.2 Value of your start-up after the first investment round

As we know, this $2,000,000 cannot be converted to cash, so you are locked with shares worth a lot on a paper that nobody will buy yet.

The only thing you can and have to do is continue working hard so that either the value of the company grows further or there is a miracle liquidity event, or both.

Let's say you are a bunch of geniuses and you smashed the goals that were set, so the pill just disappeared. Now your VC wants to invest more alongside other VC friends. They believe in you and will invest five times more, $10,000,000 for a pre-money valuation more than double the last one at $22,500,000, and a new pill. It's incredible that after just a few years you have been able to convert an illiquid $2,500 paper value into a still illiquid, still paper value, but cool $4,500,000.

Value of the company before investment	$22,500,000
New VC investment round	$10,000,000
Value of the company after investment	$32,500,000
All VC share allocation	44.62%
Your share allocation after dilution	13.85%
Illiquid valuation of your share	$4,500,000

Table 72.3 Value of your start-up after the second investment round

The company is worth over 3 times more than last time. Your shares' valuation has more than doubled, and there is a lot more value in the company, so it feels even more real that you can convert these shares into cash at this value, rather sooner than later.

I will spare you the dramatic event where all goes not so well, and the VCs take the control after exercising the new pill, because this is not the point here. The point is that if the next event is that the company gets acquired at, let's say, a cool $100,000,000 [147], then the perceived value gets transformed into real money and your 13.85% share in the start-up becomes a real $13,850,000 cash[148].

---

[147] Did you think the VCs invested for only 2 or 5% return?
[148] Minus salesmen commission and fees of all involved to make the sale. Oh… and minus tax too!

Now, tell me:

- What else will give you this return?
- Is this not money printing?

Of course this is money printing! The real money invested in this company (and let's not even discuss that it may have been someone else's debt) was $12,000,000. When it is sold at $100,000,000 it cannot be seen in another way that $88,000,000 got created. Granted, not out of thin air. Let's say out of coffee, work, and genius, but still... created! If suddenly the expected sale collapses, the company will return to work as usual. If out of nowhere, a new challenger appears with a killer-app making your product pretty useless, what could happen?

Yes, your company could sink fast, and even the $12,000,000 investment could have a "poof!" moment.

It is money printing. Entirely legal, and entirely risky.

In the past 25 years, I have lost a lot of naivety. But I still think that if I was allowed 15 lives, and played this start-up game 15 times, each time in a slightly different environment, with different people, in a different market, with different ideas, and with different luck, I am convinced that I would have got out of it with financial freedom secured within 5 years at least once or twice. Nothing extraordinary to this, just basically on par with the VCs ratios.

I still think this is a game which can be won, despite the many pitfalls awaiting your fall along the way. At the very least, it teaches a lot. Therefore, if you are up for the challenge and have an open mind complemented by good work ethics, do not look back. Just go for it!

High risk, high reward.

Step 73: money printing by flipping land

In a small French village with fewer and fewer small farms (yes, the very same village), agricultural land sells for around €0.70 per square meter, or as per the farming measure, €7,000 per hectare.

Every 5 years or there-about, as the village slowly but surely expands (it is located in a commutable distance of a mid-size city), the local municipality convenes to discuss the opportunity of converting some agricultural land into building land. A few local farmers and well-advised villagers suddenly see the price of their agricultural land move to around €20 to €40 per square meter. Let's grossly call it a x50 gain. Nothing else but profit (and taxes)!

Then, the professional builders come in, buy a large quantity of adjacent pieces of land from the local villagers, partitions the land in smaller plots, and make it ready to build, with the minimal connected infrastructure. They sell it back to new incoming villagers for them to build their house on top, at a price starting from €200 per square meter. They grossly make a conservative return of x8 on the acquired plot, although this is not all profit as they have cost to prepare the infrastructure, deal with the municipality, etc...

I have never played this game, but to me this is clearly on par with the bank's money printing. With the difference that the one printing the money is not the bank, but another invisible man sitting just between you and your local council. You have well placed land, well placed connections, and Boom! Fifty times your investment! And I should remind you that in this particular case, we are just talking about land on the fringes of a little village, not within a large city or a fast-expanding urbanisation.

Although this is the slowest of all games we have on review, and may have to be played over generations, tell me what else gives you this type of return on investment in a lifetime?[149]

---

[149] Apart from the money printer of a rare Unicorn, of course!

Step 74: other opportunities

I receive at least one email a day offering me "the best investment opportunity". Don't be jealous. If you want the same, just surf the internet and subscribe to a few email lists.

I have a brief look once a week, and if it feels interesting, I spend a bit more time to dig deeper. I tiptoed-invested a few times, but in most cases, I would find something that makes me nervous. Anyway, these daily offers give us a good opportunity to play our last financial simulation game. You already know that I did not invest in this one, but you will have to find why. Here's the opportunity with as much information as I could gather from the source.

"Your investment will give you a share-holding in the company that owns the virtual freehold (999 leasehold) and title deed of the building. This will securitise your investment and give you an asset backed holding, plus you will own part of the business which as it is shared office space and a high growth sector will be giving you returns from 12% per year"

Minimum investment	£20,000
Return on investment	12% per annum fixed
Payment terms	Paid quarterly
Exit terms	Buyback at year 5 at £21,000

Table 74.1 Investment in workspace offices

So this is what we get: we invest in a company established by supposedly reputable people. This company has the sole objective of buying and renovating one specific building around London, and then to operate it as an office space for co-sharers. Their clients will pay the service for using the facilities per hour, per week, or per month. The company will then pay quarterly dividends to their shareholders, and you will get back 12% of your paid capital per annum. They also "guarantee" a buy back at year 5 of 105% of the initial investment.

Other financial games

I asked for the full contract[150], and this is what I found in there.

> "If the Placing Shares are fully subscribed at the price of £0.10 per share, the Investors will hold 34,905,798 Ordinary Shares in the Company which will comprise 25% of the issued share capital. The remaining 75% of the issued share capital will be held by the Directors who have already issued 104,817,394 shares at £0.001. The office space will operate 100 desks at maximum capacity"

Now to your simulators! Why shall we not take it?

No, I'm not going to give you the solution just right now. It's hidden further in the Annex. For now, you need to think about this investment case and decide why you will not make it.

---

[150] Don't bother asking for a marketing brochure, you always want to see the final contract.

Step 75: to paradise with simulators

In the world of finance, we can simulate pretty much anything. And we do not need an army of accountants to do this. We can simulate all our financial futures, possible, probable, improbable, risky, worthy, and more, just from our kitchen table. We can receive opportunities and make up our mind in a few hours of internet searches and Excel spreadsheet.

And in rare but exceptionally good occasions, a few times per year at most, we implement what the simulator tells us to do.

One more deal!

I cannot stress more how these simulators have been critical to my decisions. To the point where I cannot take decisions on any important investment without first running the numbers through simulations. This process has the benefit of removing any emotional bias and just lets the numbers speak. It also creates a documented reference point for past investments. Any new opportunity can then be compared with these past benchmarks. Moving forward, it becomes easier to accept or reject opportunities based on various key performance indicators that you can improve and understand better over time.

Should you invest in property, or play in another financial game, either covered in this book or not, there are very good chances that going through simulations first will help you clarify your position and see the investment opportunity in a different light, a more analytical one.

Do not invest with just your emotional brain.

Always use simulators!

10

Leverage your life!

Look at the stars
Look how they shine for you

Coldplay

This book has an end, and we are approaching it. I sincerely hope I have been able to contribute to your knowledge, add clarity to your goals, and help you ask the right questions. But before we go our separate ways, I want to give you a most important retrospective and summary. Now comes the cherry!

Step 76: life is a journey

As I shared at the start of this book, my plan to get out of what was at the time "Metro – Boulot – Dodo"[151] was pretty simple and fast:

```
"Five years only and I will be done!"
```

Five years went by and... I was not done!!

The more I gave myself another three years, another three years, and the less I was done with it. There were two main reasons for this.

The simple one is that you cannot exit and be financially secure until... you are indeed really financially secure. This is the core of the Rat Race conundrum. But before I reconsider this question for one last time, I want to explore the second reason. I had reached a certain kind of downgraded financial security when I envisaged being debt free on my home within two years. Granted it was downgraded, but it was there for the taking. Instead, I decided to reach another milestone. Not just a financial milestone. A meaningful one. For me but also for those around me. It would have been too selfish to exit with just enough to provide a quiet life for myself. So I ran the race faster than ever before.

With this insight, the second reason is this: one may be financially secure and still not exit. One may also be financially secure multiplied by Pi, and still not exit. We need to exit knowing that we have achieved something meaningful.

The problem with exiting "too early" is that you will always wonder if you have maximised your potential. For you and for those around you. Taking a commitment to others (said or even not said but just felt) is the most powerful force of all. So, as we regularly reassess our goals, the next achievement is up for the taking, and we postpone the exit. And it goes on for a little longer. Three more years...

Until the moment when we feel comfortable enough, not just financially, but mostly having delivered enough meaningful

---

[151] The French version of the Rat Race, which would probably translate into something like this: "Commute – Work – Crash to bed".

achievements for ourselves and others we care for, that our next goal can be as valuable and meaningful out of the race as inside it.

This is when we allow ourselves to exit. Indeed, you first have to give yourself permission to take this early exit, the "financially secure first" door. This is when you can start saying:

> "Some things can change now"

Irrespective of your financial status, it can take a long time to reach this state of mind. It will take a long journey to satisfy the complex animal that you are. When people say that it's the journey that matters, not the destination, they are spot on. Without the scars, you are not a better person.

Now onto the financially secure conundrum for one last time!

You might think it was pure luck that I played the property game and managed to get out of it in a rather flattering position so far (yes so far, because nothing is gained for ever, this is for sure). But in fact, this is not what happened.

I played all of these high-risk high-reward games. All of them. With all the intensity I could possibly muster.

I traded (not very successfully admittedly) the stock market at several occasions in my life and lost enough money to know that this washing machine game is not for me to make money.

I salary sacrificed[152] a good chunk of my pay for over a decade and invested it in a retirement account that I manage directly myself (it's called a SIPP[153]), and I try to avoid trading and keep investing.

I invested a lot of time and effort in many websites and web marketing activities. It worked to a certain point, but I could not

---

[152] This is the official terminology: a salary sacrifice!
[153] Self Invested Personal Pension.

dedicate enough time to it, and in the end, I felt the affiliate marketing businesses did not align well with my personality and values.

I invested the major part of my life in start-up projects, some successful, some less so.

While doing all this, I even also worked as a freelance, designing and producing sketch videos to whomever wanted them.

And I invested in properties.

Had I been exposed to any other valuable financial game with a good enough risk-reward, I would have played it too. At the same time, and with my best efforts.

Yes, I played them all. Granted, only those games that either match your personality or for which you found the key, only those will reap the reward. For me, it was mostly properties and start-ups. But each game provided so much more in learning. It is because I played them all that I got more successful at a few of them.

Will you have the courage and the strength to try them all? Or will you pick your battles? Will you have the strength to stand-up and play again after falling? Yes, you will fall. Many times. Over and over again. It is guaranteed! Will you stand-up and continue playing, until you find the key?

It is only by playing a lot of those games that you will know which ones you are more likely to win. And all those you leave on the side are not a lost effort. If you put all your soul, skills and energy, you have the certainty that you will come out of this experience a better person. Even if you failed at the greater goal. The many lessons you will learn on the journey are gems you collect and treasure for life.

There are many rewarding games at your disposal. If you have decided that you'd like to exit the Rat Race through the financial freedom door first, you have to play the games.

Play the damn games!

Step 77: but what a journey!

What a journey we had together!

As you and I come to the end of our time together in this book, I want to express my most sincere appreciation. I am very grateful I was able to share my stories, which as a matter of fact constitute a big part of my life and who I am. Thank you for having given me your time. You could have been doing anything else instead, but you chose to stick with it. I sincerely hope you will find it rewarding. I hope to have helped you ask many questions and at the same time find as many answers for how you will or should approach your financial and spiritual goals in life.

As a "final encore", I give you here below a highlight from our journey together and what I feel is the most important message you need to keep in mind. You can come back to this condensed version whenever you need a quick refocus on what we learned together. You can also continue learning on my website www.intheRatRace.com where I maintain a growing list of useful financial simulators, to help anyone unlock financial freedom.

--

We started our journey with a rather simple and naïve approach into this world. A probing mindset saved the day by asking some simple questions. As the veil was removed, the game being played appeared more complex than initially thought. Money, the unit measure of this game, was not reliable over space and time. A reset was overdue to find out what this was all about and follow the evidences left by an invisible man who favours some to the detriment of others.

Our understanding of money from its origins has allowed us to discover that money is mostly trust in the system, and the system is massively made of debt. This accumulation of debt is nothing more than a very long list of promises from the multitude of borrowers to the multitude of lenders, to pay interest and repay capital under certain conditions (mostly interest, duration, and what the debt is secured upon). We also learned that the value of money is constantly eroded by tax and inflation. That applies to all sorts of assets acting as a store of value, otherwise referred to as capital, such as cash, gold, shares, properties, land, etc... Inflation hits certain asset classes a lot more than others. For example, cash is hit at 100%, whereas properties in locations of high demand seem to have a proven track record of more than a century of growth above inflation, thereby not only protecting their owner against loss of value, but most importantly by accelerating the owner's wealth over time. We understood that commercial banks play a key role and have a vested interest in creating new credit money which has a very inflationary impact on certain asset classes such as real estate. In bad times, central banks have bazooka powers to create gazillions of real money. We also saw that governments around the world tend to favour capital over income and tax income more than capital gain. Finally, as debt is money, we understand that debt is also helpfully eroded by inflation.

We have reviewed that our attitude, and striving each day to be a better person than we were the day before, is key to unlocking greatness. Managing stress, understanding the world around us, and learning are all part of being a better person. As much as learning is important, taking action is even more so, because there cannot be true learning without deep experience. Ultimately, who you are and who you will be will never be more influenced, positively and negatively, by the people who surround you, and by the principles which guide you. You have to expel from your inner circle all those who have a negative impact on you, whereas you have to seek and welcome those who will take you to a better path. For this, trust and shared values are essential. Before asking yourself if such or such person is trustworthy, work on being 100% trustworthy yourself. You can only do this well by discovering and deeply understanding your own values. Drawing lines in the sand help you get clarity on your values and principles. Understand what is right vs what is wrong, what is important vs what is not, what makes you smile and what makes you cry, what frustrates you and what excites you. Having sound principles in place also helps keeping the focus on what matters: the journey itself. Ultimately, your journey is way more important than any shorter-term goals. For this reason, as much as you possibly can, you should plan and design your own journey, and make sure you run it "on the right track". If you can push it even a bit further, try to understand your inner "why": your purpose.

On the road to financial freedom, you will also require a strict control over your finances. That includes a good attitude towards not taking on bad debt, being wary of fees in all their disguised forms, not wanting the latest fancy stuff, and living your life within your means and in accordance with your values. But you also have to go the extra mile and view your operational self like a company. Start tracking your income and capital as a business would do, at least once or twice a year. That includes an accurate balance sheet, a cash flow statement, an income statement, and from these financial data, a list of useful ratios which will tell you the brutal truth as to where you are in your quest to be financially independent. Finally, you have a wealth building strategy which relies on three pots. The first one, the holey bucket, is your current account leaking money every day or week as you top it up every month. Any excess from the holey bucket is automatically poured into the second pot, the barrel, which keeps your savings at the lowest possible risk. When the barrel gets full enough, you make your investment for life and keep it in the third and final pot, the lake, with all your other investments made for life.

At the start of your career, you need the best possible job and that may require working in some of the most expensive cities on earth and commute to a suburb for an affordable place to live. Unfortunately, even a perfect career is not a good bet to get you to financial freedom early, but you need this job for the leverage it can bring. As we looked into the desirability of certain types of money transactions and income, we found out that all were not equal, far from it. This research led us to find that the most desirable was passive income, followed by portfolio income, and then last is your earned income. Starting from not much more than a good job, getting to a point where your passive and portfolio income can replace your earnings required a better understanding of your human capital value, and the deeper correlation between the long-term effects of savings, debt, inflation, and risk on capital. A first model of investment showed us that investing by leveraging on debt is more powerful than investing by savings.

Acquiring properties in locations of high demand with a solid financial plan and operating them for rental returns is the safest game to play with leverage. It is also at the core of our strategy for building a stream of passive income which will progressively replace our reliance on the so called 'perfect job' and give us more freedom. By using sophisticated simulators and tracking important ratios, you can detect the right opportunities in which to invest. As your criteria get tightened up, the opportunities reduce in numbers, but at the same time, they improve in quality: you get more control and less risk. Such is the case that even when invested close to a peak market, the right opportunity remains cash flow positive during the sharpest of downturns. And even the biggest financial crisis did not make more than a temporary blip in the value of such property. We explored in detail a model showing that a couple both in employment and making a very modest 8% savings on salary and buying four similar properties (one home and three rental) over a 12-15 years period can transform an initial net worth of £35,000 into £3,500,000 within 30 years. The investments can be accelerated by saving more, such as 15% or 25%. You then have the luxury to set the cursor as you prefer: stopping your perfect career earlier and enjoying more free-time, or maximising your wealth beyond this low savings model.

I have been very direct and open with you all along. But words, advice, and even simulators, are never as transcending as action. I have shared with you a good part of my journey into property investment, wealth building and freedom seeking. You saw my naivety, mistakes, courage, and relentless drive to get out of a situation I always felt was insecure due to my choice of career path which kept me permanently on higher risk (real) and higher reward (dream).

My journey made me discover a few fundamentals in life which I have shared with you throughout many stories. The first relating to financial independence is that income is what matters. Capital can be eroded by inflation, mis-allocated by inexperience, or spent by vanity. A steady passive income for life matters a lot more, so this is what you need to engineer for yourself and your family. The second is that strong human values and grounded life principles matter even more than income, because your future passive income is just a consequence of these. Therefore, you have to work relentlessly on yourself to become a better person. And finally, the third is that a meaningful purpose in life transcends all of this. You should never lose track of purpose because it is what could deliver the most rewarding exit of the Rat Race you would ever dream of.

Lastly, I have also shared my personal experience of other financial games such as trading, investing, saving into retirement accounts, participating in exhilarating start-up projects, and more. There is no reason to pick only one game and play it blindly. All those games are here for you to play. The more variety you play, and the more regularly you play, the more likely you will get hit by so many pitfalls awaiting the fresher that you are. As a consequence, you will gain much learning from experience, and ultimately become a better person.

Acquiring financial freedom will lead you to many other important questions. How much of a lifestyle do you want to preserve? How do you want to live your future life? What is quality time to you? How much of it do you want? What will you do next? What is your purpose?

Yes, exiting the Rat Race through the financial freedom door first leads to More... More time. More questions. More introspection. More clarity on what is important vs what is not.

Ultimately, the quality of your life depends a lot on the quality of your time, the quality of the questions you ask yourself, and of the true introspection and betterment process you inflict upon yourself.

That being said, what is essential now is that you reflect and take a deep breath. I have given you a lot. But it's for you to take. It's for you to decide if you will transform this little not so significant moment of now, into a bigger and transformational one, and say as I did so many times:

> `"Something needs to change!"`

To your journey!

11

Appendix

It's the end of the world as we know it
And I feel fine

R.E.M.

At the very least, it's the end of the book, and I do feel fine about it! Thank you for your time and support, and here is the last bit…

Thank you

It's time for a few thank you. I have never been too good at this...

If in the past our paths have crossed more than an instant, it probably means that we have shared some struggles together. Most likely we shared our thoughts and efforts to resolve whatever was in front of us at the time. For your time and your effort, I want to thank you.

For a smaller list of individuals, you may have been part of the kind who backstabbed me at some point, in general for your own political agenda or your personal financial gain. Guess what, you have been part of my education, and I must acknowledge it and take the time here to thank you too. Without your nasty tricks, I would not have grown so much, and I would not either have made such a principle to stick to my values. So, thank you as well for the pain you inflicted. A better Me emerged out of this.

Now of course, there is the close circle, the one who will stay with me whatever happens. It starts with my close family, wife, children and parents, without who I could not be who I really am. Thank you all for being who you are, from the bottom of my heart.

And then, there are the rare ones. The ones who said "fuck you" to others who bullied me. Those who chose to protect me whatever happened, over a very long period of time and until now. You are a very rare breed, and you will recognise yourselves. Thank you, because you did not have to stick to your principles when faced with the surprising brutality of life, but you did. In my eyes, it makes you the most valuable people on earth. For this, I am eternally grateful.

Eric

Additional resources

The website www.intheRatRace.com will allow you to access many simulators such as those we have used throughout this book.

My promise to you is that via this website, I will continue to help you understand, through accessible and visual representations, how far away you are from getting out of this damn Rat Race.

I also promise to grant the first 50 reviewers of this book on Amazon (whatever the content of your honest review, positive or not) a lifetime free access to all simulators that will ever be made available on the website. Just send me an email at eric@intheRatRace.com with the proof of review and if you are in the first 50, I will grant you the access within a few hours or days.

For one last time…

To your journey, and to your exit from the Rat Race!

Eric Duneau

Email: eric@intheRatRace.com

www.intheRatRace.com

Solution to the investment case

First, note that the Directors allowed themselves to invest at 100 times less per shares than new investors. That's a very big red alert for me. We see here the magic of company valuations in all its splendour. On paper, the company is worth what the latest round of investors agreed to come in at. If 25% of shareholders now agree that £0.10 is the right share price, then it gives everybody else a paper share price of £0.10. Even if these everybody else invested at a fraction of this amount just a few days before.

Second red flag, the new investors will get at most a 25% share of the company, which means that even in case of a full allocation of shares, the "Directors" will keep a total control with 75% of voting rights.

Third, the investment is capped to operating one office. If they are ever successful at it, you can bet they will buy other premises through other companies, which means we will never get an upside beyond this unique office if it works well.

Then, let's try to understand the financials behind. 30,905,798 shares at £0.10, that makes a total of £3,090,579 of investment in the company, plus the Directors part of £104,817. So, at maximum investment fulfilled, we have around £3.2m of money invested. But each year, this company will need to pay dividends to the tune of 12% per share. With 139,723,192 shares in circulation, that will add-up to quite a large sum: around £1.677m.

How many desks do they need to operate to afford such a level of profit? We need a few assumptions, but a quick internet search tells us that they are unlikely to price each desk more than £600 per month. If they operate at 50% net margin (that would be a big number!), then they could get £300 profit per desk per month. They need around 465 desks[154] operating at full capacity and at full profit margin, just to pay

---

[154] £1.677m / (£300 * 12) = 465

the dividends. But they advertise being able to accommodate 100 desks. Something's gonna give!

I think they will close shop before the 5 years "guaranteed" buy back at 105% and the investors will get back in the region of 25% of the value of the offices, probably worth only £500K, and sold to the highest bidder.

Pass!

Glossary

Rat Race: willingly and consciously exchanging day after day your most valuable asset (time) against a temporary depreciating one (money) to stay in the race despite all deprivation that ensues.

Capital: the measure of your wealth, not to be mistaken by the more important measure of your financial freedom. Possessing capital helps, but only a regular passive income sets you properly on the path to financial freedom.

Debt: let's call this a negative capital, or a capital you owe someone else. Most debt is bad, but a particular type is good. The good debt is the one you leverage to secure the acquisition of an appreciating asset which will generate a net income way in excess of the interest you have to pay on the debt.

Income: money earned and flowing into your bank account to pay for your current and future lifestyle. Do not mix up capital gain with income, they are very different. Income is preferably regular, not just a consequence of luck, and is either earned from work, passive (from rent or other business), or coming from a portfolio (dividends, interest, coupons). Passive income leads to financial freedom.

Inflation: an increase in the price of goods and services which implies an equivalent decrease in the value of capital, or debt. Inflation plays a part in all financial games. Do not dismiss it.

Tax: an invention dating back a couple of millenniums which has for sole purpose to redistribute legally and regularly a chunk of your earnings or capital to a more powerful authority.

LTV: Loan to Value, or the pro-rata of the loan you take vs the total capital investment you make. Typical LTV are 60-80% but can be more. A higher LTV means a higher risk (for both yourself and the bank).

Interest only mortgage: a mortgage which allows you to defer the capital repayment at the end of the mortgage duration. You still need to have a plan for repaying this capital.

Yield: a ratio of how much money you get back from your capital over the usual period of 12 months. A 10% yield means you get back $10 over the 12 months period, out of a $100 capital. The yield gives a first indication of a return on investment, but I prefer to use many other more precise ratios, which take into account taxes, inflation, and a long list of additional reality distorting concepts.

Gross profit from operations: the gross profit you made whilst operating a business over a 12 months accounting period. This is merely the gross income deducted from all expenses incurred, although it can get a tiny bit more complicated if you either wish or have to amortise large expenses over many accounting periods.

Net profit from operations: the gross profit from operations deducted from any taxes paid (or yet to be paid) for this accounting period.

Cash on cash invested: the ratio of the gross profit made by the investment during the last 12 months accounting period divided by all cash invested at the date of investment. Of course, you could use further improved ratio, for example the net cash on cash (profit made after tax) and also the inflation proof net cash on cash (taking inflation into account, therefore valuing more any investment made in the past).

Expense coverage ratio: this is the ratio of gross income from rental activity divided by cost of rental activity. I like to see this ratio above 200%, which means my income from rental activities cover twice my costs from same activities.

Passive earnings ratio: the ratio of your gross passive earnings divided by your total gross earnings over a 12 months accounting period. If this ratio hits 50%, it means that you get half your gross income from work, half from passive income. Note that you may be taxed more on your employment than on your rental activities or portfolio income, so if you are after exact figures, you may want to look into a more accurate "Net passive earnings ratio" (the after-tax equivalent).

Freedom ratio: the sum of your portfolio and passive income divided by your total living expenses. When the freedom ratio is consistently above 100%, you are somehow already financially free and can slowly think about sunsetting your job.

References

Books

Corrigan, Joshua ; Matterson Wade. A Holistic Framework for Lifecycle Financial Planning. Milliman, 2010

Dalio, Ray. Life & Work Principles. Simon & Shuster, 2017

Dalio, Ray. Principles for Navigating Big Debt Crisis. Bridgewater, 2018

Doorman, Frans. Our Money - Towards a new monetary system. Lulu.com, 2015

Dyson, Ben ; Hodgson, Graham ; van Lerven, Frank. Sovereign Money – an introduction. Positive Money, 2016

El-Erian, Mohamed. The only game in town. Yale University Press, 2016

Flannery, Mark J. Iceland's Failed Banks: A Post-Mortem. 2009

Greenham, Tony ; Ryan-Collins, Josh. Where does money come from? New economics foundation, 2012

King, Marvin. The End of Alchemy: Money, Banking and the Future of the Global Economy. London, Little, Brown, 2016.

McLeay, Michael ; Radia, Amar ; Ryland, Thomas. Money creation in the modern economy. Bank of England, 2014

Robbins, Tony. Money master the game. Simon & Shuster, 2016

Taleb, Nassim Nicholas. The Black Swan. Random House, 2007

Websites

www.16personalities.com

www.bankofengland.co.uk

www.economicsjunkie.com

www.economicprinciples.org

www.france-inflation.com

www.ourworldindata.org

www.positivemoney.org

www.standard.co.uk

www.wikipedia.com

Index

A

attitude, 1, 53, 54, 55, 56, 114, 178, 300, 301

B

better person, xii, 58, 59, 68, 80, 297, 298, 300, 303
bucket, 8, 22, 31, 45, 109, 110, 111, 112, 144, 301

C

capital, 13, 27, 37, 43, 44, 51, 87, 91, 93, 96, 97, 98, 102, 103, 104, 106, 107, 109, 112, 126, 134, 135, 136, 138, 140, 141, 142, 143, 144, 145, 146, 147, 148, 149, 151, 153, 156, 158, 159, 167, 171, 173, 175, 176, 180, 191, 193, 194, 196, 202, 203, 204, 212, 215, 219, 221, 227, 250, 266, 287, 291, 292, 300, 301, 302, 310, 311
compounded, 6, 107, 271, 273
CPI, 4, 6, 7, 46, 47, 87, 104, 117, 118, 140, 141, 171, 173, 174, 175, 190, 192, 194, 227, 254, 255, 266, 272, 273

D

dashboard, 100
debt, 17, 18, 23, 26, 27, 30, 32, 33, 36, 38, 43, 44, 45, 46, 49, 50, 51, 54, 55, 56, 57, 72, 76, 94, 96, 103, 104, 120, 127, 135, 139, 157, 169, 170, 171, 172, 173, 175, 193, 194, 195, 196, 197, 198, 202, 203, 209, 210, 211, 212, 213, 215, 216, 218, 219, 220, 221, 222, 226, 227, 229, 230, 231, 232, 233, 234, 235, 237, 252, 273, 274, 275, 289, 296, 300, 302
desirability, 120, 121, 125, 126, 127, 128, 129, 132, 133, 134, 302

F

financial freedom, 56, 59, 60, 70, 72, 76, 110, 117, 121, 134, 135, 151, 187, 197, 207, 234, 238, 239, 244, 247, 251, 266, 278, 279, 281, 289, 298, 301, 303

G

game, 9, 41, 43, 56, 87, 92, 140, 161, 162, 189, 198, 200, 208, 211, 214, 230, 266, 267, 270, 271, 273, 277, 278, 283, 284, 289, 290, 291, 293, 297, 298, 299, 302, 303

I

inflation, 3, 4, 5, 6, 7, 21, 22, 23, 27, 28, 32, 33, 38, 39, 43, 46, 47, 55, 71, 72, 83, 84, 86, 87, 88, 89, 90, 92, 95, 96, 98, 104, 106, 112, 115, 117, 118, 119, 136, 137, 141, 147, 157, 158, 163, 171, 173, 174, 175, 180, 190, 192,

193, 194, 201, 203, 212, 227, 230, 246, 254, 255, 266, 272, 273, 275, 300, 302, 303, 311

interest, 12, 23, 24, 25, 26, 27, 28, 29, 30, 36, 38, 39, 40, 41, 43, 44, 45, 47, 51, 54, 55, 58, 77, 78, 88, 89, 90, 95, 96, 107, 121, 125, 126, 128, 130, 136, 137, 142, 143, 144, 145, 165, 166, 167, 169, 170, 171, 172, 173, 174, 177, 180, 183, 187, 190, 191, 192, 196, 202, 204, 211, 212, 219, 220, 221, 226, 228, 231, 232, 234, 254, 255, 256, 271, 273, 275, 284, 300

investment, 13, 43, 55, 88, 89, 96, 106, 110, 111, 135, 138, 142, 149, 150, 151, 153, 154, 155, 156, 157, 158, 159, 160, 163, 164, 165, 168, 172, 173, 174, 175, 176, 179, 190, 192, 193, 194, 195, 196, 197, 202, 203, 207, 210, 211, 219, 226, 230, 235, 256, 265, 266, 267, 271, 273, 274, 285, 286, 287, 288, 289, 290, 291, 292, 293, 301, 302, 308, 310, 311

invisible man, 5, 7, 9, 48, 87, 180, 229, 235, 236, 290, 299

J

job, 5, 38, 55, 56, 73, 114, 115, 119, 139, 140, 186, 199, 238, 241, 253, 281, 285, 301, 302, 312

Joe, 36, 37, 38, 47, 140, 141, 142, 143, 144, 145, 159, 160, 254, 257, 266, 273, 283

journey, xii, xiii, 9, 53, 58, 59, 72, 73, 74, 75, 79, 113, 196, 207, 263, 296, 297, 298, 299, 302, 303, 304, 307

L

lifestyle, 5, 6, 13, 57, 102, 105, 130, 141, 142, 143, 144, 145, 147, 158, 192, 197, 205, 237, 238, 239, 240, 243, 247, 255, 256, 257, 261, 262, 271, 278, 279, 280, 281, 285, 303

loan, 17, 18, 23, 27, 36, 38, 44, 54, 55, 56, 90, 94, 96, 120, 123, 124, 136, 138, 139, 156, 172, 177, 209, 210, 310

M

meaningful, 73, 262, 263, 296, 303

money, 2, 4, 5, 6, 7, 8, 11, 12, 13, 14, 16, 21, 22, 23, 28, 30, 31, 32, 33, 34, 35, 36, 37, 38, 40, 41, 42, 43, 44, 45, 46, 47, 49, 50, 51, 55, 56, 57, 59, 72, 76, 88, 89, 90, 91, 109, 111, 115, 119, 120, 121, 125, 126, 129, 132, 138, 142, 145, 157, 160, 163, 175, 180, 183, 202, 212, 226, 231, 232, 234, 246, 249, 252, 254, 257, 258, 263, 266, 267, 270, 274, 275, 278, 282, 283, 284, 285, 286, 287, 288, 289, 290, 297, 300, 301, 302, 308, 311

P

pension, 102, 121, 124, 126, 127, 128, 129, 142, 143, 273, 274, 275, 276, 284 perfect career, 115, 117, 118, 119, 140, 141, 142, 143, 145, 146, 159, 190, 254, 273, 301, 302

Phi, 71, 72, 102, 175, 193

Pi, 71, 72, 94, 95, 102, 114, 117, 119, 143, 144, 145, 175, 193, 262, 263, 279, 296

principles, xiii, 1, 8, 23, 58, 73, 74, 283, 303, 306

profit, 23, 36, 38, 54, 76, 77, 94, 95, 96, 101, 102, 112, 121, 126, 138, 139, 149, 160, 162, 170, 172, 173, 174, 175, 193, 195, 199, 224, 233, 284, 285, 290, 308, 311

purpose, iv, 97, 121, 150, 165, 240, 251, 262, 263, 264, 301, 303, 310

R

rat race, 73, 96, 97, 144, 261, 263, 278, 281, 296, 298, 303

reputation, 30, 66, 279

risk, 14, 17, 18, 23, 29, 30, 31, 32, 38, 43, 53, 70, 71, 72, 74, 89, 93, 94, 95, 104, 108, 109, 112, 136, 144, 145, 149, 150, 151, 152, 153, 154, 155, 156, 157, 158, 160, 163, 164, 173, 174, 177, 180, 186, 193, 198, 202, 203, 219, 226, 227, 233, 239, 253, 256, 266, 269, 278, 285, 289, 297, 298, 301, 302, 303, 310

S

salesman, 76, 77, 78, 82, 83, 84, 88, 89, 178, 187, 188, 279

saving, 4, 5, 32, 37, 89, 110, 114, 127, 142, 143, 144, 145, 154, 158, 176, 191, 192, 212, 253, 254, 255, 256, 272, 275, 302, 303

simulator, 113, 148, 168, 187, 188, 273, 293

T

tax, 5, 19, 20, 21, 32, 41, 54, 92, 93, 94, 95, 96, 101, 102, 105, 106, 109, 110, 118, 126, 127, 133, 135, 138, 141, 149, 160, 171, 172, 181, 184, 190, 191, 204, 215, 223, 224, 255, 266, 273, 274, 275, 300, 311

trust, 7, 8, 12, 15, 20, 22, 40, 41, 47, 58, 66, 67, 68, 74, 178, 186, 241, 300

Printed in Great Britain
by Amazon